STUDIES IN HISTORY, ECONOMICS AND
PUBLIC LAW

Edited by the
FACULTY OF POLITICAL SCIENCE
OF COLUMBIA UNIVERSITY

———————

NUMBER 509

A JUDGMENT OF THE OLD RÉGIME

BY

PAUL H. BEIK

A JUDGMENT
OF THE OLD RÉGIME

*Being a survey by the Parlement of Provence of French
economic and fiscal policies at the close of the
Seven Years War*

BY

PAUL H. BEIK, Ph. D.

Instructor in History, Columbia University

NEW YORK

COLUMBIA UNIVERSITY PRESS

LONDON: P. S. KING & STAPLES, LTD.

1944

To

D. H. B.

PREFACE

In the years before 1789 many judgments were passed upon the old régime in France. The present study, made possible by the resources of the Seligman Collection at Columbia University, is based on another, and hitherto unknown, analysis of much that was important in the pre-revolutionary economic and social structure. The magistrates of the parlement at Aix in Provence were the observers; their reflections on the France of their day, which have been the principal source of this study, are contained in the fourteen manuscript volumes of *Mémoires sur les finances* written during the period of unrest which followed the disastrous Seven Years War.

The late Professor Seligman referred to these manuscripts as " by all odds the fullest statement and discussion of the French revenues in existence," and this description is an accurate one, although in many respects the Provence memorials merely supplement Forbonnais' admirable *Recherches et considérations sur les finances de France, depuis 1595 jusqu'à l'année 1721,* from which many of their facts were taken. But the *Mémoires sur les finances* have a misleading title, for they consist not merely of an exposition and criticism of France's main taxes but also of numerous passages on such subjects as political economy, population, government, social classes, crime, and foreign policy. Indeed, they are a veritable mine of facts and opinions about the old régime.

No doubt more than one approach to this material was possible. I have chosen to study it (1) as an outgrowth of the specific historical situation which occasioned the writing of the memorials: the victory of the parlements in their dispute with the crown in 1763 and the king's request that they make constructive suggestions concerning the finances; (2) as an expression of those ideas which interested the judges most: their beliefs about political economy and their opinions of existing taxation and economic legislation; and (3) as part of a climate of economic opinion, evidence of the amount of mercantilist, physiocratic, and laissez-faire thinking current in the decade before the appearance of Adam Smith's *Wealth of Nations*. The main emphasis is thus on political economy and taxation, and especially on the former. Other ideas of the parlement, such as those about government and social classes, have been given a subordinate place in the organization of the book.

In carrying out this plan I have been greatly aided by Professor Charles W. Cole of Columbia University who has made many useful suggestions for improving the manuscript in its various stages, and in whose seminar I learned much about the history of economic ideas. I should also like to express my thanks to Professor Shepard B. Clough for his encouragement and for pertinent observations concerning the handling of the source materials; to Professors Jacques Barzun and Austin P. Evans for their criticisms of the manuscript; and to the Trustees of Columbia University for the Edward H. Perkins scholarships which made possible two years of graduate study.

PAUL H. BEIK.

COLUMBIA UNIVERSITY,
NOVEMBER, 1943.

CONTENTS

CHAPTER I

POSTWAR DIFFICULTIES FOR FRANCE; VICTORY FOR THE PARLEMENTS[1]

Tout ce que je vois jette les semences d'une révolution qui arrivera immanquablement, et dont je n'aurai pas le plaisir d'être témoin.

Voltaire, in 1764

To France the year 1763 brought peace but not harmony. The Seven Years War was ended, to be sure, but it had left behind the bitter awareness of defeat and of a lost empire. Within the ancient monarchy taxes were heavy and the government's finances were in a tangle that was none the less serious for being kept a secret. Fanned by philosophers and economists, public discussion of affairs of state was increasing. The sovereign courts of France, the parlements, were playing a dangerous game, attempting to increase their power by bidding for the support of the new public opinion. Unknowingly, these venerable courts were helping to dig their own graves, for by interfering constantly in the government's affairs they were weakening the very structure of the monarchy upon which they depended for their existence. The year 1789 was approaching, and with it oblivion for the parlements, but, like most men, the magistrates of France did not foresee their fate. For them the year 1763 ushered in a season of victory when long opposition to the king's ministers bore fruit and the parlements were finally invited to collaborate in the reformation of the French finances.

The response of one of the parlements to this invitation will be the concern of this book. From the labors of the Parlement of Provence there emerged a, set of documents containing a monumental evaluation of the French tax structure, observations on the condition of the treasury and, less extensively, on the state of society in the old régime, and an economic credo

1 Because of its frequent appearances, sometimes several times on a single page, the word "parlement" has not been italicized.

which casts some light on the political economy of an era in which the ascendency of mercantilism was being challenged by the doctrines of laissez-faire.

1. THE SORRY STATE OF THE FRENCH FINANCES

The sad story of France's empty treasury begins with the reign of Louis XIV, when the monarchy was at its height, and continues, through a century, into the years of the Great Revolution. Failure of the state's tax machinery to supply sufficient money for the expenses of government became most serious during the final years of the old régime, but to understand the difficulties which confronted Turgot, Necker, and Calonne it is necessary to examine the French finances of the period prior to the accession of the unfortunate Louis XVI. The reign of that king's predecessor and grandfather, Louis XV, is especially significant to a study of the financial causes of the revolution, for during that period certain popular notions concerning taxation and finance became embedded in the public mind; like the more frequently mentioned political ideas of Rousseau and Montesquieu, these notions were to prove embarrassing to the guardians of the monarchy during its last years. The year 1763, which marked the close of the expensive Seven Years War, furnishes a convenient window through which to view the unhealthy condition of the French finances during the reign of Louis XV.

To the officials in charge of taxation the Seven Years War was a long unhappy struggle to raise money for the support of military and naval operations. Despite France's undoubted wealth and power, the finances of Louis XV's government were not in condition for a sustained effort.[2] At the start of the war receipts were less than expenses, and as early as April, 1756, the deficit stood at over 67 million *livres*.[3] In order to

2 Charles Gomel, *Les causes financières de la révolution française* (Paris: Guillaumin, 1892), I, 5–6.

3 J.-J. Clamageran, *Histoire de l'impôt en France* (Paris, 1867–76), III, 323–325.

finance the war, the government attempted to collect as much money as possible by means of extraordinary taxes; such a policy was a natural outgrowth of eighteenth century conditions, for credit was limited and the income from ordinary taxes, which spared those best able to pay, was relatively small; the government, moreover, lacked the means of securing large loans, and repayment of those loans which were obtained had to be guaranteed by increases in taxation.[4] Extraordinary taxes were therefore collected, though not with ease, for public indignation ran high and the parlements, posing as champions of the people, delayed registration of the decrees. In July, 1756, for example, when the collection of a second *vingtième* was ordered,[5] the uproar which followed was raised by both parlements and public; numerous magistrates resigned from their posts, and in some localities justice was suspended for several months. Other and equally unpopular extraordinary taxes were ordered in 1759 by Controller General Silhouette in an attempt to increase the contributions of the privileged and rich. Privileges such as exemption from the salt tax were curtailed, taxes on luxury goods were increased, and a third *vingtième* was levied. These measures were so unpopular that the parlements registered them only after the king in September, 1759, had brought his power to bear by means of a *lit de justice*. Silhouette's tax measures having failed to check the state's headlong course toward bankruptcy, their author was dismissed from office in disgrace, and his name, once a signal for public applause, passed into the language as a synonym for shadowy emptiness. His successor to the office of Controller General,

4 Gomel, *op. cit.,* I, 9–10.

5 The *vingtième* was a tax which in theory should have amounted to one-twentieth of all incomes but which in practice amounted to less than one-twentieth, and was scarcely more than a tax on incomes from land. The *vingtième* grew out of a similar tax called the *dixième* (tenth). The *dixième* gave way to the first *vingtième* in 1749; thus the addition of another *vingtième* in 1756 meant a doubling of this tax. Later, from 1760 to 1763, there were three *vingtièmes*. See Marcel Marion, *Dictionnaire des institutions de la France au XVIIᵉ et XVIIIᵉ siècles* (Paris: Picard, 1923), p. 556.

Bertin, lasted until 1763. Although withdrawing the most unpopular of Silhouette's taxes, he managed to maintain the essence of his predecessor's program of taxing the privileged and rich; in 1760, for example, the third *vingtième* was restored, and indirect taxes collected by tax farmers were increased. Bertin supplemented these measures by borrowing heavily,[6] but in spite of borrowing and extraordinary taxes it proved impossible to pay for the war. Annual deficits of as much as 200,000,000 *livres* were not uncommon during the war years.[7]

The coming of peace in 1763 brought no conclusion to the government's financial worries, although the French nation enjoyed an increasing prosperity, punctuated, to be sure, by occasional economic crises.[8] Agriculture in particular suffered serious reverses in 1759, 1766–68, 1772–76 and 1785; in the last mentioned year occurred a serious drought which, followed by several years of poor harvests and an industrial depression, probably contributed to the outbreak of the revolution in 1789.[9] In general, however, the second half of the eighteenth century was for France a period of great economic expansion, characterized by an increased commerce, rising prices, and the beginnings of large capitalist industry.[10] Occasional economic crises might mean ruin for some and suffering for many, but the wealth of the nation as a whole was probably increasing. Despite the condition of the nation, however, the public finances of France were in a sorry state at the close of the Seven Years War. The national debt had mounted to the ominous figure of over 1,700,000,000 *livres*. Sums due at once amounted to 250,-

6 H. Carré, *Le règne de Louis XV, 1715–1774*, in E. Lavisse (ed.), *Histoire de France depuis les origines jusqu'à la révolution* (Paris: Hachette, 1909), pp. 361–365.

7 Gomel, *op. cit.*, I, 9–10.

8 Marcel Marion, *Histoire financière de la France depuis 1715* (Paris: Rousseau, 1914–1928), I, 243–245.

9 Henri Sée, *Histoire économique de la France. Le moyen âge et l'ancien régime* (Paris: Colin, 1939), pp. 212–213.

10 *Ibid.*, p. 401.

000,000 *livres*.[11] To make matters worse, current expenses of government were greater than revenues, with the result that there was an annual deficit (*déficit normal*) of about fifty million *livres*.[12]

With its finances in such poor condition, the government found the very fact of peace a source of embarrassment. Now, more than ever, it was difficult to justify before public opinion the continuation of chronic borrowing and extraordinary taxes.[13] It must be remembered that the people of France, and even the parlements, had been kept in ignorance of the true state of the public finances; they knew neither the extent of the debt nor the amount of current and wartime expenses, and could only guess at the ultimate destination of the revenues from the various taxes. What they did know, or thought they knew, was that their king had ample resources for the scattering of favors among his friends. From popular conceptions of life at Versailles it was but a step to the conclusion that the government's income, if properly managed, was large enough for its needs. The people had been promised, moreover, that the extraordinary wartime taxes would end with the war. With the arrival of peace, the government therefore found itself in the difficult position of having to demand continued sacrifices of a people who saw no reason for them. The only alternative was to tell the truth about the finances, and Louis XV's ministers did not choose to take this step.[14]

2. Awakened Interest in Political Economy

The French public in the period following the Seven Years War was becoming less and less inclined to allow political and economic developments within the monarchy to pass unnoticed. As the eighteenth century advanced the force of public opinion

11 Carré, *op. cit.,* pp. 365–366.
12 Marion, *Histoire financière,* I, 213; Gomel, *op. cit.,* I, vi.
13 Marion, *Histoire financière,* I, 213.
14 Gomel, *op. cit.,* I, vi.

in France grew increasingly greater, and came to be respected
by administrators and courtiers alike. Necker, the most popular
of Louis XVI's ministers, considered it a king ". . . at whose
voice all tremble and obey." And Necker was not alone in holding this view, for the court at Versailles, which in the seventeenth century had been aped by the people of Paris, had at last
begun to show concern over the opinions which its actions
aroused in that city.[15] Although a great part of the population
still took no interest in public affairs, there was an increasing
number of articulate people prepared to bestow their favor or
disfavor upon the ideas and events of their time. In France at
the close of the Seven Years War there were many reasons for
public dissatisfaction. Not only was taxation heavy and commerce disarranged, but to a certain extent these sacrifices were
in vain, for the nation had been defeated in war, her shipping
largely destroyed, and most of her colonies seized by a foreign
power. To many people the irresponsible gaiety of the court at
Versailles appeared unsuitable at such a time and insulting to
the public distress. By 1763 the reputation of Louis XV, who
had been forgiven so often, was damaged almost beyond repair, and satirical songs and verses at his expense were passing
along the streets. Many minds were agitated and restless, some
of them excited by the ideas of the "philosophers", who attacked church and nobles and talked of equality; others turned
their attention toward problems of social organization. Certainly there was a demand for solutions to the varied problems
faced by the monarchy.[16]

Much of the awakened public interest found an outlet in discussions of political economy, a subject which is believed by
some historians to have had its first scientific beginnings in this
period.[17] Whether scientific or not, thought on economic ques-

15 Louis Ducros, *French Society in the Eighteenth Century,* translated by
W. de Geijer (London: Bell and Sons, 1926), pp. 313–314.

16 Gomel, op. cit., I, iv–v, 13–14.

17 The upholders of this view contend that the writings of the physiocrats,
which began to appear in the 1750's, were the first scientific studies of po-

tions took great steps forward in the decades between 1750 and the French Revolution, and this period is characterized by the number and variety of its writings. In the France of that day the complex of economic ideas and practices known as mercantilism was still strong. Regulation of economic life by the state was still widespread; in industry, for example, it was necessary to keep track of numerous laws regulating dimensions of goods, quality of raw materials, and methods of construction, and to beware of periodic inspections by government agents. Disobedience to the rules sometimes meant severe penalties. Royal manufactures, in many cases, still enjoyed their privileges.[18] Craft guilds continued to exist, and even to increase in number, and additional sets of regulations for industry continued to be made as late as the 1780's.[19]

In the field of economic thought, moreover, there were still defenders of mercantilism, and it is safe to say that the writings of at least three of these men were influential in the decade which followed the Seven Years War. François Mélon (*Essai politique sur le commerce,* 1731) and a certain Dutot (*Réflexions politiques sur les finances et le commerce,* 1738) did their writing during the first half of the century. François Véron de Forbonnais wrote during the second half of the century and was more influential during that period than his predecessors. Forbonnais lived until 1800, but of his many writings the best known were probably his early ones: *Elémens du commerce* (2 Vols., 1754); the monumental *Recherches et considérations sur les finances de la France de 1590 à 1720* (4 Vols., 1758–59), which is still the best printed source of information con-

litical economy. They base their claim upon the fact that the physiocrats were believers in natural economic laws, whereas earlier economists such as the mercantilists were pragmatic in their approach to political economy. But much of the physiocratic reasoning was deductive and *apriori,* while many mercantilists were scientific at least in the sense that their thinking was empirical.

18 Carré, *op. cit.,* pp. 365–366.

19 Eli F. Heckscher, *Mercantilism,* translated by Mendel Shapiro (London: Allen and Unwin, 1935), I, 215–216.

cerning taxation in the old régime; and *Principes et observations économiques* (2 Vols., 1767).[20] By some authorities, Mélon, Dutot, and Forbonnais have been called neo-mercantilists because their emphasis was less on the accumulation of money than on its use as a means of acquiring wealth in the form of actual goods.[21] The distinction may or may not be a significant one; for the purposes of this study it is enough to note that Mélon, Dutot, and Forbonnais, by recommending the strengthening of the state by such positive actions as encouragement of economic self-sufficiency and productivity, were continuing the mercantilist traditions of Colbert.

Mélon, for example, believed that the strength of a state depended on its ability to supply itself with essential goods. Money, though extremely useful, was merely a means to this end. The enlightened legislator would therefore provide for the state's needs in the order of their importance: first, the production of vital necessities such as grain; second, population increase and the efficient use of the people in the production of goods; third, an adequate supply of money, whether metallic or paper, to serve as a medium of exchange and aid in the commercial circulation of goods. The state could become powerful by being as self-sufficient as possible. Such a policy, to be sure, would decrease commerce with other nations, but the self-sufficient state could benefit by using its commerce as a political weapon; rival states could be ruined by embargoes and their populations forced to emigrate; commerce could be maintained with weak or friendly states.[22] Mélon recognized that the increase or decrease of the nominal value of gold and silver coins could be a field for the operation of the state's economic policies,

20 René Gonnard, *Histoire des doctrines économiques* (Paris: Librairie Valois, 1921–22), I, 246. See also Paul Harsin, *Les doctrines monétaires et financières en France du XVIe au XVIIIe siècle* (Paris: Félix Alcan, 1928), p. 249.

21 Gonnard, *op. cit.,* I, 248.

22 François Mélon, *Essai politique sur le commerce,* reprinted in Eugène Daire (ed.), *Economistes financiers du XVIIIe siècle* (Paris: Guillaumin et Cie, 1851), pp. 666, 668–669.

and it was this doctrine which occasioned the writing of Dutot's *Réflexions politiques sur les finances et le commerce,* in which the author insisted that the nominal value of money should be kept constant lest commerce be disorganized.[23]

In the main, however, Dutot approved of Mélon's economic ideas and subscribed to the mercantilist doctrines. Like Mélon, he regarded money as a medium of exchange and a measure of value, and true wealth as the products of the earth and of industry. It was the duty of those in power to protect the state's interests by positive actions. Dutot believed that if the productivity of agriculture and the output of manufactures were increased the nation's commerce would be improved. Commerce in its turn should be carefully managed so that the state as well as the individuals involved would profit. The nation's surplus goods could be sold to foreigners and those necessities which it was impossible to produce at home could be imported. It was especially important that a favorable balance of trade be maintained in order that the nation might be assured an adequate supply of money. For Dutot the extent of a nation's commerce was a measure of its wealth and power; commerce should therefore be among the first considerations of an enlightened administration.[24]

Forbonnais, who served for a time as adviser to the unfortunate Controller General Silhouette, was perhaps the best-known mercantilist writer at the close of the Seven Years War. He believed that a nation could have three kinds of wealth, that produced by nature, the artificial wealth manufactured by man, and a "conventional" wealth, which consisted of metals used as a medium of exchange and a measure of value.[25] The real wealth of a state was its stock of useful things produced by na-

---

23 Dutot, *Réflexions politiques sur les finances et le commerce,* reprinted in Eugène Daire (ed.), *Economistes financiers du XVIIIᵉ siècle* (Paris: Guillaumin et Cie, 1851), pp. 786–787.

24 *Ibid.,* pp. 899–901.

25 François Véron de Forbonnais, *Elemens du commerce* (Leyden: 1754), I, 11.

ture and the arts and represented in everyday life by the conventional wealth known as money.[26] But those in charge of strengthening the economic position of a state should overlook neither real nor conventional wealth. With regard to its real wealth a strong state should be as self-sufficient as possible, and should even aim at the production of a surplus to be exported to other lands.[27] If possible, a favorable balance of trade should be obtained so that the state's supply of money or conventional wealth would be increased. Such an increase was to be desired not for the sake of the money itself but because it would stimulate production of real wealth by lowering interest rates, increasing the circulation of goods and money, and providing subsistence for a greater number of people. Thus the state with the most favorable balance of trade could be expected to be the most powerful.[28] The mercantilist views of Forbonnais and his predecessors were to some extent upheld by such critics of the physiocrats as Ferdinando Galiani, whose *Dialogues sur le commerce des blés* appeared in 1770, Voltaire in the field of letters, and Necker in his administration of the French finances.[29] But though mercantilism was to hold its influence over statesmen and administrators for some time to come, it is probably safe to say that from the 1750's on it was losing its predominance in the field of economic thought.[30]

In the decade which followed the Seven Years War the physiocrats were the dominant school of writers on economics. By no means agreed in all of their views, these men may be said to have constituted a "school" only because of similarities in the broad outlines of their thought. Earliest and most important in the group was Dr. Quesnay, court doctor of Louis XV, whose articles *Les grains* and *Les fermiers,* appearing in the *Grande encyclopédie* in 1756 and 1757, were his first writ-

26 *Ibid.,* II, 68.
27 *Ibid.,* I, 47.
28 *Ibid.,* I, 70–72, 74, 77–78; II, 125.
29 Gonnard, *op. cit.,* I, 246.
30 *Ibid.,* I, 290.

ings on economic subjects. Quesnay's *Tableau économique,* published in 1758, proved to be the classical demonstration of physiocratic doctrines. His ideas were further revealed in 1760 with the appearance of the *Maximes générales du gouvernement économique d'un royaume agricole.* Quesnay's influence on the economic thought of his day was considerably widened by the work of his disciples, one of whom was the Marquis de Mirabeau, father of the famous orator of the revolution. After writing *L'ami des hommes,* which appeared in 1758 and which was not physiocratic in its outlook, Mirabeau was won over to physiocracy, to the literature of which he added two famous books, *La théorie de l'impôt* (1760) and *La philosophie rurale* (1763). Other physiocratic writers were Mercier de la Rivière, whose *L'ordre naturel et essentiel des sociétés politiques* was published in 1767, and Dupont de Nemours, who gave the movement its name in his *Physiocratie, ou constitution essentielle du gouvernement le plus avantageux au genre humain* (1768). "Physiocracy" meant "rule of nature". Aided by the work of Dupont, Le Trosne, Abbé Baudeau, and others, the ideas of the *économistes,* as the physiocrats were at first called, received widespread attention in the years which followed the Seven Years War. The high point of physiocratic influence was reached in the 1760's, and after 1770 both the "school" of economists and the system of thought began to dissolve.[31]

The main outlines of physiocratic thought may be summed up briefly if attention is devoted to the ideas which the members of the group held in common rather than to the numerous differences of emphasis and opinion which existed among them. Fundamental to the physiocratic doctrines was a belief in the existence of a "natural order", the laws of which applied to human society as well as to the inorganic parts of nature. By careful study men could discover these laws, and even measure their workings by means of mathematics, in order that a better

31 Georges Weulersse, *Le mouvement physiocratique en France (de 1756 à 1770).* (Paris: Félix Alcan, 1910), I, 241.

society, one in harmony with the natural order, might be built.[32] Such a society would be based on the firm foundations of property rights and liberty; property rights were inviolable, and liberty could be counted upon to serve the best interests of society as well as those of individuals seeking their own betterment.[33] Government, it followed, would have little to do beyond guarding the natural order—for men could recognize the laws but not make them—, educating the people, and performing a few necessary public works.[34] But though its activities might be limited, government should have complete authority. Democratic or parliamentary forms could not be tolerated, for it was essential that the king be a despot, if only in the sense that an orchestra leader is despotic when he insists that his musicians strike no false notes. The natural order, like the laws governing music, was not a matter subject to compromise, and the only possible freedom lay in recognition of this fact.[35]

While searching for the natural order in the production and consumption of wealth, the physiocrats arrived at the conclusion that agriculture was the only truly productive calling; indeed, this proposition became the cornerstone of their whole system.[36] Agriculture alone produced a net product, that is, a net amount of new wealth remaining after all expenses of production had been paid. Other forms of endeavor were sterile; commerce merely moved things from place to place, and manufacturing simply combined or modified materials already produced. Industry and commerce were necessary and useful, of course, but with the possible exception of fishing and mining, agriculture was the only form of endeavor by which man, with the collaboration of nature, could add to his store of wealth.[37] Since they produced no new wealth of their own, people en-

32 *Ibid.*, II, 120–122.

33 *Ibid.*, II, 93–95.

34 *Ibid.*, I, 516; II, 36–37, 66.

35 *Ibid.*, II, 48–49, 55–58.

36 *Ibid.*, I, 243–244.

37 *Ibid.*, I, 261–262, 274–275, 280, 305.

gaged in industry, commerce, banking, and even the professions could remain alive only by obtaining some of the wealth
produced by agriculture; thus as people exchanged goods and
services wealth circulated among the various classes of society,
productive and non-productive alike.[38] In order that the net
agricultural product might be sufficient for the needs of everyone, it was essential that the soil be tilled as efficiently as possible. The physiocrats therefore entertained full sympathy for
the ideas on scientific farming which were even then helping to
bring about the eighteenth century "agricultural revolution".
They favored large holdings of land (*la grande culture*), believing this system to be the most efficient both for the working
of the land and for the accumulation of the large amounts of
capital so necessary to scientific agriculture. By means of increased knowledge, better tools, and careful management, large
scale agriculture would be best able to produce the surpluses
which alone added to the wealth of mankind.[39]

It is not surprising that the physiocrats, with their confidence
in natural laws, made proposals which, if accepted, would have
abolished many of the practices of the old régime. Their belief
in freedom, a natural corollary to their respect for property, led
them far along the road toward laissez-faire. Men should be
free to choose whatever form of labor or business enterprise
appealed to them, for the sum total of many individual quests
for happiness or success would be the good of society. Therefore let the farmer plant whatever pleased him and the manufacturer work without fear of restrictions. Free competition
would be regulation enough. Let commerce flow where it would,
unhindered by barriers inside or at the borders of the kingdom.
Enough had been heard of that myth, the favorable balance of
trade; a nation could not undersell its rivals without lowering
the price of provisions and raw materials and thus favoring the
sterile commercial and manufacturing classes at the expense of
the productive agriculturists; wise statesmanship would rather

38 *Ibid.*, I, 268–269.
39 *Ibid.*, I, 333, 350.

remove all barriers to trade and let the prices of foodstuffs and other materials rise to their natural levels, thus benefiting their producers.[40] In matters of taxation the physiocrats believed in a single direct tax on the revenues from land. Only the proprietors should pay, for they were the only ones who received the net product, or newly produced wealth; rent-paying tenants could not be taxed without decreasing production, for they received only enough wealth to pay their expenses; the sterile classes engaged in industry and commerce could pay taxes only by raising prices and passing the burden on to the agriculturists; indirect taxes were wasteful because of the great expenses of collection. There remained one rational solution, that of going directly to the source of new wealth by a simple direct tax to be paid by the proprietors of the land.[41] By such reasoning, the physiocrats attacked existing taxes, import and export duties, river tolls and provincial *douanes,* restrictions on industry and agriculture, craft guilds, and indeed almost the whole body of existing economic legislation. Their attempts to plan a society in harmony with the natural order were leading them toward the kind of thinking which has usually been called "laissez-faire" or "economic liberalism".[42]

The physiocrats, however, were by no means alone in their use of liberal concepts during the period before Adam Smith's *Wealth of Nations* assumed its leadership in this field. There were other thinkers whose ideas contained a good deal of liberalism, and these men, who belonged to no particular school, are difficult to classify and indeed have been variously termed mercantilists, liberals, and physiocrats. If examples of economic liberalism are sought only among French thinkers, it is possible to find Pierre de Boisguilbert, as early as the first decade

---

40 *Ibid.,* II, 17–20; I, 539–542.

41 *Ibid.,* I, 468–470.

42 "Liberalism," for example, is the term used by Professor Heckscher to describe the cluster of ideas which gradually replaced mercantilism. Thus laissez-faire replaced state intervention, while individualism rather than *raison d'état* became the basis of economic policy. Heckscher, *op. cit.,* I, 469.

of the eighteenth century, writing that it was necessary "only to
let nature act in matters pertaining to grains as one does in the
case of fountains." [43] Students of Boisguilbert have disagreed
over the question whether he was essentially a mercantilist or a
liberal precursor of Adam Smith, but there is at any rate some
reason for believing that Boisguilbert was the first to use the
now famous phrase "laissez-faire" when referring to the activities of nature.[44] In its more modern sense of allowing individuals to pursue their private interests with a minimum of
government intervention, the phrase laissez-faire was probably
used for the first time by the Marquis d'Argenson (1694–
1757), who in addition to his activities as a student of government and as the writer of a journal which has been of tremendous value to students of the eighteenth century, found time to
formulate doctrines in the field of political economy. D'Argenson believed that the principle of liberty or laissez-faire should
to a large extent be applied to agriculture, industry, and commerce, and indeed to most matters of political economy.[45]

In the world of practicality considerable impetus toward economic liberalism was given by Vincent de Gournay, a promi-
nent business man who became Intendant of Commerce, and
whose personality and ideas, during the 1750's, won him numerous disciples, the most distinguished of whom was Turgot.
Gournay, like many of his contemporaries, believed that individuals, if allowed to pursue their private interests, would serve
the general welfare. He believed that commerce was governed
by natural laws which were everywhere the same, and that no
good could come from excessive interference with these laws
by means of monopolies and government regulation. Labor,
money, and materials should therefore be enabled to circulate

43 Pierre de Boisguilbert, *Traité de la nature, culture, commerce et intérêt
des grains,* reprinted in Eugène Daire (ed.), *op. cit.,* p. 363.

44 Hazel Van Dyke Roberts, *Boisguilbert, Economist of the Reign of
Louis XIV* (New York: Columbia University Press, 1935), p. 249.

45 André Alem, *Le Marquis d'Argenson et l'économie politique au début
du XVIIIe siècle* (Paris: Rousseau, 1900), pp. 1, 81, 175–176.

under conditions which would allow a large degree of freedom and competition.[46] Under Gournay's leadership administrative practices in France were gradually modified in the direction of economic liberty. Manufacturers were allowed to produce a greater variety of products and to follow the styles, and visits by government inspectors began to resemble formalities. Because of his influence on both thought and practice, Gournay is sometimes considered by historians to be the head of a "commercial school" of economists characterized by their demands for greater freedom for commerce and industry and by their opposition to such monopolies as the India Company.[47] By some historians, however, Gournay and the other administrators with liberal inclinations have been classified as examples of a "reformed mercantilism."[48]

Another eighteenth century economist who may perhaps be classified as a mercantilist with liberal tendencies was Richard Cantillon, a man of Irish parentage who established himself as a banker in Paris in 1716. After predicting the failure of John Law's Mississippi scheme, Cantillon for his personal safety had to leave France, but he retained his business connections in Paris and managed to accumulate a fortune by speculating for the fall of Mississippi shares. At his death in 1733 or 1734 he left behind him a manuscript work entitled *Essai sur la nature du commerce en général* which appeared, without the author's name, in 1755 and which has caused him to be termed a mercantilist by some, and by others a liberal precursor of the physiocrats. Cantillon defined wealth as the nourishment, commodities, and good things of life which had their source in the earth and were given their form by labor. The intrinsic value of an object was thus determined by the earth and by the labor entering into its creation.[49] In addition to these definitions of

46 G. Schelle, *Vincent de Gournay* (Paris, Guillaumin, 1897), pp. 198–200, 203–205.

47 Carré, *op. cit.*, pp. 345–350.

48 Heckscher, *op. cit.*, I, 213–214.

49 Richard Cantillon, *Essai sur la nature du commerce en général*, reprinted for Harvard University (Boston: George H. Ellis, 1892), pp. 1–2, 33.

wealth and value, Cantillon distinguished what he chose to call the "comparative wealth" of states, which consisted of the quantities of money they possessed, and which could be increased by the development of a favorable balance of trade.[50] A nation which succeeded in accumulating a large supply of money would be powerful for a time; consumption of goods would increase and prices would rise. Eventually, however, these very conditions of prosperity would lead to laziness at home and heightened competition abroad, and equality between the fortunate nation and its neighbors would tend to be reestablished. Cantillon believed that a wise administration could and should take action to prolong the nation's enjoyment of "comparative wealth" and to guide it back to economic supremacy again when the inevitable decadence had set in.[51] Thus in his concept of alternating periods of supremacy and decline in "comparative wealth", arising out of the nature of commerce, and in his general definition of wealth, Cantillon perhaps anticipated Hume and Smith as well as some elements of physiocracy, while in his desire for positive government intervention in economic affairs he remained essentially mercantilist.

Even more closely related to the physiocrats both in time and in his beliefs was Turgot, who, while resembling the physiocrats in many respects, yet managed to maintain a certain independence and even in some ways to resemble Adam Smith. Although he began writing long before the birth of physiocracy, Turgot's most important work, *Réflexions sur la formation et la distribution des richesses,* was written in 1766, in the decade when Quesnay and his followers were enjoying their greatest influence. As Intendant of Limoges and as a minister of Louis XVI, Turgot was able to supplement his thinking on economic matters with practical experience in affairs of state. Like the physiocrats, in whose ideas he was deeply interested, he believed that people who tilled the soil produced a surplus of wealth for which those engaged in other

50 *Ibid.*, p. 244.
51 *Ibid.*, pp. 244–246, 256–257.

professions exchanged their labor in order that they might
live.[52] To both Gournay and Quesnay Turgot acknowledged an
intellectual debt, and like them, he desired free competition,
liberty for commerce, and the abolition of restrictions on industry.[53] In three respects, however, the thought of Turgot
seems to resemble that of Adam Smith more than that of
Quesnay and the physiocrats. While terming the agriculturists
a productive class, he nevertheless avoided the rather harsh
adjective "sterile" when dealing with men engaged in commerce and industry; instead, he chose the term "stipendiary"
(*stipendiée*), and although all authorities do not agree concerning Turgot's intentions, it is possible to assume that he
meant to assign to these classes a more important role than
that granted them by the physiocrats.[54] Of greater importance
is Turgot's definition of value as an expression of the varying
esteem with which men, conscious of their needs and desires,
regard nature's goods;[55] his awareness of the subjective psychological quality which much later came to be known as utility marks Turgot off from the physiocrats. Finally, instead of
criticizing bankers and banking as did most of Quesnay's followers, Turgot defended the taking of interest. Capital, he believed, was just as necessary to commerce and industry as to
agriculture, and there was no essential difference between selling the use of money and selling the use of land.[56] Thus in
many respects the doctrines of Turgot resemble those of Adam

52 Turgot, *Réflexions sur la formation et la distribution des richesses,* in
Oeuvres de Turgot, edited by Eugène Daire (Paris: Guillaumin, 1844), Section V, pp. 9–10.

53 Douglas Dakin, *Turgot and the ancien régime in France* (London:
Methuen and Co., 1939), pp. 302–303.

54 Turgot, *Réflexions sur la formation et la distribution des richesses,* in
Oeuvres de Turgot, edited by Eugène Daire (Paris: Guillaumin, 1844), Section VIII, pp. 11–12.

55 Turgot, *Valeurs et monnaies,* in *Oeuvres de Turgot,* edited by Eugène
Daire (Paris: Guillaumin, 1844), p. 80.

56 Turgot, *Réflexions, op. cit.,* Sections LXVIII–LXIX, LXXL–LXXIV,
pp. 45–47.

Smith as well as those of the physiocrats, and indeed some authorities have suggested that Smith copied from Turgot, while others have contended that Turgot copied from Smith.[57]

One final example, the philosopher Condillac, will illustrate how far the cause of economic liberalism had advanced in France by 1776, the year when Adam Smith's classic expression of liberalism, the *Wealth of Nations,* appeared. In that same year Condillac, who already had a reputation as a philosopher, published a little book called *Le Commerce et le gouvernement considérés relativement l'un à l'autre,* in which he urged the necessity for economic freedom, especially in commercial matters.[58] Condillac's doctrines had much in common with those of his better known contemporary, Smith. His concept of value was based on the subjective psychological factor of utility, which varied from person to person, but he recognized also that supply, as well as demand, played a part in determining value, since the utility of an object depended in part upon people's opinions concerning its abundance or scarcity.[59] Condillac's concept of value enabled him to declare that commerce was productive, for because of the subjective nature of value it was possible for both parties in a commercial transaction to benefit, each receiving more utility than he gave.[60] The magic of utility, by a similar process, also rendered manufacturing truly productive. Thus, although admitting that the earth was the original source of all goods, Condillac was able to conclude that farmers, merchants and artisans all added to the supply of available wealth.[61]

Despite the numerous disagreements of the economists, it is possible to sum up, roughly, the main trends in political economy in the decade following the Seven Years War. In the first

57 Dakin, *op. cit.,* p. 346, note 64.

58 Etienne de Condillac, *Le commerce et le gouvernement considérés relativement l'un à l'autre* (Amsterdam, 1776), pp. 583–584.

59 *Ibid.,* pp. 11–14.

60 *Ibid.,* p. 55.

61 *Ibid.,* pp. 53, 58–59, 66.

place, mercantilism was still very much alive, especially in the practices of the administrators. Secondly, there was in the thought of the period a decided tendency toward economic liberalism, a tendency which for the most part took the form of physiocracy. But it would be a serious mistake to suppose that all liberal economists in the France of this period were physiocrats, for there was also a shift toward liberal beliefs on the part of a good many economists and men of affairs who belonged to no particular school and who cannot be classified without injustice to the variety of their thought.

3. Awakened Interest in Taxation and Finance

Associated with the problems of political economy in the period during and after the Seven Years War, but more specific in nature and far more embarrassing to the government, was an increased public interest in France's taxes and in the condition of her treasury. At a time when the prosecution of an unsuccessful war had necessitated unusual sacrifices in the form of extraordinary taxes, it was natural that people's attention should turn to the manner in which their money was being collected and spent. The writings of such able economists as Turgot and Forbonnais naturally added to public discussion by calling attention to injustices in the existing taxes,[62] but in addition to economic works of a general nature there appeared a great many pamphlets which were aimed at a wider audience and which were bold in their demands for fiscal reform. Although often poor in quality, intemperate in language, and full of impractical proposals, this pamphlet literature testified to the existence of a fairly general dissatisfaction with the taxes of the old régime. Already imperiled by an abundance of criticism, the position of the king's ministers was made still more difficult by the actions of the parlements, which, though often unable to defeat legislation outright, at least managed to spread their favorite maxims among the upper classes and the bour-

62 Gomel, *op. cit.*, I, iv–v.

geoisie, perhaps aided by the philosophical and critical spirit of the age. It was a great handicap for the government to have its fiscal system publicly condemned by eminently respectable bodies which claimed to speak in the name of the taxpayers.[63] Louis XV's ministers were not blind to the threat of so much discussion, and by a declaration issued in March, 1764, attempted to curtail the output of writings about financial reform. Like so many other laws of the old régime, however, this one was disobeyed, and the pamphlets about taxation continued to appear.[64]

Before offering specific examples of the pamphlet material in this great tax debate, it will perhaps be appropriate to summarize the principal ideas on taxation which were being discussed in this period during and after the Seven Years War.[65] Most pamphlets of the day complained of inequality in taxation. The *taille, capitation,* and *vingtièmes* were said to be assessed in too arbitrary a manner; the *corvée* was too heavy and the *gabelle* inhumane; taxes on consumption were too numerous and heavy, and tolls on commerce within France destructive of business, while an excessive number of arbitrary and unenlightened rules shackled industry.[66] The Farmers General, a group of financiers to whom collection of many of the indirect taxes

63 *Ibid.,* I, 24–25. This sort of criticism was, in the long run, to play an important part in bringing about the downfall of the monarchy. To understand this state of affairs, it is sufficient to recall Necker's famous *Compte rendu* of 1781, which may serve as an illustration of the position into which the government tended to be driven by public criticism. Necker's *Compte rendu* may be regarded as both a cause and an effect of public opinion. It was issued for two chief reasons: to shed a favorable light on its author's administration, and to keep up the government's credit. Both of these reasons reflect a fear of public opinion, but the *Compte rendu* only made matters worse by filling parlements and public with illusions about the adequacy of the revenues. Naturally, they continued to oppose increases in taxation, and when the government was finally forced by its empty treasury to reveal the true state of affairs, the people were all the more enraged and demanded control of the finances for themselves. See Gomel, I, xxvi–xxviii.

64 Carré, *op. cit.,* p. 368.

65 Of the ideas described here, some were of course more popular than others, but it is safe to say that all were fairly widespread.

66 Gomel, *op. cit.,* I, iv–viii, 23–24.

was "farmed out", were decidedly unpopular.[67] Most economists held that the treasury was already receiving as large an income as the nation could afford to pay, and insisted that there be no further increase in taxes so notoriously vicious. This idea, by dint of much repetition, was spread far and wide, even among people who did not as a rule read either the works of the economists or the popular pamphlets about taxation; it was to be given a measure of official sanction in 1774 when Turgot, on becoming minister, informed Louis XVI that any increase in the taxes was out of the question.[68]

There were, of course, numerous suggestions for reform, and it is with quickened interest that the historian discovers that most of the writers who discussed this problem felt that a successful reform of the finances would have to be based on a complete overhauling of the whole of French society. Such talk had an ominous ring which was not overlooked by Voltaire, who on April 2, 1764 made his famous prediction of revolution: "Everywhere I see being sown the seeds of a revolution which will arrive without fail, and which I shall not have the pleasure to witness." [69] It must be remembered, moreover, that the people of France, and even the reputable economists and the parlements, had been kept in ignorance of the true condition of the nation's finances, and that potential reformers could only guess at the magnitude of the problems which their suggestions were designed to solve. In view of this fact it is not surprising that there was a widespread demand that the burdens of taxation upon the people be considerably lightened. Other popular suggestions for reform were that the privileged orders, as well as the third estate, be made to pay their share of the taxes, that there be internal and to some extent external freedom of trade, and that taxes and regulations harmful to industry be abolished.[70] The notion that collection could be

67 Marion, *op. cit.*, I, 222.
68 Gomel, *op. cit.*, I, xvii–xviii.
69 Carré, *op. cit.*, p. 368.
70 Gomel, *op. cit.*, I, iv–vi.

greatly simplified by means of a single tax also enjoyed considerable popularity; the physiocrats were not alone in recommending this reform, and it is possible that fundamental economic changes in the second half of the eighteenth century may have contributed to the vogue for a single tax on land, for rents and prices were rising while the real profits from agriculture remained more or less stationary; thus it appeared that the landed proprietors rather than the tillers of the soil were the beneficiaries of the rise in prices.[71] It should be noted, however, that the idea of a single tax, though it enjoyed its greatest popularity after 1750, was by that time far from new. As early as 1695 the economist Boisguilbert, in his *Détail de la France,* had suggested the possibility of some form of single tax.[72] In 1707 appeared Vauban's *Projet d'une dixme royale,* a book largely devoted to the author's proposal that a single tax "on all the fruits of the earth . . . and on everything which produces income for men" be used instead of the traditional sources of revenue.[73]

Of the many pamphlets which spread these various ideas about taxation in the second half of the eighteenth century several attracted so much attention that they deserve special mention as outstanding examples of their kind. One of the physiocrats mentioned above, who indeed had been converted to their doctrines by Quesnay himself, was the Marquis de Mirabeau. Perhaps hoping to become a minister, Mirabeau in 1761 judged the moment ripe for an attack on France's old system of taxes. In his *Théorie de l'impôt* he denounced the existing taxes, especially the indirect ones and those on consumption,

71 C.–E. Labrousse, *Esquisse du mouvement des prix et des revenus en France au XVIIIe siècle* (Paris: Dalloz, 1932), pp. 626–627. This suggestion, made by Labrousse, does not account for the existence of proposals for a single tax other than that on the incomes from landed property.

72 Roberts, *op. cit.,* p. 149.

73 Vauban, *Projet d'une dixme royale,* in G. Pirou and F. Simiand (eds.), *Collection des principaux économistes* (Paris: Alcan, 1933), p. 13.

and called for the abolition of tax farming.[74] Besides the assault on the tax farmers, which proved very popular, Mirabeau in this pamphlet attracted attention by other statements pleasing to the public. On the grounds that the unlimited power to tax was a threat to property rights, upon which society was founded, and a long step toward despotism, he denied that the crown possessed that power, and called for the assembling of provincial estates in order that the people might check unfair assessment and wasteful collection of the taxes.[75] Mirabeau's solution to the problems of taxation was the physiocratic one of a tax on land (*impôt territorial*).[76] Such a tax, levied on the net product produced by agriculture, would eventually yield the bulk of the nation's revenue; for though the yield of the tax would at first be small, the reform of the existing irrational financial structure would in time allow a great increase in the net product upon which the land tax was to be based. Meanwhile the needs of the government could be met by a tax on rents (*loyers*) and by some form of levy on individuals (*capitation personnelle*).[77] Mirabeau, jailed and then exiled for the expression of these opinions, nevertheless enjoyed the knowledge that his pamphlet was a huge success.[78]

Another successful pamphlet, advocating in a different way the panacea of a single tax, was Roussel de la Tour's *La richesse de l'état,* which appeared in 1763. Unlike Mirabeau and the physiocrats, Roussel de la Tour did not propose an attempt to tax the net product of the land but turned instead to a *capitation,* or tax on households. With a few exceptions, all other taxes could be swept away. In their place would be levied the *capitation,* graduated according to fortunes. All heads of families were to be divided into twenty classes according to

---

74 The Marquis de Mirabeau, *Théorie de l'impôt* (1761), pp. 115–116, 353–356, 389.

75 *Ibid.,* pp. 125, 137, 362, 400, 402.

76 *Ibid.,* p. 390.

77 *Ibid.,* pp. 391–397.

78 Marion, *op. cit.,* pp. 201–203.

their incomes, and the tax was to vary from three *livres* for those in the lowest class to 730 *livres* for those in the highest. This system, declared the author, would not only decrease expenses of collection but would greatly increase the revenues of the king. Like a good magistrate—for he was a *conseiller* of the Parlement of Paris—Roussel de la Tour assumed that all disputes over the workings of the system would be settled before the courts, after the twenty classes of taxpayers had been organized by the citizens themselves.[79] His little pamphlet provoked the writing of a host of replies, another proof of the public interest in fiscal reform.[80]

A third very successful pamphlet, and one which also proposed a single tax as a solution to the government's financial difficulties, was written by a lawyer named Darigrand, a disgruntled ex-employee of the tax farmers who became aroused by attempts to defend them against the attacks of the parlements.[81] Darigrand hastened to join the attack on the tax farmers and produced, in 1763, a pamphlet the title of which left no doubt about the author's opinions; it was called *L'anti-financier, ou relevé de quelques-unes des malversations dont se rendent journellement coupables les Fermiers-Généraux, et les vexations qu'ils commettent dans les provinces.* He condemned the existing system of taxation for its obscurity and arbitrary nature, claiming that it encouraged fraud and evasion, built great financial fortunes, and harmed the nation's economy to the extent of four times the value of the income received by the king. Throughout his pamphlet Darigrand defended Roussel de la Tour's *La richesse de l'état* and contended that in view of the disastrous effects of the existing financial system a single tax would be a decided improvement. He believed that the single

79 Roussel de la Tour, *La richesse de l'état* (1763), pp. 4-7, 27-28. The *capitation,* of course, was not a new idea. This tax on families had existed, in its modern form, since 1695. Although supposed in theory to reach everyone, it rested very lightly on the privileged classes.

80 Gomel, *op. cit.,* I, 24.

81 Marion, *op. cit.,* p. 221.

tax could be based on the *taille* and the *capitation,* thus reaching incomes from land and those from other sources as well, and like Roussel de la Tour he wanted participation by the citizens themselves in the levying of the taxes, with disputes settled before the ordinary courts.[82]

These pamphlets attacking the existing financial system did not, to be sure, have the field entirely to themselves but met at least some opposition. There was, for example, the *Réponse à l'anti-financier,* a pamphlet which ridiculed the single tax, and which was probably inspired by the ministry. A writer named Navau, in his *Financier citoyen* (1757), boasted of the spirit of good faith with which the Farmers General performed their services to the state. There is, indeed, some reason for believing that the tax farmers of the late eighteenth century were more moderate in their profit taking than those of an earlier era, but this virtue, if it existed, went unnoticed by the French public of the period, and the Farmers General continued to be unpopular. Despite all opposition, demands for financial reform, and especially for a single tax, continued to be made. Seductive in its simplicity, the single tax also offered an opportunity for striking a blow at tax farmers and financiers, and like many of the proposals for financial reform at the close of the Seven Years War it appeared to call for no immediate sacrifices.[83]

4. The Claims of the Parlements

Troubled by lack of funds and by widespread public discussion of political economy in general and of public finances in particular, the French monarchy at the close of the Seven Years War was further embarrassed by the actions of its own parlements, which, posing as spokesmen and defenders of the people, tended to make the collection of taxes more difficult and

82 Darigrand, *L'anti-financier, ou relevé de quelques-unes des malversations dont se rendent journellement coupables les Fermiers-Généraux, et des vexations qu'ils commettent dans les provinces* (Amsterdam: 1763), pp. 56–57, 84–87.

83 Marion, *op. cit.,* pp. 200–204, 222.

the discussions of the fiscal system more significant. In the France of 1763 there were twelve parlements; a thirteenth, that of Lorraine, was to be added in 1775. The most important of these was the Parlement of Paris, which had developed gradually out of the courts which the French kings of the Middle Ages had gathered around them for the purpose of discussing public affairs, dispensing justice, and going over their accounts. Time and the demands of a more complicated administration had led to the splitting of these medieval gatherings into three parts: the *Conseil,* for political affairs; the *Chambre des comptes,* for financial matters; and the Parlement of Paris, for judicial decisions. Of these three the parlement became the most influential, partly because in a society where everything was subject to legal action the dispensers of sovereign justice held great power, and partly because the amount and difficulty of its work necessitated a permanent organization and an able membership. The provincial parlements, whose duties within their various jurisdictions paralleled those of the Parlement of Paris, were the outgrowth of a compromise between the centralizing tendencies of the crown and the spirit of decentralization and local autonomy. Before being joined to the royal domain, most of the great fiefs had had courts of their own. As a means of winning the loyalty of the provinces, many of these courts were erected into parlements similar to the one at Paris; thus the provincial parlements were outgrowths of the high courts of justice of the annexed fiefs. Both at Paris and in the provinces the judges were at first appointed either by the crown or by the courts themselves, but in time the government's need for money and the judges' desire for security led to the sale of offices and to the *paulette,* a tax the payment of which made the offices hereditary. The purchase of offices and titles made of the magistrates a formidable caste, the *noblesse de la robe,* who were in a sense the proprietors of justice.

By the second half of the eighteenth century the parlements had become more than mere "sovereign" courts established to render justice in the name of the king. The fact is that by this period they had developed the view that they were the rightful representatives of the nation, the tutors of kings and the fathers of the state.[84] They claimed to exercise this position as representatives of the nation in the absence of the Estates General, though there is good reason for believing that the parlements' oft-repeated faith in the Estates General was not entirely sincere, for there was little danger that the government would call the Estates; and when it finally did, the parlements apparently had no intention of giving over completely their own right to register the laws.[85] The basis for this sizable claim on the part of the parlements was historical in nature. The French monarchy, they held, was "monarchical" and "legitimate", that is, founded on laws rather than despotic. This assertion was safe enough, for the crown itself admitted its truth on more than one occasion, but the magistrates went further. The Parlement of Paris, they said, was the direct descendant of the ancient general assemblies of the nation which dated back to the earliest days of the monarchy; thus in their view the Parlement of Paris, together with the other parlements, which were one with it, represented the nation at least in the interval when the Estates General were not in session, and therefore had the power to consent in their name to the legislation issued by the crown.

This argument was by no means new, for it had been advanced at the time of the sixteenth century religious wars and again during the Fronde. It was revived once more in the 1750's, when for the first time in the eighteenth century the parlements presented emphatically their interpretation of their origins. Whether historically true or not, the claim constitutes a significant portion of eighteenth century constitutional history. There is, however, good reason for holding that the parle-

84 Marcel Marion, *Dictionnaire des institutions de la France aux XVIIe et XVIIIe siècles* (Paris: Picard, 1923), pp. 422–424, 427–429.

85 Roger Bickart, *Les Parlements et la notion de souveraineté nationale au XVIIIe siècle* (Paris: Alcan, 1932), pp. 250, 252, 254.

ments, in claiming an unbroken chain of institutions binding them to the earliest general assemblies of the nation, were on very uncertain ground. The most ancient link in the chain, the assemblies described by Tacitus, did exist as bodies with the right to decide all important affairs. It is also true that the Parlement of Paris, at a much later date, gradually split off from the *Curia regis,* or king's court, and by the beginning of the fourteenth century had become a separate body with a specialized function. It should be noted, however, that the *Curia regis* did not represent the nation and did not agree in its name to the formation of the laws; and it would be a very difficult task indeed to justify joining the *Curia regis* to the early general assemblies by an unbroken chain of representative institutions.[86]

In the second half of the eighteenth century, however, the parlements were doing their utmost to establish themselves as the legal representatives of the people. Another of their doctrines, likewise based on history, was the theory of the "classes". According to the magistrates, the parlements of France constituted a single indivisible body, for the provincial courts had been formed simply by detaching them from the Parlement of Paris for the sake of convenience. Again it is necessary to qualify the interpretation advanced by the magistrates. It is true that as the kingdom grew in size jurisdictions similar to that of the Parlement of Paris were established; but a good many of the provincial courts, such as that of Besançon in Franche Comté, were not simply broken off from Paris but were continuations of seigneurial jurisdictions which had existed before the annexation of the provinces in question to the crown.[87]

The device by which the parlements attempted to participate in the name of the nation in the formation of the laws was called registration. Originally registration had been nothing

86 *Ibid.,* pp. 255–256, 261–265.
87 *Ibid.,* pp. 266–267; Marion, *Dictionnaire,* p. 427.

more than a means of conserving the laws by reading them publicly and writing them down in the registers. Gradually the parlements developed the practice of "verifying" the laws by discussing them; when such a discussion revealed some flaw or inconvenience in a law or the fact that established precedents had been broken, the judges would inform the king by means of "remonstrances" and would await his response before completing the registration. This was a useful practice, and the prestige of the king was safeguarded by keeping the remonstrance secret. The king, on his part, was not supposed to interfere with the discussions. Beyond this point, however, the parlements and the king came in time to disagree. The parlements began to claim that they could refuse registration until the king took into account the changes they had proposed. The king, of course, insisted on his right to order registration—either in person by *lit de justice* or through an intermediary—and to be obeyed without further arguments; for the monarchical régime rested on subordination of all individuals and bodies to the king, in whom resided both responsibility and sovereignty.[88]

This dispute over the position of the parlements did not, of course, appear suddenly at any particular time. All through the seventeenth and eighteenth centuries there were intermittent struggles between the parlements and the royal power, the parlements having an advantage during minorities or in periods when the royal power was in feeble hands, and the kings having the upper hand when they were fortunate enough to have such ministers as Richelieu or Colbert, or when they themselves were powerful, as in the case of Louis XIV. In the eighteenth century Louis XV displayed occasional bursts of energy in his relations with the parlements, but for many reasons, not all of them associated with the personality of the king, his reign witnessed the gradual weakening of the royal power, and the parlements were very successful in advancing

[88] Bickart, *op. cit.,* pp. 267–269.

their claims. With one exception, the sovereign courts emerged victorious from all their conflicts with the royal power after the middle of the century. That exception occurred in 1771 when Chancellor Maupeou broke the power of the parlements and reorganized the whole judicial system; but even that crushing victory was only temporary, for Louis XVI later recalled the old parlements by a fateful order which, in the opinion of some historians, ruled out the possibility of reforms needed to preserve the nation from revolution.[89]

Whatever their relation to the revolution, the claims of the magistrates, and the energy with which they upheld them, offered a constant threat to the traditional character of the monarchy. To insist that registration represented the consent of the nation to the law, and to deny the right of the crown to force registration, was to make the passage of legislation dependent on the consent of the nation. Thus the parlements were dividing the legislative power between king and nation, a tendency certainly not in harmony with the traditional nature of the monarchy; for tradition had it that the king, holding his power directly from God, was responsible only to him, and that his sovereignty on earth was complete and indivisible. If the parlements were to have their way, they, as representatives of the nation, would have the right to amend and the power to veto legislation proposed by the king's officers; thus the judges were demanding for themselves a considerable amount of legislative power. This interpretation, whatever the intentions of its authors, tended to aid the growth of the doctrine of popular sovereignty. In addition, moreover, to the practice of supporting doctrines which aided the forces of change, the parlements by their stubborn resistance to enforced registrations considerably weakened the efficiency of the traditional monarchy. By such measures as suspension of service and collective resignations they fought to have their way. Every little conflict was magnified by the theory of "classes" which held that all of the parlements of France were members of the same body, and after 1755 an at-

89 Marion, *Dictionnaire*, p. 424.

tack on one parlement meant a fight with all of them. As a last resort, to be sure, the king could still resort to *lettres de cachet* and other forceful means; but in the eyes of the public such methods served only to make martyrs of the courts and a despot of the king.[90]

A dispute with the "parliamentary league", as it came to be called, was not to be lightly undertaken, for the judges wielded tremendous influence in the places where it counted most. Their position as judges lent weight to everything they said, while their remonstrances, printed and widely distributed, went far toward shaping public opinion in an age which had no political press. Thus occurred the novel spectacle of resistance to the will of the king taking on a semi-official character. As judges, the members of the parlements moved in circles frequented by men of property and were surrounded by a numerous and articulate clientele of inferior judges, lawyers, and clerks. Aside from their professional position, moreover, the magistrates were members of a class influential in its own right. Although in many cases descended from wealthy middle-class families, the judges in the parlements as a rule formed a special class, the *noblesse de la robe,* by virtue of the judicial offices which they owned. Most of them led the lives of nobles and enjoyed noble privileges such as exemption from the *taille* and from the lodging of soldiers. During the eighteenth century the usage was established of demanding of all applicants for parliamentary office four quarters of nobility, with the result that entrance into the judicial nobility became difficult for the newly rich. Even at Paris, where great financial fortunes usually outshone all others, the judges managed to hold their own in a glittering and expensive society, and considering the environment in which they lived the provincial judges were as wealthy as those of Paris. The magistrates in the parlements were of course paid salaries, but these were little more than interest on the price of their offices; in addition to salaries they received *vacations* and *épices,* fees paid by the litigants; very often the

90 Bickart, *op. cit.,* pp. 271–273, 275–278.

king granted them gifts and pensions, especially in cases where a conflict of opinion had arisen between crown and parlement. Thus the magistrates, as judges, as nobles, and as representatives of a wealthy class, were firmly entrenched in the social structure of the old régime. It is not surprising that people listened when they spoke, and regarded attacks on the parlements as evidences of despotism.[91]

Although the parlements helped to lessen the monarchical authority and contributed to the triumph of the idea of national sovereignty, their reward for this role was political oblivion. To the parlements the beginning of the great revolution meant the end of their place in the public life of the nation.[92] Why the magistrates thus lent their strength to the forces making for revolution is an historical problem difficult to solve. Certainly they did not foresee the conclusion toward which they were helping to push the *ancien régime*. Most historians, in dealing with this problem, have handled the parlements roughly, treating them as the victims of blindness and error, narrowly intent on defending their privileges and property rights against the onslaughts of reform. For example Aulard, the great historian of the French Revolution, speaks of the parlements as a school for an aristocratic kind of republicanism, but a school in which the magistrates taught in spite of themselves,

> . . . for they were the adversaries of every serious attempt at reforming the *ancien régime*. They wished for their own profit to preserve the *status quo*. If they paved the way for the Revolution, and, indirectly, for the Republic, it was not only because they belittled royalty by the fact of their dis-

91 Henri Carré, *La fin des parlements* (*1788–1790*), (Paris: Hachette, 1912), pp. 1–10, 15; Bickart, *op. cit.,* p. 278.

92 Bickart, *op. cit.,* p. 279, and Conclusion. Many of the judges lost their lives and property in the revolution. Many became *émigrés*. Of the survivors or their sons Napoleon appointed about one hundred and fifty to administrative and judicial positions and in so doing helped to pave the way for the Restoration, for many of them deserted him when his star had set. For an account of this period in the lives of the parliamentarians, see Henri Carré, *La fin des parlements,* chapters V and VI and Conclusion.

obedience, but also because they prevented the Monarchy from evolving, and from founding new institutions in accordance with the spirit of the times.[93]

Henri Carré, the historian of the decline and fall of the parlements, has this to say: "As proprietors of lands and offices, the magistrates must combat every reform threatening property." [94] Marcel Marion, writing of the resistance of the parlements to the government's tax program in the 1760's, passes the following severe judgment on the magistrates.

> . . . In their resistance, concern for the public welfare was entirely missing, and in striving against the treasury it was neither the liberties of the people nor the good order of the finances but only the privileges of their caste which they were defending: their opposition was as little disinterested as it was enlightened, and this must deny them the sympathy of history.[95]

As a final example, here is the conclusion of Roger Bickart, a student of the political ideas of the parlements.

> . . . The rebellion of the *grandes robes* lacked even the excuse of generosity and unselfishness. It is clear, in fact, that underneath a liberal exterior the parliamentarians hid the narrowest possible social conservatism, the most rigid political egoism. Just as, while apparently defending the public liberties, they sought to preserve the privileges of their caste, so, under the pretext of assuring the nation the exercise of its rights, they were merely concerned with monopolizing political power for their own benefit.[96]

93 A. Aulard, *The Revolution under the Monarchy, 1789–1792,* Vol. I of *The French Revolution, a Political History, 1789–1804,* translated from the French of the Third Edition by Bernard Miall, 4 vols. (London: T. Fisher Unwin, 1910), p. 106.

94 Carré, *La fin des parlements,* p. 20. It should perhaps be noted that in this passage Carré is speaking of the 1770's in particular.

95 Marion, *Histoire financière,* I, 206.

96 Bickart, *op. cit.,* p. 279.

In passages such as these the role played by the parlements has again and again been reviewed and found wanting. It is, to be sure, an easy matter to find individual magistrates renowned for their justice, integrity, and learning; names such as Harlay and Daguesseau are great names in French judicial history. But by most historians the parlements as a whole have been condemned for the manner in which they faced the mounting problems of the old régime.

Whatever their motives, the parlements in the years during and after the Seven Years War threw themselves ardently into the great debate over the public finances. By their resistance to new taxes and by their demands for fiscal reform, made known in their remonstrances, they undertook to defend the taxpayers against the demands of the treasury. Sincere or not, they played the part of reformers and friends of the people, and they played it aggressively, especially in the provinces, where distance seems to have emboldened them. In the opinion of Marcel Marion, the parlements, besides being selfish, were completely unfitted for the task of planning fiscal reforms.[97] Rightly or wrongly, however, the parlements, along with the economists and pamphleteers, succeeded in making known to the public their views concerning the condition of the nation's finances.

It would be a mistake, of course, to assume that the opinions of all twelve parlements concerning the finances were exactly the same, or even that all the members of any single court were in complete agreement. Some ideas, however, were repeated so often and in so many places that they may be regarded as typical of the arguments advanced by the magistrates in their numerous conflicts with the crown. One opinion, widely believed by both parlements and public, was that France was exhausted by the weight of the taxes and by vicious methods of assessment and collection, that the limit of her endurance had been reached, and that additional taxation would be useless and intolerable.[98] Another conviction which the magistrates shared with the gen-

97 Marion, *Histoire financière*, I, 205-206, 209, 215-216.
98 *Ibid.*, I, 209; Gomel, *op. cit.*, I, 21-22.

eral public was that the gains of tax farmers and of financiers who loaned money to the government were excessive. Many of the judges apparently could not bring themselves to regard the property of *rentiers* and holders of government contracts as genuine wealth, equal in importance to landed property. They were as suspicious of "financial fortunes" as they were respectful in their attitude toward real estate, and this distrust was so strong that it even colored their opinions about the public debt. Payment of the government's debts, in the opinion of many of the parlements, was of secondary importance; the primary obligation of the king was the subsistence of his subjects, and to neglect that vital need in order to pay other debts was to undermine the very foundations of the state. Several of the parlements even suggested that if a choice had to be made between taxing the people further and neglecting to pay the king's debts to *rentiers* it would be better not to pay the *rentiers*.[99]

Specific criticisms of the taxes of course varied from court to court, as did the details of suggested reforms. In September, 1759, for example, the *cour des aides* at Paris [100] complained that there were too many laws about the taxes, that the gains of the financiers were excessive, and that poor people were the most heavily taxed. The court proposed a fixed and certain law about the tax on real estate, a proportional and not too arbitrary law for taxing persons, and a uniform law for taxing consumption.[101] In 1763 the Parlement of Rouen (in Normandy) stated that the remedy for the financial troubles of the state was not in increasing taxation but in exact knowledge of the state's expenses and resources. Accounts of the income and debts of the kingdom should be sent to the parlements. The state's ex-

---

99 Marion, *Histoire financière*, I, 233–235; Gomel, *op. cit.*, I, 16–18.

100 Though the *cours des aides* (courts having jurisdiction over cases pertaining to the *aides* and to some other taxes) were in many cases joined to the parlements (for example at Rennes, Rouen, and Grenoble), the *cour des aides* at Paris was not joined to the Parlement of Paris. This example has been included because the *cour des aides* at Paris was as outspoken a critic of the finances as any of the parlements.

101 Gomel, *op. cit.*, I, 16–18.

penses should be divided into classes, with each class having a definite purpose and a definite income to meet its needs; money should not be diverted from one class to another and all expenditures should be accounted for. There should be a single tax, but its collection should be left to the provinces themselves.[102]

As might be expected from their political opinions, the parlements by about 1760 came to believe that they themselves were the agencies through which the government's financial problems could be solved. In remonstrances which were daily becoming bolder in tone they advanced beyond the mere consideration of weight and distribution of taxes and questioned even the taxing power of the crown. They wanted not only to vote on the taxes but also to have a hand in their allocation and collection and to supervise the government's spending of money. In 1760, for example, when Controller General Bertin ordered the collection of a third *vingtième*, together with other increases in the taxes, the Parlement of Paris declared itself unable to register the new legislation until it was certain that the money was really to be spent in the interest of the state and until the arbitrariness in the taxes had been corrected. The parlement also demanded economy in the expenditures of the king and a "fixed and legal order in the finances." In May, 1760, the Parlement of Rouen even went so far as to request the calling of the Estates General.

> . . . Return to us, Sire, our precious liberty; give us back our Estates; it is of the essence of a law that it be accepted . . . the right to accept is the right of the nation . . . this right still stands, and Your Majesty recognizes it by sending edicts to the magistrates, who, in examining them, can take the place of the people. Exercised in the absence of the Estates by those whom the nation regards as depositories of legislation, this sacred and imprescriptible right can be exercised by them only . . .[103]

102 Marion, *Histoire financière*, I, 218.
103 Quoted in Marion, *Histoire financière*, I, 207.

Later in the same year, the Parlement of Rouen went even further and insisted that fiscal laws were not obligatory unless registered by all of the parlements of the kingdom, constituting the Parlement of France.[104] By such arguments the magistrates directed the full force of their political theories against the financial programs of Louis XV's ministers.

5. THE VICTORY OF THE PARLEMENTS IN 1763

Far from existing in a vacuum, the opinions of the parlements concerning politics and taxation were given expression on many occasions when the magistrates opposed with all their power legislation of which they disapproved. During the Seven Years War the parlements fought new taxes and loans from the very beginning. Desperate as France's situation was, the government from 1756 on was scarcely able to collect a tax or negotiate a loan without facing an uproar designed by the magistrates to put the crown in the wrong in the eyes of the public.[105] When the Seven Years War was finally ended, the parlements became more vehement than ever in the expression of their opinions and in the exercise of their power. Controller General Bertin, who had weathered the storm for four years, now had to face another great attack. To the treasury the coming of peace meant only further embarrassment, for it was now necessary to put an end to certain extraordinary taxes, such as the second and third *vingtièmes* and the supplements to the *capitation,* which had been justified as war-time measures. Faced with the loss of much income, Bertin decided that he must at least keep two of the *vingtièmes* and make certain that these were effectively collected on all landed property. This was the aim of the edict of April, 1763, which suppressed the third *vingtième* and the supplements to the *capitation,* but which maintained the first two *vingtièmes* for another six years and ordered a careful census of all landed property, even that of the privileged classes, so that the remaining *vingtièmes* could be

104 Marion, *Histoire financière,* pp. 206–207.
105 Gomel, *op. cit.,* I, 14–15; Marion, *Histoire financière,* I, 209.

proportionately assessed. Although the edict denied any intention of touching "well-established" privileges, the nobility and clergy were alarmed, and with reason, for it was evident that some attempt to revise existing privileges would be made.[106]

Immediately the parlements launched a campaign against Bertin. The Parlement of Paris would register Bertin's edict only at a *lit de justice,* and those of Toulouse, Grenoble, and Besançon agitated violently against the new legislation. At Bordeaux the parlement went so far as to treat the tax collectors as swindlers, calling them "an army of enemies of the public peace" and hinting at the desirability of confiscating the property of the financiers. In various parts of France the royal governors who had been ordered to secure the registration of the edict were threatened with arrest by the parlements and had to surround themselves with guards. At Rouen the governor attempted to attend a session of the parlement, only to find that at his approach most of the magistrates had walked out in a body. *Lettres de cachet* in hand, the governor forced a few remaining officials to register Bertin's legislation, but when the other members of the parlement next met they attempted to nullify the registration. Ten members were exiled and a great many resigned.[107] Thus the new legislation was everywhere halted or delayed by the activities of the parlements. War with England gave way in 1763 to something resembling civil strife at home.

Louis XV, who had a profound sense of the importance of a king of France, was far from indifferent to the revolts of his sovereign courts. Stirred by their outbreak in 1763, he took immediate action. In a series of *arrêts du conseil* in August and September of that year he suppressed all remontrances which had been published and forced registration of the legislation

106 Marion, *Histoire financière*, I, 213. Bertin's program had other details, but the continuation of the *vingtièmes* was perhaps the most menacing part from the standpoint of the privileged classes, for it resembled to some extent the land tax of the physiocrats.

107 Carré, *Le règne de Louis XV*, pp. 366–367.

rejected by the parlements. His position with relation to taxation was simple. As he said to a delegation from the Parlement of Paris in August, 1763, "It is my business and mine alone to decide whether the financial aid which I demand is real and absolute. The doubts which some people raise concerning the utility of the plans which I have proposed can only delay the relief which I wish to procure for my people." [108] Thus the king defended his theoretical right to tax as he saw fit. But Louis XV was not the man to hold fast to a difficult position for very long; he preferred to give way rather than to fight; giving way he found easy, so long as it was only his ministers or his financial affairs that were attacked. This was the situation in 1763. Apparently the king did not feel himself personally menaced by the actions of the parlements, and so he presently yielded to their urgent demands.[109]

Thus the Fall of 1763 found the crown retreating from its original position. By the Declaration of November 21, 1763, Louis XV withdrew Bertin's unpopular April edict. The declaration also assured the people that it was the king's intention to rule "not by his authority alone, which he holds from God and which he will never allow to be lessened, but also by love, justice and observation of the rules and usages wisely established in his kingdom." He had recognized that "although there was need for changes in the system of taxation, one could not begin to make such changes without great care, because of the justifiable fear which they would cause, because of delays in the collection of the taxes, and because of other inconveniences of various kinds." The king therefore invited his parlements, *cours des aides,* and *cours des comptes* to express to him their views concerning the possible means "of perfecting and simplifying the imposition, distribution, collection, use, and bookkeeping of everything related to his finances, and of giving to all the said divisions the form least oppressive to his subjects." [110]

108 Quoted in Gomel, *op. cit.,* I, 22–23.

109 Marion, *Histoire financière,* I, 225.

110 This and the two preceding passages of the declaration are quoted in Marion, *Histoire financière,* I, 226–227.

For the carrying out of this plan of reform, *lettres patentes* of November 21, 1763 established a commission of four *conseillers* from the Parlement of Paris, two from the *cour des comptes,* and two from the *cour des aides*. This commission was to collect and summarize the recommendations sent in by the courts of France. "Our intention," declared the king, "is to give to the said commissioners such communications as shall be necessary in order that they may . . . indicate to us what they consider to be the most proper means for easing the people's burdens and establishing better order in everything related to our finances." [111]

Besides inviting the parlements to suggest financial reforms the Declaration of November 21 ordered a number of specific changes of a nature calculated not to arouse the anger of the judicial caste. There was to be a census of property, but its rules had to be verified by the courts before the actual work was begun. The second *vingtième* was not to be collected after January 1, 1768. From the product of the first *vingtième* there was to be raised an annual amortization fund of twenty million *livres;* any surplus was to be joined to the product of the second *vingtième* and to certain other funds and used for the payment of arrears.

As the year 1763 drew to a close Louis XV made still another concession to the parlements by dismissing Bertin and replacing him with L'Averdy, a *conseiller* of the Parlement of Paris. It was the first time a *conseiller* had been made Controller General. The choice of this man, a well-known Jansenist who had played an important part in the trial of the Jesuits and who knew little or nothing about the finances, was obviously an effort to appease the judicial caste. [112]

Thus at the end of the year 1763 the parlements emerged victorious from their struggle with the royal power, with one of their own kind in the office of Controller General. L'Averdy,

[111] Quoted in footnote of Marion, *Histoire financière*, I, 227.

[112] Carré, *Le règne de Louis XV,* p. 267; Marion, *Histoire financière*, pp. 226–227.

like his predecessors, was to feel the weight of judicial displeasure, but this trouble could not be foreseen in 1763. For the time being, at any rate, the parlements were riding high. The strength of their position can be seen in the fact that they were slow to register even the Declaration of November 21, which was nothing if not a concession to them. Unsatisfied despite their victory, the parlements attached conditions to their registrations of this declaration. Most of them declared that the first *vingtième* could be collected for no longer than ten years after the peace, and that the two *vingtièmes,* during their existence, could be levied only according to the actual rolls then in effect; they insisted, in other words, that the present inequality in the assessment of these taxes must continue.

But by far the greatest victory of the parlements was given them by the Declaration of November 21 itself. After years of opposition, after all their demands for reform, the magistrates were now being invited to tell the king what to do about "the imposition, distribution, collection, use, and bookkeeping of everything related to his finances." A special commission was to be formed to collect the opinions of the magistrates. As for the proposed register of landed property, to which there had been so much opposition when it was ordered by Bertin, it was still to be made, but only according to rules approved by the parlements. For better or worse the courts had advanced from the role of critics of the king's financial affairs to that of collaborators in their administration.[113] As though this were not enough, the government in the Spring of 1764 attempted to give the parlements a monopoly of the position of financial reformers. By a declaration issued on March 28 "all others" were forbidden to print, publish, or spread any projects concerning the reform of the finances. "Just as memorials wisely assembled by our courts can be useful to this great aim, so memorials and projects written by people without character, who make them public instead of sending them to the persons capable of judging them, can be . . . harmful . . . and prevent the good

113 Marion, *Histoire financière,* I, 228, 230–232.

which we would be able to effect with the aid of the memorials dictated by the enlightened zeal of the magistrates." [114] In this way the government tried to silence all other participants in the great debate over the taxes. The parlements had won their fight and must be heard. Not so with the rest of the people; their time had not yet come.[115]

The victory of the parlements in 1763 was not to be permanent, however. For a time, to be sure, it appeared that L'Averdy, the new Controller General, would be a true reformer. He won praise from economists in December, 1763, by authorizing provisionally the commerce in grains from province to province; and in July, 1764, the commerce in grains was made free within the kingdom, and imports and exports were even allowed, subject to a light duty. But France's financial problems were not solved. L'Averdy established no new taxes, but he had to increase the old ones. By means of a complicated system of amortization funds the government was able to announce each year the amortization of several million *livres,* but meanwhile new debts were being contracted.[116] Abbé Terray, on becoming Controller General in December, 1769, found the financial situation desperate, and began to make plans for declaring the state bankrupt, a scheme which in the opinion of at least one authority added twenty years of life to the *ancien régime.*[117]

Meanwhile the king had again decided to be firm with the parlements. In 1768 René-Nicolas de Maupeou had become Chancellor, and both Maupeou and Terray were determined to put an end to the meddling of the parlements in the affairs of the king and his ministers. Both men were political opponents of Choiseul, the powerful Secretary of State, and when in December, 1770, Louis XV disgraced Choiseul, his action was tanta-

114 Quoted in Marion, *Histoire financière,* I, 230.

115 But pamphlets on the finances continued to appear, for under the old régime arbitrariness was corrected in practice by administrative neglect, and the most severe prohibitions were not always enforced. Gomel, *op. cit.,* I, 24.

116 Carré, *Le règne de Louis XV,* pp. 367–368.

117 Gomel, *op. cit.,* I, 30–31. The authority mentioned is Marcel Marion (*Histoire financière,* I, 247).

mount to declaring a preference for Maupeou and Terray, who wished to make war on the parlements, rather than for Choiseul, who favored revenge against England.[118] Already the campaign against the parlements had begun. In an edict of November 27, 1770, they were ordered to submit to the will of the king even when their remonstrances were ignored. Maupeou on December 3 caused an edict to be issued forbidding the parlements to use the terms "unity", "indivisibility", and "order" with reference to the magistracy. In a *lit de justice* of December 7, 1770, the king reaffirmed the doctrine that he held his crown from God and that remonstrances could not be used as a form of resistance to the authority of the crown. The parlements, unable to accept these absolutist assertions without abandoning all of their recent gains, resisted by means of protests, remonstrances, and resignations. But Maupeou was ready for them. After exiling the members of the Parlement of Paris and replacing them with a new court, he proceeded in 1771 to overhaul completely the judicial organization of France, abolishing *épices,* the sale of offices, and interference by the courts in matters of administration.[119] So ended the period which had begun in 1763, during which the parlements had enjoyed increased power and the opportunity to meddle with the administrative affairs of their nation. This power and this opportunity were to return to them once more—during the reign of Louis XVI, when judicial opposition played a large part in forcing the convocation of the Estates General in 1789—and their conduct on that occasion was to be suicidal.

118 Carré, *Le règne de Louis XV,* pp. 386, 390–391.
119 *Ibid.,* pp. 394–403; Gomel, *op. cit.,* I, 32–34.

CHAPTER II

THE PARLEMENT OF PROVENCE AND THE PROBLEM OF FISCAL DISORDER

Augmenter la richesse nationale est la première loy de la finance bien entendue.

Parlement of Provence, *Mémoires*, XIV, 72.

In the period of increased influence which followed their victory in 1763 the French parlements accomplished little or nothing toward solving their country's financial problems. The Declaration of November 21, 1763, had invited suggestions for reform, but there is little evidence that the parlements made use of this opportunity. From the very first they hastened to safeguard their own interests. Before registering the Declaration of November 21 most of the parlements took care to specify that the first *vingtième* was not to last for more than ten years after the coming of peace; they insisted that the proposed census of the kingdom's real estate be made according to rules formulated by the magistrates themselves, and they declared that this project was not to endanger the immunity of noble lands from taxation. By such actions they annulled in advance any reforms which might have come from the Declaration of November 21.[1] As it turned out, the proposed inquiry into means of improving the nation's finances amounted to so little that it is difficult to find any reference to it whatever in most histories of the period. A few memorials, which it is quite possible that nobody read, were the outcome. Apparently the courts were slow to send in their recommendations, and the king's ministers took care not to encourage them.[2] The inquiry, to be sure, was extended to

1 Alphonse Jobez, *La France sous Louis XV* (*1715–1774*), Vol. VI (Paris: Librairie académique, 1873), pp. 129–130.

2 J.-J. Clamageran, *Histoire de l'impôt en France* (Paris: Guillaumin, 1876), III, 387. A. Vührer, *Histoire de la dette publique en France* (Paris: Berger-Levrault et Cie, 1886), I, 501.

foreign lands, where French ambassadors were asked to collect information about taxation, and in some cases special missions were sent to study foreign tax systems.[3] But in France itself the investigation did little more than annoy the tax collectors. The parlement at Rouen in Normandy used it as an excuse for interfering with the collection of taxes and for keeping the administration from learning anything about the condition of landed property, and in 1768 the *procureur général* was able to boast that the proposed register of landed property had been abandoned in that province. Indeed, the inquiries about landed property were given up entirely, so great was the fear of the parlements.[4] There is little evidence that most of France's sovereign courts interpreted the Declaration of November 21, 1763, as anything more than a political victory for themselves.

There was, however, at least one parlement which accepted the government's invitation and set out to plan the reform of the French finances. This was the Parlement of Provence.

1. Province, Parlement, and Crown

Provence lay in the south-eastern corner of France, between Dauphiné and the Mediterranean, Italy and the Rhône. It was an ancient land. Tradition had it that the city of Marseilles had been a Greek colony as early as 600 B.C., and the very name Provence was said to come from the words *Provincia romana*. Under the Roman Empire the territory around Marseilles, Aix, and Arles became an important center of learning and civilization. Rome's decline brought successive waves of conquerors: Visigoths, Ostrogoths, Franks, and even Arabs from Spain. Provence became a part of Charlemagne's great empire, and after his death

3 The results of this inquiry are given in Vol. I of Moreau de Beaumont's *Mémoires concernant les impositions et droits en Europe*, 4 Vols. (Paris: Imprimerie royale, 1768–69). The other three volumes deal with the taxes in France. It is quite possible that some memorials sent to the government by the parlements were used in writing this book, but the writer is aware of no evidence to support this possibility.

4 Marcel Marion, *Histoire financière de la France depuis 1715*, I, 231–233.

passed through many changes of fortune, emerging in the ninth
century as a kingdom, one of whose rulers even managed to
become emperor. During most of the Middle Ages, however,
Provence was ruled by her counts, and it was one of these,
Charles III, who on his deathbed late in the year 1481 be-
queathed Provence to his cousin Louis XI of France.[5]

Although joined to France, Provence in the old régime retained an identity of her own. If the last of her counts, surrounded by agents of the French king, willed his territories to
Louis XI, he nevertheless requested that Provence be allowed to
keep her political individuality, her constitution, estates, and special privileges. Louis XI and after him Charles VIII, agreed
to these conditions, and in return the provincial estates in 1482
and again in 1486 swore loyalty to the crown of France. This
union of Provence with France was in theory a personal union.[6]
French kings were also counts of Provence, and only the use of
this title was to validate legislation pertaining to the province.
Moreover, royal decrees were not to be valid in Provence until
they had been registered by the *Conseil royal*, the ancient royal
court of Provence, which later became the parlement; the members of this body, as well as all important officers of Provence
were to reside in the county.[7] In many respects, the province preserved the appearance and even the reality of a free and independent *pays*. Although French became the official language,
Provençal continued to be spoken by the people. The provincial
estates continued to meet until 1639, and although they were
replaced after that date by the *assemblée générale des com-*

5 J. Marchand, article "Provence", pp. 849–852 of Vol. 27 of *La grande
encyclopédie, inventaire raisonné des sciences, des lettres et des arts,* sous la
direction de Mm. Berthelot, Ch. Langlois, (and others). 2nd ed. (Paris:
Société anonyme de la grand encyclopédie, 1886–1902).

6 Raoul Busquet, *Histoire des institutions de la Provence de 1482 à 1790*
(Marseille, Typographie Barlatier, 1920), pp. 3–7.

7 *Ibid.,* p. 9. The constitution of Provence, which was based on precedents
formulated by the estates over a long period of time, had many other provisions, but these were the most important. They illustrate the strong desire
to avoid absentee administration of the province.

munautés, an assembly consisting largely of representatives from the towns and therefore less likely to oppose Richelieu's policies, this body retained the right to assess Provence's taxes and to supervise the spending of the proceeds. Contributions to the Royal Treasury of France were made by means of a *don gratuit* granted by the assembly. The sovereign court of Provence, first in the form of the *Conseil royal* and later as the parlement, was able to retain its prestige and authority.

With the passage of time, however, the tendency toward centralization within the French monarchy was increasingly evident in Provence. A new superstructure of centralized administration was added to the ancient institutions of the county. Governors and Lieutenants General took the place of the ancient courts; after 1660, moreover, there was always an intendant in Provence, and these "king's men" were able gradually to assume most of the real power, directing the assemblies, supervising municipal administration and the judicial bodies, and controlling the finances. Provence became a *généralité* as well as a province, and the addition of new nation-wide taxes such as the *capitation* and *vingtièmes,* collection of which was supervised by the intendant, considerably decreased the reality of Provence's claim to be autonomous in matters of taxation.[8] Throughout the old régime the people and officials of Provence remained extremely jealous of the "rights" guaranteed them under their constitution, but the French kings, by scrupulously observing a few principles of that constitution, were able in the long run to destroy all the rest. The French kings continued to call themselves counts of Provence and were careful to have all legislation registered by Provence's sovereign court; but while thus saving appearances they succeeded in introducing whatever other legislation they desired, even when that legislation violated the less carefully guarded institutions of the province. Under a cloak of legality they modified the administration of the province and altered bit by bit its principles of public law.[9]

8 Marchand, *op. cit.,* p. 854.
9 Busquet, *op. cit.,* pp. 9–11.

In justice to the crown it should be stated that Provence was probably well-administered during the reign of Louis XV. The intendants, usually natives of Provence, worked with the *assemblée des communautés,* and for the most part succeeded in furnishing good government. There is evidence that the administrators even looked with favor upon many of the reforms suggested by the eighteenth century philosophers and economists. But public opinion in Provence, as in the rest of France, remained unsatisfied in the face of disorder in the nation's finances, military defeats, and the vacillating direction of policy from Versailles.[10]

Discontent with the conduct of Louis XV's government was usually expressed by Provence's sovereign court, the parlement, which was founded in 1501 and met for the first time at Aix in 1502. The parlement was not a new court set down in Provence by the centralizing monarchy, but merely a continuation of an older institution of Provence, the *Conseil royal,* sometimes called the *Grand conseil* or *Conseil éminent;* as such it merely replaced the *Conseil royal* at the head of the complicated and ancient inferior jurisdictions in Provence. The *Conseil royal* had a long history of its own, for it was descended from the ancient royal council or court which had met with the counts of Provence or with their representatives. Under the presidency of the *Grand Sénéchal* of Provence, the *Conseil royal* stood at the head of the many inferior judicial jurisdictions in Provence, acting sometimes as court of appeal and sometimes hearing cases directly; the *grand sénéchal* was also the executive officer in the county, next to the counts in importance, and the *Conseil royal* also handled matters of administration.[11]

10 Paul Gaffarel, article "La fin de l'ancien régime", in Part I of Vol. III, pp. 146, 151–153 of *Les Bouches du Rhône. Encyclopédie départmentale publié par le Conseil Général avec le concours de la Ville de Marseille et de la Chambre de Commerce sous la direction de Paul Masson.* (Paris: Librairie Honoré Champion, 1932–37).

11 Busquet, *op. cit.,* pp. 51–55, 57–59. Louis Wolff, *Le Parlement de Provence au XVIIIᵉ siècle. Organization, procédure.* (Aix: B. Niel, F. N. Nicollet, 1920), pp. 4–5, 7–8.

Thus in 1501 when King Louis XII of France replaced the *Conseil royal* by a parlement he instituted no sharp break in the history of Provence. During subsequent centuries the crown tried to model the Parlement of Provence after the other parlements, particularly that of Paris, but though it came in time to resemble the other sovereign courts of France, the parlement at Aix never lost the imprint of its past and of the institutions and usages of Provence. To the very end of the old régime the magistrates at Aix considered themselves champions of their province's historic constitution, and especially of the principles that all legislation sent to Provence had to be registered by the parlement, and that *Provencaux* should be judged in their own courts, according to Roman law and the ancient statutes of Provence.[12]

In the 1760's the Parlement of Provence still retained a strong sense of its important mission as a sovereign court, second to none in its jurisdiction. The judges at Aix rendered justice faithfully, according to the forms prescribed by the statutes of 1667 and 1670, but they had not forgotten the rules peculiar to their ancient province, and in many important cases they gave these precedence over the laws of France. Like the *Conseil royal* before them, they combined administrative with judicial duties.[13] Despite the progress of centralization in the monarchy the parlement remained a powerful instrument for the defense of local traditions and interests.

Counting only the most important officials, the *présidents à mortier, conseillers, avocats généraux,* and *substituts,* the Parlement of Provence in the eighteenth century consisted of from sixty to seventy magistrates.[14] At the head of this body was the *premier président,* charged with the responsibility of maintaining order and harmony in the parlement and representing its point of view in dealings with the king. The office of *premier président* was especially important in Provence, and

12 Wolff, *op. cit.,* pp. 1–3, 10–11, 13.

13 Wolff, *op. cit.,* p. 516.

14 Marchand, *op. cit.,* p. 853.

serves to illustrate the overlapping of judicial and administrative duties in the parlement and in the province. In Provence the *premier président* was also *intendant de justice,* and as such represented the interests of the crown in the province. Thus the *premier président* was both head of the parlement and chief executive officer in Provence, and had the difficult task of reconciling the interests of the province and its parlement with those of the king. It was a peculiar combination of duties, but it had its precedents, for in former times the *Grand Sénéchal* of Provence had also combined the duties of chief executive officer with those of head of the *Conseil éminent.* The *premier président* and *intendant* was appointed by the king, who usually chose the man indicated by the parlement. As the king's representative, he could be counted on to defend the interests of the crown in Provence; as head of the parlement, however, he would not allow its rights or those of the province to be decreased. It was a useful compromise for a province whose citizens had attacked the first *intendant* sent by Richelieu in 1631, forcing him to flee from his house by way of the chimney.[15]

Next in importance to the *premier président* came eight or more *présidents à mortier,* so-called because of their "mortarboard" hats. One of these magistrates took the place of the *premier président* when he was absent. Every hearing at the parlement had to be presided over by a *président à mortier.* These *présidents,* in addition to their judicial duties, were sent on administrative missions in the various parts of the province, and even journeyed to Versailles to explain the parlement's point of view to the king.[16] The main body of the parlement consisted of about forty-five to fifty *conseillers* who acted as judges in civil and criminal cases which came before the court and who also did administrative work in Provence. Custom allowed these judges to submit reports concerning any abuses which they had seen or any prosecution which they thought should be made; thus every judge was an important public offi-

15 Wolff, *op. cit.,* pp. 57–64.
16 Wolff, *op. cit.,* pp. 64–68.

cial in Provence. The deliberations of the *conseillers* were shared to some extent by *véterans* and *survivanciers,* retired judges who had been allowed to keep their honors and some of their duties.[17] Lower in the judicial hierarchy than the *conseillers* but important because of their duties as the king's representatives in the parlement were the members of the *parquet.* These officials, a *procureur général,* his deputies, and several *avocats général,* were supposed to watch the conduct of the magistrates and the parlement's admission of new members; it was their task to get the king's legislation registered by the parlement and to intervene in all cases where the royal *domaine* was involved. They also had innumerable other duties of a judicial and administrative nature, such as inspecting the inferior courts, prosecuting criminals, protecting public order and morality, taking charge of frontier administration, hygiene, and security of streets, defending the crown against libels and sedition, and to some extent supervising education. The members of the *parquet,* like the *premier président,* tended to divide their loyalty among province, parlement, and crown; they claimed that whatever they did was in the king's interest, but as holders of purchased offices and residents of Provence, they often defended province and parlement against the very legislation which they were supposed to support.[18] In addition to the officers already mentioned, the Parlement of Provence had a member, the *avocat et procureur des pauvres,* whose duty was to defend the interests of people too poor to afford their own lawyers.

Like all courts the Parlement of Provence was attended by a large number of minor officials and employees of the court. There were clerks, ushers, doorkeepers, a medical attendant, a jailer, and an executioner. Finally, not joined to the court but of necessity working with it, were the *avocats* and *procureurs,* counsels and attorneys who defended the interests of their clients in cases tried by the parlement. *Avocats* and *procureurs*

17 Wolff, *op. cit.,* pp. 74–78.
18 *Ibid.,* pp. 80–82, 91, 97–110, 512.

had to meet certain professional requirements set by the parlement. The corporation of *avocats* in eighteenth century Provence usually numbered about one hundred men, while that of the *procureurs* had an average membership of between thirty and forty.[19]

The work of most French parlements was divided among chambers which by a process of evolutionary development had become specialized organs for dealing with various kinds of cases. In the Parlement of Provence there were six chambers: *grand'chambre, tournelle, enquêtes, eaux et forêts, requêtes,* and *vacations,* and some cases were handled by special commissions belonging to no particular chamber. In actual practice, however, most of the work of the parlement was done by the *grand'chambre* and the *tournelle;* the other chambers, which had for the most part been formed as a result of the king's desire to sell offices, had few responsibilities.

The *grand'chambre,* which had originally been the whole parlement, reserved for itself the most important political and judicial functions; it believed itself competent to interfere in any phase of the social, economic, political, or judicial life of Provence, and claimed the right to govern the province in the absence of the royal governor. It shared its own work with the *tournelle,* the chamber second in importance, leaving it most criminal cases and the administration of prisons. On especially important occasions, when it was necessary to consider matters which concerned the parlement or the province as a whole, all of the chambers met together: for example, when the king ordered registration of important edicts his representatives in Provence had to face the *chambres assemblées* of the parlement.[20] Because the magistrates of the parlement formed a corporation having its own treasury, debts, and assessments, they elected each year a group of commissioners to look after the common funds and the parlement's administrative organiza-

19 *Ibid.,* pp. 148–152, 155, 157–162, 513.
20 *Ibid.,* pp. 261–264, 289–291, 515.

tion. Decisions of these commissioners had to be approved by the *chambres assemblées*.[21]

The Parlement of Provence was made up of magistrates who had purchased their offices and therefore considered them, like their land and homes, to be private property. Many offices had remained in the hands of the same families for generations. Venality of offices had originally been prohibited in Provence, but the king's constant need for money, coupled with the natural desire of the judges to perpetuate their honors, had overcome constitutional scruples. By the late eighteenth century, to be sure, venality of offices was widely recognized as immoral. The magistrates in Provence did not dare defend it openly, but contended that it was a necessary evil, since the only alternative was to expose justice to a system of arbitrary appointments influenced by the king's favorites.[22]

By the eighteenth century admission to any parlement as a *conseiller* automatically made a man and his descendants members of the nobility of the robe. This rule was of little importance in Provence, for membership in the court at Aix had become the monopoly of a local nobility of long standing; it had become virtually impossible for members of the bourgeoisie, grown rich in business or financial ventures, to enter the parlement; indeed, the magistrates made it a rule to exclude "shopkeepers". The magistrates themselves formed a caste in which an intellectual élite, whose families had been nobles of the robe for generations, sat side by side with nobles of the sword. Candidates for admission to the parlement were carefully investigated with regard to both family connections and wealth, and he who lacked either nobility or the wealth necessary for living in the manner expected of magistrates had virtually no chance of acceptance. By the eighteenth century the magistrates of Provence had become a new aristocracy, almost indistinguishable in social position and way of life from the nobility

21 *Ibid.*, p. 515.
22 *Ibid.*, pp. 21, 23–24, 509.

of the sword, and it is safe to say that the judicial power had become closely related to the ownership of property.[23]

Like members of the judicial caste in other parts of France, the magistrates of Provence enjoyed numerous privileges and material advantages which they viewed as positive rights associated with their offices. They were exempt from certain taxes, the *taille, lods et ventes* (duties on transfer of certain kinds of property), *franc fief* (a duty paid by those holding certain kinds of noble land), and to a certain extent the salt tax. They were exempt from military service and from the quartering of soldiers. In addition to their *gages,* which resembled salaries but were actually revenues attached to the offices according to their original price, like the interest on a loan, the magistrates received *épices,* or fees for their services. To some of them the king granted pensions for special merit or long service.[24] Despite their material advantages, however, the magistrates of Provence scarcely profited financially as a result of their enviable positions. In addition to their original investments in their offices they were subject to a number of duties which had to be paid if their titles to the offices were to be kept clear, and they also had to contribute to the treasury of the parlement itself. Thus the honor of being a magistrate was very high-priced indeed, and could by no means be regarded simply as a way of increasing one's fortune.[25]

For those whose families and fortunes met the rigid requirements of the judicial caste, admission to the parlement was an easy matter, and it was therefore not uncommon for new magistrates to be mere youngsters who knew little of law or Latin. Apparently this system of admissions did not seriously harm the quality of the parlement's work, for newly admitted magistrates were required to serve for several years in

23 P. Albert Robert, *Les remontrances et arrêtés du Parlement de Provence au XVIII siècle, 1715-1790* (Paris: Rousseau, 1912), p. 15. Wolff, *op. cit.,* pp. 15-21.

24 Wolff, *op. cit.,* pp. 222-225, 514.

25 Wolff, *op. cit.,* pp. 38-39, 509.

a minor capacity where they had ample opportunities for learning the law and where they could make no serious mistakes.[26] There is, on the whole, good reason for believing that the character and ability of the magistrates at Aix were of unusually high quality during much of the eighteenth century. The period from 1751 to 1771 was an especially brilliant one for the Parlement of Provence, and two of its members, J.–P. François de Monclar (*procureur général,* 1732–73), and J.–F. André Leblanc de Castillon (*avocat général* after 1741) had reputations throughout the French kingdom and even beyond its borders.[27] The parlement, by a kind of division of labor, had members especially fitted to deal with economic, philosophical, historical, and theological problems.[28] In general the integrity of the magistrates was high; in the eighteenth century there were few examples of magistrates accepting improper gifts or departing from the tradition of judicial impartiality, and those who did were dealt with severely by their colleagues. In both civil and criminal cases most of the magistrates at Aix tended to be liberal in the sense that they avoided lengthy and excessively formal or legalistic trials. Torture was seldom used in Provence, and individual liberty was shown considerably more respect than in many of the other parlements of France.[29]

It is the conclusion of M. P. Albert Robert, one of the most careful students of the Parlement of Provence in the eighteenth century, that the activities of the magistrates at Aix were characterized above all by concern for the public welfare.[30] It is quite possible that Provence, with its somewhat isolated geographical position and its powerful traditions of autonomy,

26 Wolff, *op. cit.,* p. 510.

27 Busquet, *op. cit.,* p. 110; Robert, *op. cit.,* pp. 42–46.

28 Robert, *op. cit.,* p. 660.

29 Wolff, *op. cit.,* pp. 246–248, 516.

30 Robert, *op. cit.,* p. 660. Robert and Wolff are, to the knowledge of this writer, the best authorities on the Parlement of Provence in the eighteenth century. Both agree concerning the high ability and integrity of the court. The writer has found no authority to refute these statements.

was fortunate enough to possess a magistracy superior, at least, to many of the other parlements of France, upon which the verdict of history has been rather severe. The magistrates at Aix were apparently sincere in their desire to honor and respect the king, to give him aid when he needed it, and to set a good example for the rest of the people; thus the parlement did not hesitate to borrow money in order to aid in the payment of debts contracted by the crown, and in the conflicts between the parlements of France and the royal authority the magistrates at Aix tended, more than the other courts, to uphold their dignity as judges and to refrain from rabble-rousing.[31] On the other hand, the magistrates insisted that it was their duty to tell the king the truth at all times, even when that truth was unpleasant; they refused to remain silent in the face of what they considered to be evil conditions in the kingdom. They contended that the king should respect their important function, for to undermine the parlements would be to undermine the laws of the land. Above all they considered it their duty to uphold at all costs the interests and privileges of Provence, even in the face of the king's displeasure. This strong conviction, based on a sense of Provence's history and institutions, gave the parlement at Aix a certain individuality which set it off somewhat from the other sovereign courts.[32] Whether or not the Parlement of Provence was less narrowly selfish than the other parlements, it is certain that the magistrates at Aix had a strong sense of duty toward their province and their king. It does not follow that their judgments concerning the public welfare were correct.

Rightly or wrongly, the Parlement of Provence became associated in the second half of the eighteenth century with the political activities of the "parliamentary league", led by the Parlement of Paris. Like the other sovereign courts, the Parlement of Provence tended to be Jansenist and Gallican in its religious views, and therefore defended Jansenists and attacked

31 Robert, *op. cit.*, pp. 656–657; Wolff, *op. cit.*, pp. 244–245.
32 Wolff, *op. cit.*, pp. 244–245, 514, 516–517.

priests who refused to grant them the sacraments. Following
the lead of the Parlement of Paris, the court at Aix attacked
the Jesuits and expelled them from its jurisdiction in 1763. The
fight against the Jesuits marks a turning point in the history
of the French parlements in the eighteenth century, for it was
during the "Jesuit affair" that the association of sovereign
courts became firmly welded together and therefore became a
powerful instrument of opposition to the royal power.[33]

In the struggles between the parlements and the crown over
taxation the magistrates at Aix came to stand side by side with
the other sovereign courts. During the period of Cardinal
Fleury's influence (1726–43) Provence had had few complaints about taxation, for Fleury, besides being economical,
was a native of Fréjus and until his death remained fond of
Provence.[34] After Fleury's death, however, the War of the
Austrian Succession continued to increase the government's
deficit, and the Seven Years War made France's fiscal condition worse and worse. Controllers General came and went; new
taxes, such as the *vingtièmes,* tended to come and to remain.
Like the other sovereign courts, the Parlement of Provence
fought the new tax legislation edict by edict, preaching order
and economy in the finances, writing remonstrances, and finally
registering only when concessions had been made or when
force had been brought to bear. The Parlement of Provence
did not, to be sure, play a leading part in the resistance to new
taxes; it registered them much more readily than the parlements at Paris, Bordeaux, Toulouse, Grenoble, and Besançon.[35]
But it played its part in the game of opposition and obstruction
which resulted in the downfall of Silhouette and Bertin; and
when in 1763 the crown gave way once more before the onslaughts of the judicial caste and issued the Declaration of November 21 inviting the sovereign courts to participate in the

33 Busquet, *op. cit.,* pp. 110–113.

34 Robert, *op. cit.,* pp. 68–70.

35 Busquet, *op. cit.,* pp. 111–112.

reformation of the finances, the Parlement of Provence had a share in the victory.[36]

2. The Provence Memorials

The Parlement of Provence accepted the invitation given in the Declaration of November 21, and in 1764 named an extraordinary commission for the purpose of preparing memorials about the various taxes collected in the province and generally on all questions pertaining to the finances.[37] Little is known about this commission [38] but they evidently set to work with a will, for in the space of two, or perhaps three years they managed to turn out fourteen thick folio volumes of manuscript entitled *Des mémoires envoiés à M. le Contrôleur Général des finances par le Parlement de Provence, en vertu de la Declaration du Roi du 21 N^{bre} 1763.*[39] These memorials were to be the

36 The Parlement of Provence was also to share the downfall of the judicial caste when Maupeou made his reform in 1770–71. Like the other provincial parlements the court at Aix supported the Parlement of Paris in its fight against Maupeou and was suppressed in 1771, to be replaced by a new court. It was reestablished, along with the other parlements, by Louis XVI's edict of 1774. It met for the last time on August 9, 1789, and was definitely suppressed, along with all the old jurisdictions, in 1790. Busquet, *op. cit.,* pp. 113–115, 118–119, 121.

37 Robert, *op. cit.,* pp. 90–91.

38 Robert mentions its existence but in writing his book apparently knew nothing of its membership or the extent of its work.

39 This title, without alterations of punctuation or spelling, is taken from the table of contents for the whole fourteen volumes, at the end of Volume I. The full title given in that place actually begins *"Table Générale des volumes des minutes, des mémoires envoiés* etc.", a fact which seems to indicate that the fourteen manuscript volumes are a first draft, and that the authors did not yet know how many volumes there would be. The title printed by hand on the outside of each volume of the memoirs is simply *Mémoires sur les finances.* The present writer is unable to say exactly how many years were taken to assemble the memorials. The year 1765 is written on the title page of Volume I. In Volume XII the year 1766 is referred to as "this year", and in Volume XIV the wording on pages 63 and 121 seems to indicate that that volume was also written in 1766.
Whether the volumes of memorials were ever actually sent to the Controller General is a question which will be discussed later. The fourteen

parlement's contribution to the complete economic and fiscal reform of the state. In their eyes the Declaration of November 21 meant that the king had asked their advice concerning the best means of increasing the wealth of the state and assuring the happiness of the people.[40] Magnanimously, but with obvious confidence both in their right and in their ability to institute reforms, the magistrates of Provence opened their first memorial with an indirect reference to the recent conflict between parlements and crown.

> It happens only too often that the best of princes, their confidence betrayed, are led into errors by the very measures which they have taken as means of learning the truth. This difficulty need not be feared today; the wisdom of the mon-

manuscript volumes are now in the Seligman Collection at Columbia University. The writer has been unable to trace their whereabouts in the years before their purchase by the late Professor Seligman. In a memorandum about some of the items in his great collection, Professor Seligman stated that the existence of the Provence memorials "has hitherto not been known", and the writer, who has been unable to find any references to the memorials in books about the French finances, the parlements in general, or the Parlement of Provence in particular, believes this statement to be correct. As we have seen, P. Albert Robert's *Les remontrances et arrêtés du Parlement de Provence* mentions the commission which wrote the memorials but shows no awareness of the existence of the memorials themselves. Like so many other documents of the old régime, the volumes of manuscript may have been misplaced or stolen during the great revolution.

Professor Seligman, in his memorandum, calls the Provence memorials "by all odds the fullest statement and discussion of the French revenues in existence." Certainly the Parlement of Provence did a remarkable piece of research in assembling such a vast body of material; and anyone reading the *mémoires* will be left in no doubt of the authors' erudition and familiarity with the best eighteenth century works on political economy and public finance.

40 *Mémoires sur les finances,* Volume VIII, pp. 11–12. Throughout the remainder of this study all footnotes referring to the Provence memorials will indicate only the volume and page numbers. This note, for example, would simply be "VIII, 11–12". Since the identity of the authors of the *mémoires* is unknown, and since it is assumed that the parlement as a whole approved their conclusions, the terms "parlement", "magistrates", "judges", and "commission" will be used interchangeably in referring to the authors of the memorials.

arch has safeguarded the supreme grandeur against the surrounding snares. If fidelity and truth were banished from the rest of the land, they could still be found in this great corporation of magistrates which the king has been pleased to question concerning the administration of the finances.

The time has come to establish facts which have almost always been falsified, to verify complaints which have often been stifled and occasionaly exaggerated, and, what is no less essential, to establish the fundamental maxims which must serve as the basis for all financial operations in the common interest of the sovereign and his subjects . . . It is in this spirit that we shall carefully develop the maxims of statesmanship which appear to us to be the most reliable, in order that they may be clarified by objections, corrected if necessary, or adopted.[41]

In undertaking this project, the Parlement of Provence apparently hoped to work in collaboration with the other members of the "corporation of magistrates", for they urged that their memorials be sent to the other sovereign courts of France for additions and corrections.[42]

The original plan of the Parlement of Provence was to write no less than five memorials. The first of these was to be a description of the worst abuses in taxation, evils the reformation of which should be undertaken at once. The second memorial would be a kind of census of all the taxes collected in Provence, and the third would describe municipal administration in the province. In the fourth memorial the magistrates promised to demonstrate the advantages of a uniform system of administration for the whole kingdom, and to show how such a system could be established. The fifth and last memorial was to discuss the assessment of the taxes and the problem of paying the nation's debts.[43] Thus it was the intention of the Parlement of Provence to launch a full-dress attack upon the chief financial problems facing the France of their day.

41 I, 1–3. In this, and in all other translations from the *mémoires,* the only changes have been occasional changes in capitalization and punctuation.
42 VI, 528–530.
43 I, 18–19.

Whether or not this impressive program was ever completed remains a mystery, but it appears likely that it was not. The fourteen folio volumes of memorials which came, at last, into the possession of Columbia University contain only the first and second sections projected by the parlement. It is possible, of course, that the other three memorials may have existed, or may still exist. One might guess, on the other hand, that by 1766 or 1767, with fourteen volumes behind them, the Parlement of Provence may well have decided that the none too cordial relations between the king's ministers and the parlements did not justify the continuation of their task. There is some evidence that the first two memorials, or at least parts of them in the form of abstracts, were sent to the Controller General.[44] But the condition of Volume XIV, which is unbound, badly organized, and poorly paged, seems to indicate that the great undertaking was drawing to a close.

Whatever may have been the fate of the memorials during the reign of Louis XV, and whether or not additional ones were written, the existing fourteen volumes constitute a rich mine of information about the economic opinions of the Parlement of Provence in the years which followed the close of the Seven Years War.[45] They contain opinions about most of the

44 It will be recalled that the full title given in Volume I began with the words "Des minutes, des mémoires envoiés à M. Le Contrôleur Général des finances." In the margin of Volume III, p. 1, is the following notation: "Il y a 376 pages du mis au net envoyés le 10 Xbre 1764." Again on the first page of the second section of Volume XIV there is a reference to an abstract of the memorials: "tome 14 de la minute et tome 9 du mis au net."

45 This material is organized in an almost unbelievably confusing manner. In their main outlines the memorials are simple enough: Volumes I and II contain the first memorial concerning the evils most in need of correction; the rest of the volumes contain the second memorial, which, despite the announced intention of the authors, is an attempt to discuss all the main taxes of France. Within each of the two memorials, however, no heading can be depended upon to tell exactly what follows; and that condition, though confusing, is a source of great variety and richness, for the authors, after setting out to discuss a tax, very often proceed to unburden themselves of general convictions concerning such elements of political economy as tariffs, manufacturing, commerce, population, the proper use of money, and the vices and virtues of state intervention in economic enterprise.

taxes of France, though the authors originally intended to leave that subject for their last memorial. There are also numerous discussions of political economy, for the authors refused to divorce that subject from the problem of taxation. Indeed, one of the most significant facts about the memorials is that the magistrates turned a discussion of the finances into a great examination of the accumulated legislation, and particularly the economic legislation, of the old régime. In effect, the memorials written by the Parlement of Provence give their answer to the Declaration of November 21, 1763, concerning what should be done for France. It is the purpose of this study to examine that answer in more detail.

3. THE DILEMMA IN THE FINANCES

Examining the condition of the French finances at the close of the Seven Years War, the Parlement of Provence found certain troublesome facts. Like most people they believed that the coming of peace should mean the lightening of taxation. Statesmanship as well as humanity, they insisted, demanded that the government adhere to the old maxim that the people should be allowed to breathe in time of peace. In wartime people suffered doubly, having to pay heavier taxes while production and commerce were interrupted, and unless a nation was allowed to recover its prosperity when peace returned, a new war would find it exhausted and impotent.[46] Yet France was deeply in debt. The parlement was ignorant of the amount of this debt, and made haste to stress this fact as a prelude to asking for information, but they admitted that the debt existed.[47] They hastened also to express their sympathy for the French people, faced with the problem of paying the enormous current expenses of the state, as well as the arrears and interest on the debt. Worse still was the prospect that the greater the debt, arrears, and interest payments became, the greater the

46 I, 49–51.
47 I, 107–108, 113.

expenses of financial administration and tax collection would be.[48]

In the opinion of the parlement the French people were too exhausted to go on paying the extraordinary wartime taxes. For this reason most of the items in the government's program, expressed in the Declaration of November 21, were faulty; the declaration was, to their way of thinking, little better than a temporary measure.[49] Like most of the parlements, they were suspicious of the proposed register of property, which they accused of being a slow and expensive project. The amortization fund of twenty million *livres* was inadequate and was therefore a slow poison to the state; the idea of amortization was sound, to be sure, but a fund of twenty millions was just big enough to make the taxpayers suffer, and yet too small to pay the debts of the state, since such items as arrears and interest would all but use up the fund without making more than a trifling headway against the debt itself. Thus the people would suffer and the nation's production would be handicapped, and all to no avail. In fact, actual harm would be done, for the inadequate amortization would make the nation poorer by exhausting the provinces through taxation.[50] As for the taxes ordered by the Declaration of November 21, the parlement predicted that however necessary they might be they could not be collected unless the government came to the rescue of the people, for the taxes were harmful and actually tended to decrease the ability of the people to pay money into the treasury.[51]

Unfortunately the existence of debts and the exhaustion of the taxpayers were not the only evils which the parlement felt called upon to point out, for they also believed that the administration of the government's finances was faulty. In past years the excessive expenses of the government had placed a strain on the nation's tax structure. In order to increase the

48 I, 42–43.
49 I, 25.
50 I, 25–27, 103–108, 113–115.
51 I, 27.

revenues harmful operations had been undertaken, and these operations had been defended by false principles. In the opinion of the parlement the false principles had been given lasting life by a few people who turned them into dogmas in order that they might profit from the disorder in the finances. The situation, moreover, was a vicious circle, since new needs of the treasury caused the false operations and principles to be used all the more. As a result, the finances had become "a complicated science, the mysteries of which are impenetrable, except to a few of the initiated who profit by the public misfortunes." [52]

Thus the Parlement of Provence, on setting out to examine the condition of the French finances, found certain faults which obviously needed correction: the state was in debt; the taxpayers were suffering and could not be asked to pay more; and the very system of handling matters of taxation and finance was faulty in structure, and was being made more so by the everlasting need for money. These unhealthy conditions presented the parlement with a trying dilemma. What was to be done? Obviously, for one thing, the debt should be paid. "France will never see order perfectly established in her finances unless the Royal Treasury is set free from all debts; it is the best means of preparing the way for a truly paternal government and a patriotic administration (*administration citoyene*)".[53] But with the nation in such an exhausted condition, how could the debt be paid without doing serious harm to the economy and to the people? "However indispensable may be the adjustment of the finances in order to assure and hasten payment [of the debt], it is expedient not to rush matters, considering the actual condition of the kingdom, similar to that of a sick person whose exhaustion demands that he be allowed to regain strength before risking remedies." [54] The situation was a dilemma. The parlement was convinced that the burden

52 I, 4–5.
53 I, 16.
54 I, 19–20.

of taxation should be made less heavy on the backs of the
people; yet on the other hand the existence of the public debt
seemed to indicate that the collection of taxes could not be
diminished.[55]

4. A FUNDAMENTAL PRINCIPLE

Faced with the twin evils of inadequate revenues and exhausted taxpayers, the parlement sought a solution by striking
at what they considered to be the roots of the difficulty. They
were convinced that the form of assessment and collection of
the taxes was faulty, and like so many other people in the
France of the 1760's they considered the possibility of a sweeping change in the whole tax structure. But at this point they
began to tread warily. One can only guess at their motives:
perhaps, like other members of the judicial caste in other parts
of France, they were not unaware of danger to their own privileges and property; already they had opposed the project of a
register of all landed property in France. Whatever their motives, the magistrates preferred not to hasten a decision about
the distribution of the taxes.[56]

Reform of the methods of assessing and collecting the taxes
was not to be abandoned completely, but was merely to be postponed for a while so that the unhealthy economic system could
regain its strength. Thus there were two jobs to be done: the
existing faulty system of finances had to be made less burden-
some and the plans for a new system drawn up. The parlement
insisted that both of these jobs should be done at the same time,
which was equivalent to saying that relief for the taxpayers
should come first; for the planning of a better system of taxation would require a large amount of research, and it was this
research rather than the immediate institution of a new tax
system that the magistrates recommended.[57]

The most pressing problem was the need to make easier the

55 I, 20.
56 I, 20–21.
57 I, 28–29.

lot of the people, and in the opinion of the parlement everything else was secondary to that necessity.[58] Thus they refused
to be encouraged by the government's plan for an amortization
fund of twenty million *livres*. So long as the yearly budget was
balanced, they argued, there was no need for excessive worry
about the amortization of the debt. Indeed, the fund of twenty
millions would make necessary the continuation of taxes which
were harmful to the economy of the nation. Since the rescue of
the provinces from such taxes was the most vital need of the
moment, and since in any case there was no prospect of paying
the debt for many years to come, it would be better to diminish
the amount of the amortization in order that agriculture and
commerce might be encouraged. Faced with the problem of
France's debts and inadequate revenues, the parlement actually
recommended that the amortization fund be decreased in size
and that the weight of the taxes be made lighter.[59] They did
not regard this view as paradoxical, but insisted that it would
be possible to give the people relief from taxation and at the
same time find sufficient resources for the needs of the state.[60]

In justification of this point of view the parlement called
upon a principle which, by their own admission, was the core
of their thought concerning the financial problems facing the
France of their day. This principle was more than just another
suggestion about the finances. Given what they chose to consider as facts—that the government needed money, that the
taxpayers were exhausted, and that the system of taxation was
faulty,—the magistrates took their stand on the high ground
of political economy. France's debts must indeed be paid, and
the treasury must be filled by means of taxation; but the first
step toward the attainment of these ends should be, not the
crushing of the forces of production, but their liberation.

The parlement recognized that complaints were often made
with justice against the government's taking too much money

58 I, 102–103.
59 I, 106–107.
60 I, 109–110.

from the people by taxation. But their main concern, they insisted, was with regulations which prevented the people from getting money in the first place. Reform of such regulations was the real problem. Its solution would prepare the way for reform of the actual processes of taxation.[61] True, the government had creditors anxious for their money. But the best security that these creditors could have would be the increased wealth of France. For "the national wealth is the state's security for the taxes, and the security of creditors for the sums which are owed them: their common interest demands that work be done to increase the value of their security." [62] Was it not, after all, easier to tax a rich nation than a poor one? [63] It should therefore be to the benefit of everyone to see that the nation was allowed to become rich; and the great obstacle in the way of the production of wealth was a mistaken policy with regard to taxation and regulation of economic enterprise. If everyone would recognize this fact, the unwise operations would soon be abolished.[64]

Again and again in the course of their fourteen volumes of memorials the magistrates returned to this principle, which is perhaps best summarized in the following quotation.

Now is the time to apply the general principle which is the touchstone in the administration of the finances: every tax which diminishes the productivity of the earth or of the arts, or which weakens the nation's advantages in the balance of its trade, is a blind and murderous operation. It is just to tax people who profit or reap; it is foolhardy, unjust, and absurd to prevent them from profiting and reaping.

An author well versed in these matters has said very aptly that the public revenue, or the taxes, are merely the result of a kind of discount deducted from the incomes of individuals. The discount cannot be large unless there is an increase in the

61 I, 762–763.
62 I, 47–48.
63 XIV, 80.
64 I, 281.

mass of individual incomes which make up the national income; it is impossible to maintain the public revenue while diminishing the national income by restricting consumption, by annoyances placed in the way of commerce and obstacles preventing production.

We insist on this capital point, which is the summary of all our memorials, and we are aware of no other maxim in finance than to increase the national income in order to draw from it abundant resources without harming the body of the state.[65]

In this way the parlement justified their view that the relief of the people was the most pressing problem, the one to be faced at once. "To increase the national wealth is the first law of intelligent finance." [66]

The parlement's acceptance of this principle had implications which are vital to an understanding of their thought. By adopting as their major premise the maxim that an effective financial system must be based on a healthy economic system, they at once widened the financial problem into a problem of political economy and took upon themselves the task of telling how to increase the national wealth. The prospect of outlining a plan for encouraging the economic well-being of France was certainly far from unpleasant to the parlement. Of the five memorials which they planned to write,[67] it is probable that only two were actually completed, but both of these contain a great deal of opinion about general economic matters. The first

65 IV, 825–828. A note in the margin of the memorial refers to *"recherch. sur les fin.* T.2.p.164." It is a reference to François Véron de Forbonnais' *Recherches et considérations sur les finances de France, depuis 1595 jusqu'à l'année 1721* (Basle, 1758, 6 Vols.). The book was published without the author's name, and it is possible that the magistrates of Provence, who refer to it often throughout their memorials, did not know the author's name. Forbonnais' exact words were "En effet les revenus publics sont-ils autre chose que le résultat d'une espèce d'escompte prélevé sur les revenus particuliers? Lorsque l'incertitude des propriétés anéantit le travail et les consommations, il est absolument impossible que le produit des revenus publics se soutienne."

66 XIV, 72.

67 I, 22–23.

memorial is avowedly a discussion of the worst taxes and regulations in France as a whole, viewed mainly from the standpoint of their effect on the economy. The second, though in
name merely a description of Provence's taxes, turns out on
closer inspection to be nothing less than a description of the
principal taxes in France, in which is included a large amount
of economic opinion.

Judging from what they actually wrote, then, the parlement
was by no means unprepared to discuss matters of political
economy. One can only speculate concerning their reasons for
including so many discussions of how to make France rich. It
is quite possible that, faced with the difficult problems of budget
balancing and the apparent need for more taxes, they preferred the easier theory that a France delivered from oppressive taxes and regulations was the first objective in a program
of financial reform. Such a solution would undoubtedly have
appealed to a group of men wishing to avoid further heavy
taxation on property, whatever their motives. Moreover, since
legislation concerning taxes was so closely bound up with matters of economic regulation and general economic policy, it is
not surprising that the magistrates were quick to discuss political economy as well as taxation. The question of tariffs, for
example, was closely allied to the question of the advantages
and disadvantages of free trade. Certainly much of the material in the Provence memorials is negative in nature; that is,
the authors in telling how to solve the financial problems by
making France prosperous hastened to point to the need for
tearing down a great many economic regulations and financial
practices of the old régime. Whether their motives were narrowly selfish or unselfish and statesmanlike, this tendency to
urge the removal of objectionable legislation is an outstanding
characteristic of the memorials.

Because the magistrates chose to examine existing legislation not merely where it touched matters of taxation but also
where it concerned economic policy, their fourteen volumes of
mémoires may be viewed as an evaluation of the legislation of

their day from two points of view. There was, in the first place, the problem of seeing that France was prosperous and that the sources of revenue were not dried up by faulty governmental policies; and secondly there was the problem of tapping those sources properly, in such a way that adequate revenues were obtained without harming the sources themselves. Both of these problems were closely allied to the principle which the magistrates themselves described as the essence of their memorials: the principle that it would be easier to tax a rich nation than a poor one and that the first law of the finances was to increase the national wealth. Because of the negative character of so much of what they had to say, however,—in other words because they found so many obstacles in the way of France's prosperity—the problem of making France wealthy received more attention than the problem of how to tax properly. At any rate, the memorials contain many more opinions on how not to tax than positive descriptions of a good tax system.[68]

It is true that according to the words of the magistrates themselves neither of the two essential actions, relief for the people and the planning of financial reform, should have priority over the other. Both tasks were to be undertaken at the same time.[69] In actual practice the removal of oppressive taxation was to begin at once, while the launching of a new financial system was to await the results of a careful research project, toward which the magistrates considered their memorials to be an important contribution. Judged by their actual recommendations, therefore, the most immediate concern of the parlement was the removal of legislation oppressive to the taxpayers and

68 Perhaps if the full five *mémoires* planned by the parlement were available it would be possible to form a more complete idea of what the judges recommended in the way of a tax program to solve France's pressing need for money. It is possible, on the other hand, that the parlement's ideas on this subject, either out of distaste for more taxes or for some other reason, remained unformed. In that case the bulk of their opinions concerning the problem of the French finances were concerned with their oft-repeated principle that the most important problem was to increase the national wealth.

69 I, 28–29.

to the economic system, a program in keeping with their comparison of France to a sick person who needed a chance to regain his strength before being given strong medicine. Meanwhile, the plans for a better financial system could be drawn up, in preparation for the day when the nation would be healthy enough to make the change. The projected financial system was to be characterized by order, uniformity, and rationality. The magistrates viewed the existing system as a haphazard affair, the parts of which had been added one after another without regard for symmetry or proportion, and they were determined either to reform or to replace it.[70] A reasonable method of taxing could be found only by examining the whole problem of the finances in its entirety. At the risk of making some mistakes, the parlement was prepared to undertake this task, and they expressed the hope that the other parlements would aid them.[71]

But even in discussing the need for a complete system of finances, the magistrates turned again to general criticisms of the France of their day. Just as they had turned from the problem of France's debts to the necessity for making the nation rich, so now they went on to insist that the finances could not be reformed unless the state were reformed as well.[72] The people and the government, they pointed out, tended to influence each other constantly.[73] In the sixteenth century, for example, King Francis I had managed, by appointing zealous men, to pay his debts and to accumulate a treasury surplus; such a policy of economy had been possible in that period because the people of France believed in sound principles.[74] The eighteenth century, however, was not so fortunate, for a widespread change of morals was reflected in and endangered the state; the existence of such qualities as thirst for money, love of pleasure, incapacity, laziness, and complacency was a con-

70 I, 30–31.
71 VI, 528–530.
72 I, 205–206.
73 I, 151–152.
74 I, 154–155.

stant threat to the government's finances; men strong enough to serve the public good in spite of personal unpopularity were becoming rare.[75] "The spirit of interest and venality, which in former times destroyed the most celebrated peoples on earth and which is current in the nation, constitutes an almost general conspiracy against economy in the finances, and one which must be crushed." [76]

This need for moral reform, in the opinion of the parlement, justified even wider demands than those they had made thus far. They contended that a complete system of finances, desirable as it was, could only be brought into being as part of a general system of legislation and government. There should therefore be a uniform system of political and moral regulations of the kind best suited to the genius of the nation. Such an immortal work, they urged, would win for the king a place in history superior to that of all other great legislators.[77]

> In the existence of states the passage of time always brings on a critical epoch when, in order to prevent decadence, it would be necessary for the government to examine all parts of its legislation and administration; but there is no example of a sovereign having such foresight; without calling a halt, men follow the ancient ways, and the evils increase by degrees until the whole perishes. The time has come to erect a dike against the torrent which is carrying us away . . ." [78]

Doubtless the magistrates, emboldened by their recent successes, were enjoying the vision of such a great reform, supervised to a large degree by the parlements of France.

The Parlement of Provence thus responded to the Declaration of November 21, 1763, by embarking upon a great criticism of the old régime. Given an opportunity to suggest means

75 I, 161–162.

76 I, 166–167. This passage exemplifies the prophetic, Old Testament kind of language often used by the parlement in its memorials.

77 I, 154–159.

78 I, 159–161.

of financial reform, the magistrates widened their analysis to include matters of political economy, and even called for a general reform of the state. The dilemma in the finances—need for money and yet exhaustion of the taxpayers—appeared to indicate reform of the faulty tax structure; but the parlement insisted that such reform be accompanied, and even preceded, by relief for the people, on the ground that the first law of the finances was to increase the national wealth. They recommended, therefore, that the national wealth should be increased by liberating the forces of production from the bondage imposed on them by unwise taxes and regulations. That accomplished, there would remain only the task of planning a uniform system of finances for the purpose of tapping the national wealth without danger of drying up its sources. But by formulating such aims, the parlement made necessary the consideration of national affairs other than the finances. Making the nation wealthy meant determining economic policies, and the parlement insisted that the general plan of financial reform was inseparably allied with a reform of the whole system of legislation then in effect in France. Far from quailing before the magnitude of such problems, the magistrates proceeded with zest to record their opinions in the fourteen volumes of *Mémoires sur les finances*.

CHAPTER III

POPULATION AND STATESMANSHIP

Nous finirons cet essay sur la population par ce beau mot de l'illustre Mr. Hume: Là où il y a plus de bonheur et de vertu avec le gouvernement le plus sage, il y a plus de peuple.

Mémoires, I, 506.

In recording their suggestions for a better France, the magistrates of Provence found it necessary to treat at some length the subject of population. Their analysis of the financial problems facing the nation pointed to the need for relief of the taxpayers and for a general program of legislation in order that the state might be reformed and made more wealthy. Such a program required a careful study of population problems, and the parlement went so far as to say that the very art of government could be understood as the treatment of the population.

> . . . We extend our lands by increasing their productivity, and the sovereign whose power must be judged according to the number of his subjects and their accomplishments multiplies men by making them more useful. The great art of government can be reduced to these two points: increase the population and make the best possible use of it. These two aims are in a sense one; for if one makes good use of people they multiply, and if the population increases noticeably, considering the quality of the soil and climate, it is a sign that the administration is good. Ordinarily a society is peopled only to the extent that it is happy.[1]

Besides serving as a sign that the people were being wisely governed, a large population was to be sought as a source of positive benefits to the king and to the state. Population was "the glory and strength of kings", for men were the most precious of possessions. Indeed, the whole economic system was closely linked to the number of people in the kingdom.

1 I, 250–251.

The finances could not be reformed unless commerce was made to flourish, and the success of commerce rested upon the extent of agricultural prosperity. Agriculture, in its turn, depended upon a numerous population, for in the words of the magistrates themselves, "agriculture and commerce are the two mainsprings of the national wealth." Population was therefore a vital subject if the great reform undertaken by the parlement was to be completed. In the financial system of France every practice harmful to population had to be corrected without delay, for taxes cutting into the subsistence of families were a crime against the state.[2]

The magistrates apparently had no fear that the population of France might become too large. They argued that more men meant more production: for a greater number of people would mean greater competition for subsistence, and this competition would have the good effect of forcing men to find new means of making a living. Population increase would have the further advantage of reducing superfluous consumption by non-productive classes and enlarging consumption by workers; necessity would force a better distribution of the goods produced, and the state would benefit.[3]

The parlement's opinions about population thus supported their general thesis that the people and the national economy needed rescuing from a great deal of legislation harmful to their well-being.

> . . . If all men join in recognizing that the population is the glory and strength of kings, if their wealth depends upon that of their subjects and that of their subjects upon multiplication of the kinds of occupations, which in turn multiplies the means of subsistence, there will be great haste to reform operations which are at the same time harmful and unjust, operations which exhaust the provinces, alter the organization of the state, and obscure the majesty of the government.[4]

2 I, 240–242.
3 I, 443–444.
4 I, 655–656.

Because the subject of population was so closely related to the need for reform, the magistrates treated it at some length. Two principal themes appear again and again in their discussions of population: the importance of collecting all available facts, and the need for fostering the well-being of the people.

1. THE IMPORTANCE OF FACTS ABOUT POPULATION

The parlement believed that there should be an answer to the vital problem of how large a population the national resources could support. At the beginning of the eighteenth century Marshal Vauban, whose writings were familiar to the magistrates,[5] had expressed the opinion that the France of that day was capable of nourishing 25,500,000 people. The magistrates made no comment concerning the accuracy of this figure, but they believed such estimates to be extremely useful, and they were convinced that the France of their own day would be able to support a much larger population if only agriculture were improved and commerce extended.[6]

Unfortunately there had been so little interest in the vital subject of population that the exact number of people in France was not even known. Some people claimed that the nation had become strangely depopulated since the reign of Charles IX, and that despite increases in territory the population had declined from 19 million to the low figure of 16 million. The parlement doubted the accuracy of this estimate. Vauban had set the population at 19 million, while others said 17 million and most authorities, according to the magistrates, believed that there were 16 million people in France. The author of *Le détail de la France*[7] had set the figure at 15 million, and the

5 The maréchal de Vauban is best known in the field of economic thought for his *Dixme royale*, which was published in 1707. Vauban was in general a mercantilist, though some of his beliefs, such as his statement that the real wealth of a nation consisted of goods needed by the people, have caused him to be considered by some people a forerunner of the physiocrats.

6 I, 251–252.

7 This book was written by Pierre de Boisguilbert, a magistrate from Normandy, and published anonymously in 1695. Boisguilbert criticized some of

pamphlet *Financier citoyen*[8] favored an estimate of 20 million. Another writer, whom the magistrates did not name and whom they suspected of purposely exaggerating all the advantages of France, set the figure as high as 24 million.[9]

The magistrates themselves believed that the figure was somewhere between 16 and 20 million, and they were far from satisfied with its magnitude.

> . . . We believe France to be a little better peopled than is usually supposed, infinitely less peopled than it should be, and proportionally less than it was in the days of Charles IX. That fact is all the more remarkable, considering the ample increase in navigation and commerce, the more skilled industries, the better police regulations, and the more firmly established interior peace; some malignant cause must have counterbalanced all these advantages, and that cause is not difficult to find. We believe, moreover, that the same causes which have prevented population increase have brought about in great numbers of the people a decline in vigor and strength which makes them less capable of carrying on their work and resisting ill health.[10]

At this point in their memorials the magistrates did not choose to say more about the evil influences which were causing the population to be less sizeable and less energetic; but their reference to the existence of such influences tended to support their general thesis that the people were suffering and needed relief from badly conceived taxes and economic regulations.

The parlement was unable even to give the exact population of their own province. The judges were inclined, for example, to be amazed at the estimate reported by M. de Boulainvilliers

the mercantilist notions. For example, he wanted free export of grains and, unlike most mercantilists, thought that agriculture was the most important branch of national production.

8 See Chapter I, section 3. The author of this pamphlet, which appeared in 1757 and which defended the tax farmers, was named Navau.

9 I, 253–256.

10 I, 256–258.

in a collection of the memoirs of the intendants,[11] an estimate which credited the Provence of 1658 with 228,487 households and 1,006,976 people. Whatever its population may have been in the seventeenth century, insisted the parlement, the Provence of the 1760's did not have nearly so many households or individuals. Vauban's estimate of 639,895 people for the year 1700 was far more to their liking.[12] Their own estimate, made by multiplying the number of births (or deaths or marriages) in a given year by a ratio expressing the number of living people for each birth (or death or marriage), set the population of Provence at 700,000 people. The ratio which they used was itself only a rough estimate, however, and the parlement, far from being satisfied with their own work, claimed to be presenting it only as an example of what needed doing by more expert hands.[13]

For why depend on guesses when an actual count could be made? Turning to history, the magistrates pointed out that the Romans had had a census of persons and of inheritances. They hastened to add that France had no need for a census of inheritances; but the population should be counted, and a suitable procedure would be that recommended by Vauban and patterned after the practices of the Chinese: there could be one inspector for each fifty families, visiting each family four times a year. Such a plan would aid in preventing vagrancy and begging, and would place hardships upon neither the inspectors nor the people. Again following the lead of Vauban, the magistrates pointed to the uses which such a census would have. The king's own interest demanded that he look after the well-being of the people so that they would increase in numbers. A yearly census would allow the monarch to know exactly the wealth and strength of his kingdom. In the population figures

11 This would be the *Etat de la France,* edited by Boulainvilliers, which was published in 1737. It was a six volume collection of memoirs written by the various intendants of France.

12 I, 361–362.

13 I, 343–363.

he could see the good or bad effects of legislation, and could act accordingly.[14]

Following this train of thought, which they owed to Vauban,[15] the magistrates found in the population statistics possibilities for a veritable science of government. In their enthusiasm they came perilously close to giving their sovereign some good advice about his personal life.

> . . . This continual attention to the accidents which disturb the order of propagation and to the causes which favor it is the study most worthy of a king : if there is any pleasure which can compensate a generous soul for the boredom, emptiness, and servitudes of supremely high position, it is without doubt the sovereign's delicious pleasure in seeing families which owe him their existence, their subsistence, and their happiness, increase and multiply because of his care, in enjoying the spectacle of the general well-being which he himself brings about, and in exciting transports of affection and gratitude in all the courts.

> . . . This so satisfactory study is at the same time the most instructive one for a government. There, as in a faithful mirror, it can see at any time its faults and its successes. It will recognize good and bad policies by their effects, and it will proceed from the effect to the propagation, what accidents disturb it, and how they could have been prevented by vigilance.

> . . . Population is a reliable thermometer in affairs of state; its variations, whether large or small, rapid or slow, have various causes which the statesman must distinguish. Temporary disorders must be distinguished from progressive and habitual disorders; epidemics, famine, and taxes depopulate, but in different ways. There are cases of rapid depopulation which are immediately noticeable and which quickly spread,

14 I, 261–269.

15 The authors of the memorial do not cite a particular work by Vauban, but by using his name in their text they acknowledge that the idea of a yearly census as a means by which the king might examine the good or bad effects of legislation was his.

others which become apparent later and only gradually, and which are more lasting and destructive.[16]

The parlement, prompted by Vauban, was thus able to picture the king and his ministers studying the population statistics, separating out long term trends and random variations, and applying their knowledge to the betterment of the lot of the people.

From these statistics could be constructed a complicated machinery of statesmanship. The parlement, not satisfied with a mere census to get knowledge of total population, recommended also the collection of statistics about marriages, the birth rate, average length of life, and population density. By keeping track of the number of marriages in the nation as a whole and in its various divisions the king and his ministers could accumulate evidence concerning the true condition of the people; for prosperity and sound morality would cause the number of marriages in a district or in the nation to increase, while misery or immorality would have the opposite effect. The birth rate, recorded by means of the lists of baptisms, could serve in a similar manner. Subject to some variation because of differences in climate, the birth rate in the various parts of France should be fairly constant; the appearance of signs of sterility in a district or in the nation would be a symptom of misery or declining morality, and in either case the government would stand accused of faulty legislation or of neglect. Another means of measuring the well-being of the people would be a quotient indicating the average length of life in France or in a part of France. This quotient could easily be found by dividing the number of inhabitants of the section in question by the average number of deaths per year. It would then be possible to draw up lists of the places with the highest death rates, and steps could be taken to remedy the causes of this unfortunate condition. In Provence, for example, the average length of life

16 I, 269–273. This passage is apparently the authors' own interpretation and expansion of Vauban's suggestion that a yearly census be taken.

could be said to vary considerably from place to place; the magistrates believed that men lived longer in the mountains than in *la basse Provence,* but that because of north winds and poverty suffered by the mountaineers the average length of life was probably still greater in *la Provence mitoyenne.*[17] The government should also keep statistics of population density, in order that administrators might be warned in time to take action when, as in the case of the mountains of Provence, poverty led to emigration, or when a decline in population occurred for other reasons.[18]

In addition to serving as a thermometer for testing the national well-being, the statistics of population were essential for the straightening out of the financial muddle. The parlement believed that the population figures were a springboard to knowledge of such factors as national consumption of goods and national income, factors which were necessary to the proper planning of taxation.[19] Since the "public income" of the government, based on the taxes, depended on the national income, it was necessary to know the size of the national income in order to know how big the public income could safely be made, or in other words how heavy the taxes could be.

But in making such estimates it was essential that the meanings of the terms used be clearly understood. The magistrates chose to define national income (*revenu général*) as the value of all the annual productions of the earth and of the arts, minus whatever was purchased from foreign lands for the purpose of bringing about that production. Evidently they did not mean the "net product" in the physiocratic sense. Speaking of the attempt of an anonymous writer to estimate the net product from agricultural production, the magistrates expressed the opinion that such estimates were too difficult when the national income itself was unknown.[20] By their own definition the na-

17 I, 273–275, 342–343.
18 I, 275–276; XI, 386, 393.
19 I, 276–277.
20 IX, 341–344.

tional income was produced mainly by agriculture and manufacturing. Internal commerce could not be included, for properly speaking it was merely exchange of products of the earth and of manufacturing. A shoemaker, for example, might exchange shoes for grain or for money with which to buy grain. The shoes and the grain, products of farmer and shoemaker, were additions to the national income, but their exchange would add nothing. By the same reasoning, which took no account of what was later to be called "utility", the magistrates decided that the materials used for the repair of houses, but not the rent, could be included in the national income. Foreign trade, on the other hand, could add to the national income, which could thus be increased by renting a house to a foreigner, or by a favorable balance of trade.[21] In the opinion of the magistrates mining, which took valuable metals from the earth, and fishing, which took wealth from the sea, also added to the national income.[22]

Thus by the term national income the parlement apparently meant the yearly amount of wealth produced in France or obtained for the benefit of France. Unlike the physiocrats they considered manufacturing as well as agriculture productive, but the element of productivity was not the essence of their concept of national income; the magistrates of Provence, without discussing whether or not it was productive, made it clear that they considered foreign commerce capable of adding to France's national income; the physiocrats likewise admitted that by means of trade one nation might gain wealth at the expense of another, but they nevertheless insisted that only agriculture was productive. The parlement's "national income" is thus a much broader and at the same time a less abstract and theoretical term than the physiocratic "net product" from agriculture.

There remains, however, the problem of whether the parlement meant by national income the gross yearly amount of

21 IX, 341–343, 374–376.
22 I, 551–552; IX, 345–346.

wealth produced or received by France, or that sum minus the costs of producing or obtaining it. The Provence memorials are not entirely clear on this point, but apparently the magistrates wished to exclude the costs of production from their concept of national income. We have already seen that they defined national income as the annual productions of the earth and of the arts minus whatever was brought in from foreign lands for the purpose of bringing about that production, and that they considered a favorable balance of trade capable of increasing the national income. They also stated that the amount of wealth used for the nourishment of horses used for luxury or convenience could be counted as part of the national income, but that wealth used for the upkeep of animals necessary to agriculture could not be included. Likewise the seeds sown by the farmer should never be counted as part of the national income, since they were part of the annual tribute paid by man in order to bring about reproduction.[23]

This care to eliminate the cost of production can be more clearly seen in the method by which the parlement proposed that the national income be measured. This method explains also the great importance which they attached to population, for it was the means by which the population figures could be made to serve the aim of putting order into the finances. Population and consumption were, in the opinion of the magistrates, the two keys to knowledge of national income. After the people in the nation had first been counted, the average amount of wealth consumed by these people was to be estimated. This average yearly consumption, multiplied by the population, would give the amount of wealth consumed yearly by the people of France. In the opinion of the parlement this yearly consumption was almost exactly equal to the national income. A few adjustments would of course have to be made. To the yearly consumption should be added the amount of precious metals and stones that the nation had managed to add to its store during the year. The amount of wealth spent on the nourishment of luxury animals

23 IX, 345–346.

(but not that spent for necessary animals or for such costs of production as seeds) should be added. Unlike that of his necessary animals, the goods consumed by the peasant would be included in the annual consumption and consequently in the national income. Any increase in the nation's reserves of capital should also be added. With these few adjustments the national consumption during a year might be considered substantially the same as the national income for that period.[24]

In the opinion of the parlement existing estimates of France's annual consumption were only tentative, at best, and at worst were almost criminal in the way they misled the public concerning the people's ability to pay taxes. One of the least objectionable estimates was made by the writer Navau in his *Financier citoyen* (1757). Setting the population of France at 20,000,000 people, 14,000,000 of whom lived in the country and the rest in towns, Navau used estimates of the average yearly consumption of city and country people as a means of figuring the total annual consumption of wealth in France. This he estimated to be approximately 2,000,000,000 *livres,* half of it produced by the earth and half by manufacturers. The parlement was not in complete agreement with the conclusions of the *Financier citoyen,* and pointed out that much of the 1,000,000,000 *livres* worth of wealth supposedly produced by manufacturing must have come in the last analysis from the earth or from animals nourished by the earth. The judges also criticized the author's failure to consider the possibility of a favorable balance of trade, though admitting that at the time

24 IX, 344–346, 350. Thus the parlement, like the physiocrats, would estimate the net product from agriculture; but unlike the physiocrats they would add to it the wealth produced by manufacturing. The memorials left by the magistrates are rather vague on the subject of how to compute the net product from manufacturing; raw materials imported from foreign lands were to be subtracted from the total annual consumption of the nation, but nothing was said about raw materials not imported. The present writer assumes that the magistrates had in mind some sort of net product for manufacturing, but cannot be certain, for the memorials left by the parlement are not always complete and consistent on every point.

of writing France's foreign trade was too small to add much to the national income.[25]

Another estimate of France's consumption with which the parlement was familiar appeared in a book on the decline of England's foreign trade, an anonymous work which had been translated from English into French.[26] According to this book France had a population of about 20,000,000 people, whose average consumption was about 100 *livres* a year and whose total yearly consumption was about 2,000,000,000 *livres*.[27] The magistrates were also familiar with the article *Les grains,* which appeared in the great Encyclopedia in 1756. The article was written by none other than Dr. Quesnay, but the magistrates of Provence either did not know, or failed to see any importance in this fact, for they refer in their memorials only to the authors of the Encyclopedia and to the title of the article. Like the *Financier citoyen* and the English work on decline of trade, the article on grains estimated the consumption, or amount of wealth spent annually by the French people at about 2,000,000,000 *livres*.[28]

This oft-repeated figure of 2,000,000,000 *livres* was, according to the parlement, the most commonly held idea of the extent of the national income. An anonymous writer, whose two articles appeared in the *Journal de commerce*[29] in 1761 and 1762, drew the parlement's fire by making estimates which exceeded this sum. In his first essay this writer estimated that the land of France produced each year wealth amounting to 3,141,297,158 *livres* and that the average yearly consumption of a population of 20,000,000 was a little more than 150 *livres*

25 IX, 363–364, 375–376.

26 The full title of this book, which does not appear in the memorials, was *Essai sur les causes du déclin du commerce étranger de la Grande Bretagne.* (2 Vols., 1757.)

27 IX, 364–367.

28 IX, 375.

29 The *Journal de commerce* was a monthly publication begun in 1759 and published in Brussels (sic). It managed to continue under various names until 1763.

per person. This estimate of what the author called the *revenu territorial,* or income produced by the earth, was based on a computation of wealth consumed in France each year; the author divided the population into families of five and the families into various classes according to the amount of wealth which they possessed; then, after estimating the number of families in each class and the amount of the earth's products consumed annually by families in the various classes, he was ready to compute the national yearly consumption of goods produced by the earth. Much to the annoyance of the magistrates of Provence, this same anonymous author made France appear even more prosperous in his second article, published in 1762. Aiming this time at national income (*revenu général*) and not merely at income from land (*revenu territorial*), he increased his estimate of the population from 20,000,000 to 24,000,000 people, and set the national income at 3,600,000,000 *livres* per year, of which only 500,000,000 *livres* were produced by industry.[30]

To the Parlement of Provence both the arguments and the statistics offered by this anonymous author were made suspect by his statement, at the end of his first article, that in view of the obvious size of the nation's income it was wrong to complain about the weight of the taxes in peace time. Where, asked the magistrates, had the writer seen harvests which yielded such a tremendous income? Certainly other economists had not given France credit for so much agricultural production. The anonymous writer, on the other hand, had set an absurdly low figure for industrial production, and had certainly overestimated the consumption of rich people by failing to consider that the livings of many poor servants should be included in the expenditures of the rich. The consumption of poor people, moreover, was set at a figure which was much too high, for to state that the average yearly consumption of Frenchmen amouted to 150 *livres* per person was to stray far from the truth. The parlement stated that in Provence, where they had made a careful

30 IX, 351–359, 376–377.

investigation of several villages, many families of peasants had only 45 *livres* a year per person, or between two and three *sols* a day per person, on which to live once the taxes had been paid to king and seigneur. It was very difficult to make any estimate whatever of the consumption of some poor people who managed to exist below the level of subsistence and whose children lived part of the year on the fruits of the fields. In the eyes of the parlement the anonymous writer in the *Journal de commerce* stood condemned as one who did not seek the truth but meant only to persuade the people that the taxes were not too high.[31] Righteously the magistrates cried out against such practices. "Have these cruel writers who find that the taxes are not excessive examined carefully the condition to which the consumption of thousands of men who are our fellow-beings and our brothers has been reduced?" [32]

The magistrates of Provence were themselves inclined to accept for the time being the commonly held notion that the national income was about 2,000,000,000 *livres*. In their opinion this income included wealth produced by both agriculture and manufacturing. Although admitting the possibility that some wealth might be added to the nation's store by a favorable balance of trade, the judges set no figure for wealth obtained through foreign commerce, perhaps because they considered the amount negligible. In their opinion manufactures produced about 800,000,000 *livres,* while wealth produced by the earth amounted to 1,300,000,000 or 1,400,000,000 *livres.*[33]

But the mere act of making estimates of their own did not satisfy the parlement, and they proposed that an end be put to the shocking conditions of ignorance which allowed such matters as the population and even the area of France to be subjects for dispute. Three great problems of political arithmetic demanded solution if the nation was to have an efficient administration. The facts about population should be determined,

31 IX, 359–363, 367–373, 376–377.
32 IX, 368.
33 IX, 373–374, 382–383.

the amount of the national production should be accurately calculated, and the people's consumption of wealth should be measured. In that direction lay the way to a true science of finance.[34]

There is some evidence that the parlement was sincere in demanding this collection of facts. As has been pointed out, the
writing of their memorials on the finances extended over a
period of years, probably from early in 1764 to somewhere in
1766 or 1767. In Volume I of their memorials the judges spoke
of the need for a complete table of facts about population in all
the generalities of the kingdom, and promised to assemble such
a table for the territory under their jurisdiction.[35] In Volume
IX of the memorials, probably after a considerable period of
time had passed, the magistrates were able to state that they
had begun work on this collection of facts and that they had
assembled during the past year a list of the births, deaths, and
marriages in all the parishes of Provence. At this time they
were still requesting that the work be made general throughout
the whole of France. They hoped that their example would be
followed by the other provinces and that material would be
added concerning such items as the number of animals in each
parish, the number of plows, and the kinds of land under each
kind of cultivation. Thus there would be a census, complete
with vital statistics and kept up to date. There would be tables
for both production and consumption in every parish of France.
These records would be renewed annually, and would enable the
king at any time to see at a glance the condition of any part of
the kingdom.[36]

2. TREATMENT OF THE PEOPLE

The Parlement of Provence, it will be remembered, believed
that the art of government consisted of increasing the number
of people and making good use of them. The facts about population were a mirror in which could be seen the success or

34 IX, 379–382.
35 I, 364–365.
36 IX, 380, 383–384.

failure of governmental policies, but population was more than a mirror or a measuring rod; it was an actual source of wealth and power. In writing their criticisms of existing legislation the parlement was concerned both with the people's well-being and with their careful treatment as a means of strengthening the state.

The magistrates recommended strongly that the government do everything in its power to encourage the increase of the population. In their opinion all wise government policies, by fostering the well-being of the people, would have this effect, but they did not limit their discussion to such general considerations alone. They believed, for one thing, that the institution of marriage should be given as much encouragement as possible. Celibacy "by true virtue or special grace" was admirable but rare; the much more common practice of simply neglecting to marry was harmful to the morality of the nation. Encouragement of marriage was by no means an easy problem, however. The experience of the Romans testified that the mere passage of laws was not enough, and there was good reason for believing that the need for encouraging marriages by positive legislation was a symptom of decadence which could not be halted by lawmaking. The magistrates believed, on the other hand, that laws to encourage child-bearing might have a favorable effect, for here the problem was to remove the fear of parents that they would be unable to support their children. Population grew best when there was a fairly equal distribution of wealth. Extreme inequality of fortunes caused luxury and waste in the lives of some people and misery in the lives of others, and such conditions would have to be reformed if the population was to be increased.[37] This kind of thinking, like the parlement's reflections about the financial problem, pointed in the direction of political economy, for if economic prosperity was necessary to population growth the magistrates would have to recommend means of improving the economic system.

37 I, 424–431.

In addition to the encouragement of large families, the parlement believed that there should be a mild and paternal policy toward illegitimate children. They believed that there were a great many such children in France, and that it would be foolish not to make them useful to the state. Children of uncertain parentage were by no means always the products of debauchery, for many were the offspring of poor people who had preferred to abandon them rather than to watch them starve, while others were victims of the unfortunate legislation against Huguenots, which allowed them neither to emigrate nor to be married by Protestant ministers. Although protesting their willingness to sacrifice the good of the state to the good of religion, the magistrates none the less insisted that the anti-Protestant legislation was regrettable, and even contrary to natural law; the legal fiction that there were no more Huguenots in France had two harmful effects: the increase of illegitimate children, and the decline in the total population. Some remedy should be found for this condition which was sacrificing the good of the state, morality, and humanity to blind prejudice and superstition. The government should adopt a benevolent policy toward children of uncertain parentage, treating them as legitimate wherever possible and in any case not degrading those who were clearly illegitimate. Each child should be given a normal upbringing, in which the state would take the place of the father and would pay for his or her support in the home of some reputable family. After learning to become useful laborers and housewives, the children would add to the productivity of the nation.[38]

The parlement's humanitarian attitude was not extended to the institution of slavery, from which the magistrates did not shrink as a means of increasing the population. For certain kinds of work, such as mining, they favored the purchase of slaves from the nations at war with the Barbary States. The

38 I, 431–442. After page 439 of the memorial there is a mistake in paging. There are two sets of "430's". If the pages were numbered correctly, this reference would be 431–452.

children of these slaves would be brought up as freemen and would add to the population.[39]

Associated with the parlement's desire to increase the number of people were their opinions about the distribution of population. The magistrates had a strong dislike for Paris, and suspicion of the metropolis left its mark on their memorials. Conversely, they favored the rural areas as places where people ought to live. They lamented the fact that since 1698 the cities of France had enjoyed a considerable increase in population. In their opinion big cities such as Paris and London decreased the total number of people in a nation; Paris, for example, swallowed up every year thousands of people from the rest of France, for because of its low birth rate and high death rate it was constantly in need of new recruits, who came from the provinces and in many cases were not replaced. The magistrates believed that the rural population, rather than that of cities, should be encouraged.[40]

Instead, however, the government had constantly favored Paris at the expense of the provinces, and the magistrates of faraway Provence resented bitterly numerous laws and regulations which they believed to be proof of this discrimination. The Paris butchers, for example, were forbidden to buy meat within twenty leagues of the city, except at certain specified points. The purpose of this law was to make easier the taxing of goods entering Paris, but the parlement claimed that in practice the law forced farmers to make long journeys with their goods and to sell them in crowded markets at low prices. The magistrates also objected to the privilege that some townspeople had of paying fewer duties on wines, and contended that the people in towns, being more prosperous, ought to pay more rather than fewer duties and taxes.[41] Another sore spot with the parlement was the centralizing tendency which caused so many matters of administration and finance to be decided upon

39 I, 429–430.
40 I, 298–307, 428–431; IV, 628–629.
41 V, 603–604, 606–607.

at Paris; the government's policy, they argued, was contradictory and inconsistent, for it forbade the building of new houses in Paris, and yet collected in the city all sorts of establishments which necessitated more dwelling places and an increased personnel. One small example was the home for injured soldiers; the parlement admitted that this was a splendid structure, but insisted that the soldiers would be happier and better cared for if given small pensions and allowed to live in the provinces.[42] The parlement's jealousy and suspicion of Paris extended far beyond their opinions about population. This attitude appears often in the memorials, mingled with the judges' dislike of financiers, antipathy toward financial fortunes, and concepts of government.

Not only the number of people, and where they lived, but also the conditions and manner of the people's lives concerned the parlement. The wise statesman should interest himself in the quality as well as in the quantity of the population.[43] Idleness, in the eyes of the parlement, was a danger to the state, for it tended to lead to vice and crime and thus to undermine public order and security. For this reason, and to increase the amount of productive labor, it was desirable that the number of religious holidays be reduced. Vagrancy should be abolished outright; it was virtually certain that those who spent money without having any source of income were criminals. Genuinely poor people, on the other hand, should be cared for by the state and put to work at productive labor, instead of being allowed to learn the ways of beggars and vagabonds. The magistrates did not believe that paupers were very numerous. A bureau in each parish could keep track of those who were out of work or who had more children than they could support; where necessary these people could be given enough bread for subsistence, and the furnishing of raw materials would enable them to be of some positive use to the state.[44]

42 VI, 755–757; VII, 467–470.
43 I, 424–425; VII, 850.
44 I, 444, 487–492.

The parlement believed that criminals should also be made useful to the state. The magistrates' opinions about the treatment of crime contained a mixture of humanitarianism with their usual beliefs about population, and may be considered typical of what is usually termed "eighteenth-century thought". They were humanitarian, they were optimistic, and they demanded a complete and rational plan of reform. In their opinion existing penalties for the various crimes were to a large extent out of date and inappropriate. Many of them, like the ferocious but ineffective punishments for illicit trading in salt, were rendered useless by their very severity. The parlement was convinced that the existing treatment of crime was harmful to population, and urged that the king supervise the writing of a great penal code which would combine and reform all the ancient scattered laws of France.[45] In their memorials they took pains to expound their own philosophy of crime and punishment. Penalties should be for correction, precaution, or example. If possible the criminal should be reformed, or at least should be allowed to become no worse; in such cases the penalty should be determined according to the age or circumstances of the person involved. When there was no hope of correction the criminal should be deprived of citizenship and placed where he could no longer harm society; even so, the criminal should not be totally lost to the state; his punishment should fit his crime, and he should be made to do useful work; such men and women should be allowed to marry, and their children should be freed and sent to the colonies. The death penalty should be avoided as much as possible, for criminals should be made to serve the society they had harmed; moreover both humanitarianism and the more practical purpose of keeping the people in awe of the death penalty demanded that it be used sparingly.[46]

Thus the parlement, true to their tendency to seek larger and larger issues, saw fit to include in their memorials about

45 I, 492–498; IV, 330–331.
46 I, 498–504.

the finances pronouncements concerning the morality of the people.

> . . . May the police stamp out vice at its sources! May men be invited to work and turned away from idleness! May games of chance never be tolerated! May begging be abolished! May vagrants and vagabonds be forced to settle down and go to work! May the constabulary be increased by a third! May first offenses be either corrected paternally or punished severely according to the circumstances! May a distinction be made between acts committed through indigence or debauchery! May punishments vary without any guilty person going unpunished! Crimes will then become more and more rare in the nation.[47]

It will be recalled that the parlement, in addition to stating the need for a complete and uniform system of finances and for a reformed and equally uniform penal code, urged that Louis XV win a place among the immortal legislators of all time by preparing "a complete system of legislation and government" which, among other things, would encourage morality in the people.[48]

> . . . Among the laws which influence morality and contribute to the formation of the national character we include those which cause religion to be respected and clergymen to be revered, the all-important regulations concerning the education of youth, the laws which maintain paternal authority and, through it, respect for old age, two excellent principles of morality; the form of tax collections, which can corrupt both exactor and debtor if it is disorderly; the correct administration of the courts of justice; the austere discipline which must be observed by the magistracy, and the con-

47 I, 504–505.

48 See Chapter II, section 4, or I, 154–155, 158–159. The judges made a distinction between the constitution of France, which they considered sound, and the proposed system of legislation. "Nos lois constitutives et fondamentales sont excellentes, le temps ne les a point vieillies; mais nous manquons de cette partie des lois qui forme des hommes, les moeurs en tenoient lieu autrefois, elles ne suffisent plus . . ."

sideration which it is just to grant to this estate; the care to occupy the troops with public works; the universal abolition of begging; the regulations which discourage inactivity and invite labor; the laws which favor marriage and fecundity in marriages, those which punish first crimes severely, which make infamy feared, which curb chicanery and bad faith; those, finally, which tend to heighten the lustre of the nobility and to subject them to the most severe rules of honor, nothing being more just than to demand the greatest example of virtue from an order which has distinguished and hereditary privileges.[49]

The parlement was also concerned that the people be allowed to work at the right occupations. Just what the right occupations would be, they had no desire to say, for they believed that men were capable of choosing their own professions. A just government would see to it that men had a chance to work at something in keeping with their estates, their fortunes, and their education, for otherwise people would leave the country; but it was not the government's place to force men into certain kinds of work.[50] In the thought of the magistrates, freedom in the choice of professions was thus combined with respect for the social order. Although in many respects desirous of greater liberty for the people, they were far from being levelers. Indeed, they were in many ways reactionary; they were not so much defenders of the *status quo*, which contained wealthy financiers and absentee landlords of whom the magistrates did

[49] I, 155–158. It will be noted that this quotation speaks of punishing first crimes severely, while the preceding one recommended a flexible policy. Both passages appear in Vol. I, but are widely separated. It must be remembered that the memorials were written by a committee, and are therefore not always entirely clear and consistent. On the whole, however, few such cases of apparent contradiction appear in the 14 volumes. In the present case all the evidence indicates that the considered opinion of the parlement was the humanitarian view of crime and punishment already described, for that view is carefully explained both in Vol. I and in Vol. IV. The sentence asking severe punishments for first offenses appears only once, early in Vol. I, when it may be presumed that the committee was still speaking in general terms and was not yet ready to outline in detail their views about crime.

[50] I, 443–444; XII, 878.

not approve, as they were reformers who wished the ancient social structure purified of such recent growths; yet even this description is only partially correct, for the judges, like so many of their contemporaries, preferred their own definitions of what was traditional in France, and did not hesitate to demand the abolition of laws and practices which they disliked. One of the parts of the old régime of which the magistrates approved was the hierarchy of classes, and though they wanted men to engage in useful and productive occupations they also wanted this hierarchy preserved.

This point of view is illustrated in their remarks about the nobility of France, an estate which they considered especially important because it was supposed to set an example of honor and virtue, qualities without which the monarchy would perish.

> . . . Without morality, honor perishes and there is no longer any monarchy; virtue is much more necessary to it than is commonly supposed. Republican patriotism is often a convulsion of self-love; it takes honor and genuine virtue to love a legitimate dependence, to preserve high courage and a noble heart, to know how to be submissive and yet free, a faithful subject and a citizen. Corruption of morals can lead only to a despot and either slaves or rebels. Heroic patriotism is to be found in monarchies.[51]

The position of the nobles should thus be protected in order that they might contribute to the preservation of the monarchy and its combination of freedom with a sense of obligation to society. But the talents of the nobility should not be wasted. Indeed, inactivity among the nobles was especially harmful, for it led the rest of the people to associate idleness with honor. It did not follow that the nation had to seek wars as a means of making use of the soldierly qualities of the nobility, for such a remedy would be worse than the disease. Those nobles who wanted a military career should be allowed to have it, but there was no reason why the rest of the nobles should consider peaceful oc-

51 I, 481–482.

cupations disgraceful. Nothing was as dishonorable as idleness. Why should not the nobles take part in the administration of justice, in municipal administration, or in the administration of the finances? What could be more necessary and noble than the honorable conduct of the nation's financial affairs? Even the sight of a noble remaining at home and managing his own estate was becoming much too rare. In the opinion of the magistrates any occupation which served the state and did not aim at self-enrichment was worthy of the nobility.[52]

Wishing to preserve the prestige of the nobility and at the same time to increase their usefulness, the parlement suggested a plan of reform. There should be in every province an organization to catalogue the noble families and watch over their conduct. Young nobles would be given a strict training to inspire them with the importance and obligations of their position. Aid would be given to noble families in need of it, and any breaches of honor would be punished. Purchase of titles of nobility would be stopped, and the dignity of the estate would be kept superior to that of mere wealth. Below the rank of the nobility would be a second order of families who by reason of their excellent services to the state would be considered candidates for entrance into the nobility. A record of their merits and services would be kept, and from time to time the most illustrious of them would be admitted to noble estate. By this curious plan, at once old-fashioned and progressive, the parlement apparently hoped to preserve the social hierarchy by giving it once more a justification for its existence.[53]

The magistrates also had a healthy respect for the worth of the bourgeoisie, and considered them superior to the rest of the third estate. The bourgeoisie, or at least those with well-established families, they looked upon as an extremely useful class which furnished "officers to the army, orators to the bar, and judges and magistrates to the courts." Such solid citizens

52 I, 472–480.
53 I, 482–487.

should not be treated as the equals of those whom the parlement did not hesitate to call "la plus vile populace." [54]

But whatever the estates to which men belonged, an important principle of population demanded that men should not be wasted in useless or harmful occupations. Observing the society of their day, the parlement saw evidence that this principle was being violated. Collection of taxes required the services of far too many men. A great many employees were used by the Farmers General for collection of the salt tax, regulation of the tobacco monopoly, and indeed for all other branches of their business; according to the parlement's estimate, the wages of employees of the farm amounted to a yearly total of over 5,000,000 *livres,* a sum greater than that spent by some princes for their entire military establishments. Since too many of these men were unnecessary and were thus engaged in non-productive activity, it was fair to assume that the goods which they might have been producing were lost to the state. As we shall presently see, the parlement did not even consider the work of the financiers themselves especially beneficial to the nation. All such useless activities were wasteful of population.[55]

What was true of tax collections was even true of the administration of justice in France. The magistrates of Provence did not hesitate to say that there were far too many courts of one kind or another, and far too many judges. This condition was in part the product of the regrettable practice of selling too many offices, judicial and otherwise, merely to get money for the treasury. The reform of a part of the judicial system would increase the efficiency of the rest. The magistrates, themselves the owners of judicial offices, may have been influenced by the fact that creation of new offices tended to reduce the value of those already in existence. At any rate, they attacked the great number of offices sold rather than the principle of the sale of offices.[56]

54 XII, 876–878.

55 I, 456; IV, 821–822; XIV, *Ferme de tabac.* This last is one section of the rather chaotic and unorganized Vol. XIV, and has no page numbers.

56 I, 456–459; VI, 565–566.

Another walk of life in which the precious manpower of the nation was being to some extent wasted was the army. The judges were inclined to agree with some political writers, whom they did not take the trouble to name, who stated that not more than one per cent of the population of a nation should be soldiers. Throughout Europe this rule of thumb was being violated. Everywhere there were too many soldiers, and this condition, even from a military point of view, was bad for the rest of the population, who tended to become soft and useless. In the opinion of the parlement there should be no offensive warfare, and for the defense of the *patrie* every citizen should become a soldier. From the point of view of economics the excessive size of military forces was harmful to production. A large army meant that recruiting had to go on perpetually, taking away men from agriculture and industry. Once in the army many of these men became forever useless as workers; they were crowded together in towns, where their lives of debauchery unfitted them for productive labor. Often soldiers deserted and were lost to the nation completely.

The parlement suggested that these conditions be remedied by the creation of a national legion made up of retired soldiers and of all citizens capable of bearing arms. Each province would have its legion, which would be ready to spring into action wherever defense of the nation was needed. With such a body of men in existence the regular army could be much smaller; numerous forts would not be needed; the soldiers could live in camps, away from the evil influence of cities, and could be paid well and made to labor at useful public works. After a service of a certain number of years, the regular soldier could be retired from the service and could return home, where he would be a useful citizen, father of a family, member of the proposed national legion, and a good influence on the martial spirit of his children and neighbors. Such a plan would lessen desertions, increase population and production, improve morals, and prevent the loss of soldiers as workers and citizens.[57]

57 I, 459-467.

In the opinion of the parlement the militia, as well as the army, was harmful to population, and had the additional disadvantage of being unjust and oppressive. This view is not surprising, for of all the practices of the old régime the conscription of men for the militia was one of the most unpopular. The magistrates, with their curious habit of looking backward into the past for some reforms and recommending very progressive measures for others, considered the system of conscription much inferior to the older method of taking only volunteers into the militia. They pictured "all the young men of the parish, frightened and trembling", being herded together and forced to draw lots, with the result that those chosen for the militia were regarded as victims, while the remainder considered themselves free of all responsibility for military service. Those chosen were not necessarily the ablest, and the effect of such a system on the martial spirit of the nation was lamentable. Conscription, moreover, was unjust, for it placed on the poor the burden of defending the nation, a task which had formerly belonged to the possessors of property. The magistrates considered it an evil tendency that at the very time when the military and other services attached to the fiefs of the nobility were falling into disuse the third estate was being loaded with more and more annoying services. They were aware, of course, that in former times everyone had been subject to military service, but they contended that the forcing of one part of the subjects to sacrifice themselves for the rest could be justified only in times of extreme peril to the state, and never as a permanent measure.

From the point of view of population, moreover, a conscripted militia had the same evils as a large regular army. Skilled artisans were taken from their work and farmers from the soil; families were broken up; to escape from the militia men ran away to other lands; population and production declined. Were not these the effects of extremely unwise treatment of the people? The remedy, according to the parlement, lay in the same national legion of citizens and retired soldiers which they had suggested as a means of reducing the size of the regular army. This legion could take the place of the militia and thus make the defenders of France citizens and free men instead of slaves chosen by lot.[58]

The same objections which applied to the militia also applied to the coast guard, which by laws of 1746 and 1748 had been made into a standing body of men, also chosen by conscription.[59] But although complaining about wasted manpower in the army, militia, and coast guard, the parlement regretted that there were not more sailors in the service of France. At a time soon after the Peace of Paris (1763) it is not surprising to find them expressing the opinion that the destiny of Europe would be decided on the sea. There can be little doubt that the magistrates were prompted by memories of the recent war when they wrote that weakness in sea power was wasteful of both property and population, since it led to heavy losses of both men and ships.[60]

Thus the Parlement of Provence believed that a growing and well-treated population was a necessity if France's financial problems were to be solved. Facing these problems at the close of the Seven Years War, they insisted upon broadening out their inquiry and suggesting general reforms which would keep open and stimulate the sources of wealth, so that eventually those sources could be tapped and the nation's finances mended. In the carrying out of this plan population was an important factor, for several reasons: it might be viewed as an end in itself, since the art of government consisted of multiplying men, treating them well, and making good use of them; but

58 XII, 855–870, 874–876, 883–885, 894–897.

59 XII, 835–839, 847–848. It should be noted that these objections on grounds of population were not the only ones. The permanent forces of militia and coast guard had to be supported by taxes on the provinces. The Parlement of Provence contended that their province had always been exempt from military taxes in time of peace. It would be foolish to overlook this fact as a source for their numerous objections to militia and coast guard, but it does not follow that the population arguments were merely rationalizations. See XII, 856.

60 I, 468–470.

these activities were also means of increasing the wealth and power of the state; and because it was so closely related to government, population could be used by statesmen to measure the success or failure of their policy. Population was interdependent with the economy of the nation, upon which depended the resources of the public treasury. It was therefore of vital importance that the means of subsistence be increased and that no obstacles be left in the way of the growth of agriculture, industry, and commerce, the topics which we shall consider next.

CHAPTER IV

AGRICULTURE

On a dit avec beaucoup de raison dans les derniers temps, honorez et protegez l'agriculture, elle est l'état naturel de tous les hommes, la mère nourrice de tous, et l'occupation du plus grand nombre. . . .

Mémoires, I, 391.

In the opinion of the Parlement of Provence the improvement of agriculture was one of the best means of increasing France's population and national wealth and thereby helping to solve the financial problem. The magistrates attached great importance to agriculture. It was, to be sure, dependent upon population, but population was in its turn dependent upon agriculture, and the two together were "the mainsprings of the national wealth." Agriculture, moreover, was the "natural state" for all men, and those engaged in tilling the soil, amounting in the opinion of the parlement to seven-tenths of all Frenchmen, constituted an especially important segment of the population.[1] Although France's colonies were valuable and should certainly not be neglected, the most useful form of conquest was at home and consisted of improving agricultural methods; for just as a wise king could multiply the value of his population by making them more useful, so might he in effect extend his territories by increasing their output. Agricultural products loomed large on the list of those which nations were fortunate to possess. In order to be self-sufficient a nation needed grain, livestock, and iron, and if it was fortunate enough also to have wine, salt, hemp, and fish nothing remained to be desired.[2] The magistrates professed to have no regrets over France's relative paucity of gold and silver mines. Agriculture and commerce were France's real mines, and if they could be made to flourish, the nations with gold mines would be like slaves kept by France for digging the precious metals out of the earth.[3]

1 I, 241–242, 391–392.
2 I, 249–251, 551–552.
3 VII, 428.

114

1. Agriculture and the Other Forms of Production

Agriculture thus assumed a high place among the various forms of economic activity. It was not a predominant place, however, for the parlement did not take the physiocratic view that agriculture was the only form of endeavor which produced wealth. The judges made various pronouncements concerning the relative importance of agriculture, industry, and commerce, and though agriculture and commerce, if judged by the attention given them in the memorials, were especially important, manufacturing, fishing, shipping, and mining were not neglected. In considering the parlement's attitude toward these forms of enterprise it is essential to distinguish between the importance of an activity and its character as a producer of wealth. Like the physiocrats, the magistrates of Provence attached importance to a great many forms of economic activity, but it does not follow that they considered all of these forms productive of wealth. It is therefore desirable to determine, if possible, which kinds of economic activity the parlement believed to be really productive.

Wealth, in the opinion of the judges, consisted not merely of money or precious metals but of material things that could be consumed. The more a nation consumed, the richer it was. True riches were such things as grain, livestock, and iron.[4] Attention has already been called to the parlement's definition of national income as the value of all the annual productions of the earth and of the arts, minus whatever was purchased from foreign lands for the purpose of bringing about that production. Internal commerce could not add to the national income, for it consisted only of the exchange of products already produced, but foreign trade, on the other hand, could swell the national income provided the balance of trade was favorable to France. Mining and fishing could likewise add to the national income.[5]

4 I, 551–552, 573.
5 See Chapter III, Section 1.

As used by the parlement, the term national income was not synonymous with the term production of wealth, and it would be a mistake to use the two interchangeably. Although the magistrates did not make an explicit statement concerning this point, one cannot do justice to their use of terms without distinguishing between wealth produced by Frenchmen and wealth merely obtained by clever trading with other nations. According to their use of the terms "wealth" and "national income," the Parlement of Provence may be said to have considered agriculture, manufacturing, mining, and fishing as activities productive of wealth. Internal commerce was not productive, and neither was foreign commerce, though the latter was capable of adding to the national income.[6] Thus the chief difference between the view of the parlement and that of the physiocrats on the question of productivity was that the magistrates assigned a productive role to manufacturing. Even so, they valued the wealth produced annually by agriculture at 1,300,000,000 *livres*, while that produced by manufactures amounted in their opinion to only 800,000,000 *livres*. Since they set the total national income at about 2,000,000,000 *livres* per year, the amount of wealth produced by mining or fishing or obtained through foreign trade must have been negligible.[7]

Quite apart from the question of the productivity of the various forms of economic activity was the question of their importance. Concerning this subject the parlement was outspoken, and there is no need for any guesswork whatever. The judges noticed that some economic writers tended to praise commerce and to neglect the importance of agriculture, while others feared that the protection given to commerce would harm agriculture, and still others were afraid that manufactures, by taking away laborers from the soil, would decrease the pro-

6 The parlement, it must be remembered, was concerned chiefly with the national income and not with the more abstract problem of productivity. This fact is probably sufficient to explain their failure to make an explicit statement concerning productivity and foreign commerce.

7 IX, 382–383.

ductivity of agriculture. With all these various defenders of specific interests, who saw only a part of the picture of France's economic life, the magistrates were in disagreement. The key to a complete and well-rounded picture was interdependence. Agriculture was the basis of commerce, for it furnished the raw materials. Commerce, in its turn, aided the prosperity of agriculture: the commercial city of Marseilles, for example, was of great service as a market for agricultural products, and England, a great commercial nation, had a flourishing agriculture as well; moreover the value of agricultural land was raised by commerce, which tended to increase the circulation of money.[8] Manufacturing was also of benefit to agriculture, for artisans were customers for the farmers; the tanners of hides made use of the livestock grown by the farmers. Conversely, agriculture tended to suffer when industry declined. In Provence, for example, the decline of the tanning industry had led to a long train of results: livestock growing had declined; people ate less meat and more grain; the soil, overworked and underfertilized, had become less productive.[9]

The parlement believed that this obvious interdependence of agriculture, industry, and commerce should be recognized by economic policy. There should be no attempts to protect one form of activity at the expense of any of the others; to protect commerce at the expense of agriculture would be to harm them both; to aid agriculture by sending artisans back to the soil, as recommended by some people, would also be harmful. The magistrates insisted that agriculture, industry, and commerce should all be favored, and though they devoted less time to mining and fishing they believed that these deserved encouragement as well. The effect of such a wise policy would be to increase population, with all the benefits which a large population implied. "Men will spring from the bowels of the earth and will convert the very stones into gold." [10]

8 I, 445–448; X, 397–398, 439–440.

9 I, 446–449, 564, 571–572.

10 I, 446–449, 454, 468–470; VII, 429–430.

2. THE LAND AND ITS PROPRIETORS

The Parlement of Provence was aware that disputes were carried on by some of their contemporaries concerning what was the best form of agriculture. One of the debatable issues about which the magistrates expressed opinions was the question of *grande* and *petite culture,* which had important implications both for agricultural methods and for land ownership. Unlike the physiocrats and the upholders of the "agricultural revolution" in England, such as Arthur Young, the Parlement of Provence disagreed with the defenders of *grande culture,* who wanted cultivation of large blocks of land, with the aid of horses, and who believed that these large-scale operations would lead to greater efficiency and a larger output.[11] The judges took the opposite view that agriculture would be more prosperous and have a greater output if the holdings of land were small rather than large, and they favored the splitting up of large properties among several proprietors. They were aware that their opponents based their argument on the assumption that a single large proprietor would not consume his whole output and could therefore market a surplus; numerous small proprietors, on the other hand, would consume most of their output, leaving little or no surplus. But in the opinion of the parlement this worship of a surplus did not take into consideration the importance of population as a factor in the national well-being. They believed that a state was rich in proportion to what it produced and consumed. If agriculture supported many people rather than a few, so much the better; industry and commerce would be stimulated and everyone would benefit.[12]

The parlement, moreover, had little faith in the efficiency of large-scale farming. The greatest proprietors were the noble-

11 It is interesting to note that the Marquis de Mirabeau, who at first opposed *grande culture* but was won over by Quesnay, came originally from Provence. See Weulersse, *Le mouvement physiocratique en France,* I, 53–57, and Carré, *Le règne de Louis XV,* pp. 354–355.

12 I, 403–408.

men, the church, and the king. Noblemen, they alleged, did not
as a rule manage their estates with skill and care; too many
of them were careless absentee landlords, who left their properties without repairs, or turned them into useless parks and
hunting preserves. Church lands, to be sure, were in some cases
carefully tended by orders of monks, but on the whole they
suffered the same neglect and careless exploitation as the lands
of the nobles. Rural property which belonged to the king was
even less productive. Repairs could be made only at great expense, and in many cases those in possession of the land feared
to make improvements lest the property, legally inalienable from
the crown, be taken from them.[13]

Between these large holdings and the very small ones was a
group of medium-sized properties which in the opinion of the
parlement were for the most part efficiently handled. Their
owners were many of them middle-class business men and entrepreneurs of all kinds. These men had more land than they
needed for their own consumption. They exploited it by means
of hired labor, under their own management, and produced a
surplus for the market. The magistrates considered this kind
of farming desirable because of its efficiency.[14] It is quite possible that they themselves, members of an aristocracy of wealth
and talent, legally nobles and yet representatives of the highest
standing to which the bourgeoisie could aspire, were also
holders of this kind of agricultural property. If such was the
case, however, the magistrates did not allow their own agricultural property to distract them unduly; they mentioned the
medium-sized bourgeois holdings only briefly, and did not
assign them an importance superior to that of the smaller
peasant lands.

The little properties farmed by the peasants formed a third
class of agricultural holdings, which the parlement considered
to be the most carefully cultivated and productive of all farm
lands, superior in this respect to the estates of the nobles and

13 I, 407–408, 388–390, 421–423, 478–480; III, 446–447.
14 I, 417–418.

even, to a lesser degree, to the medium-sized bourgeois farms. The judges believed the small peasant proprietors to be of great importance to French agriculture. Many peasants whose plots of land were too small for subsistence worked a few months out of each year for the proprietors of large or medium-sized holdings, and thus formed a precious and necessary supply of labor. These day laborers also managed to add to their incomes by working at home on crude manufactures which they sold at low prices to merchants. Numerous families, living in this way by a combination of farming, day labor, and home industry, added to the production and population of the state. Thus it would be a mistake to consider them inefficient simply because they produced little or no agricultural surplus.[15] Again it is possible to see in the opinions of the parlement what may be a reflection of their own economic interests, for if they were concerned about the preservation of a cheap labor supply, especially in domestic industry, they might be expected to favor the existence of small proprietors who were also laborers and artisans. Without a detailed analysis of the properties held by the magistrates it is impossible to do more than speculate about such matters. The only certainty is that the members of the parlement were for the most part wealthy men, and that they were in constant association with other men of property.

Whatever their motives, the magistrates insisted that agriculture would be more prosperous if the lands were as much as possible in the hands of those who actually farmed them. They had nothing to say against the proprietors of medium-sized holdings, who managed their own properties, but they believed that steps should be taken to split up the great holdings so that the peasants would be the proprietors of the lands which they farmed. The parlement was not averse to seeing noble lands, that is, lands to which certain privileges were attached, pass into other hands and lose their privileges. When such a change took place the lands were usually better cultivated, and began to contribute their share of taxes to the state. Thus the reforms

15 I, 417–420.

which they had in mind meant placing most of the land in the
hands either of peasants or of proprietors who managed their
own holdings, employing day laborers to do the work.[16]

This desire to split up large holdings of agricultural property
appears radical at first glance, but the parlement was not radical
in any Jacobin sense; indeed, their ideas about land-holding
illustrate the curious mixture of economic progressivism and
antiquarian concern for feudal institutions which appears so
often in their memorials. The magistrates hastened to state that
the fiefs of the hereditary nobility were necessary to the monarchy. They had no intention, moreover, of despoiling the nobles
of their property; as judges and wealthy men they had a great
respect for property rights, and believed that if the peasants
were to be made proprietors the nobles would have to be in-
demnified. In framing specific proposals of reform, the parlement therefore allowed their respect for property rights and
for the feudal nobility to temper their desire for smaller agricultural units. They suggested that the peasants could be made
proprietors under a system of quit rents, payable to the nobles,
and they even ventured the opinion that the *banalités* (requirements that the peasant use, for a fee, the noble's mill, winepress,
bakeshop, and so forth) were not as evil as they had been
painted, and might be continued. It should be noted, moreover,
that the magistrates did not suggest that the large holdings be
turned over to the peasants exclusively, but also spoke of putting
more land into the hands of owners who would better understand farm management and the direction of day laborers; thus
they favored not only the peasants but also the owner-managers,
many of them middleclass, of the medium sized holdings. The
parlement stated clearly, moreover, that large estates could not
be done away with entirely, for some of them would have to be
retained in order that there might be employment for day
laborers and a surplus for the consumption of merchants and
artisans.[17]

16 I, 408–416, 420–423.
17 I, 415–416, 420–421; XIV, *Ferme de tabac* (no paging).

The method by which the parlement recommended that at least a good many of the large estates be broken up is further evidence of their respect for property. They did not believe that the government should use force against proprietors who insisted on keeping their large holdings; even if various owners decided to join together their properties the government could not prevent such action. The proper method of achieving the change toward smaller holdings lay not in force but in encouraging the proprietors to take of their own accord steps in keeping with the welfare of the state. In Provence, for example, there were laws which tended to split up large estates without threatening property rights. Noble lands could not be sold without becoming non-noble and losing their privileges, including that of exemption from taxation. Such a law would appear at first glance to prevent alienation of noble land, but Provence had overcome the difficulty by means of a rule called *compensation,* which allowed the nobility to ennoble lands of a value equal to that of the lands which they had sold; the seigneurs were not afraid to sell their noble lands, for they knew that they could acquire others. In actual practice, however, this generous rule tended to split up the great estates. Nobles tended to wait before purchasing more land, sometimes because they lacked the money, and sometimes in the hope that they might purchase more land than they had sold; for the rule of *compensation* allowed the ennobling of lands equal in value to those which had been sold, and if those lands rose in value, even after the sale, their original owner might claim that his right to purchase and to ennoble property had been extended proportionally. Very often, however, those nobles who delayed their purchases of more land never made those purchases at all. Thus Provence's non-noble lands increased in amount, paid more taxes, and were better cultivated.[18] The magistrates believed that such indirect methods could succeed in breaking up large inefficiently managed estates without any violation of property rights.

18 I, 405–406, 410–414.

The parlement's desire to avoid the use of force against proprietors arose in part from respect for property rights and in part from the associated belief that proprietors should be allowed to follow their own interests. It was true that a proprietor, if left alone, would seek his own advantage, but this was as it should be. The magistrates contended that if all proprietors were allowed to do what they considered best for themselves the well-being of the state would result.

> We believe that it is to the interest of agriculture, and consequently to the interest of the state, to allow the cultivator to choose what he wishes to plant in his fields; all prohibitions appear to us to be unreasonable, unjust, and contrary to the right of property. . . . Property must be respected and the cultivator must be given the freedom to sow his field as he pleases because his interest is a reliable guide and the general welfare demands that he follow it.[19]

This outburst of liberalism was of course aimed at the numerous regulations which restricted agricultural activity in the old régime. The parlement condemned in advance anyone who might attempt to argue that some of the restrictions were for the good of the state.

> The interest of the state, which has sometimes been used as an argument against this trustworthy maxim derived from the right of property, is always fictitious and ill applied and directed by special interests of power or greed, which are the two usual sources for these prohibitive laws.[20]

Thus in the realm of agriculture the parlement strongly recommended economic individualism and a policy of laissez-faire. Like most supporters of those ideas, however, they were forced, when dealing with specific problems, to recommend that a few precautions be taken for the protection of the public welfare. Once those precautions had been taken they were prepared to endow the remaining liberty with the sanction of natural law.

19 XIV, *Ferme de tabac* (no paging).
20 XIV, *Ferme de tabac* (no paging).

Their conclusions concerning the problem of forest lands furnish a good example.

> It is necessary that the fleet be able to retain for itself the timber needed for construction. It is necessary to prevent the careless cutting of trees and clearing of the land from carrying away the soil or causing floods; these two requirements being fulfilled, the liberty which is in conformity with natural law is equally to the interest of the state.[21]

If proprietors would serve the general welfare when left free from all but a very few restrictions, one might very well wonder why the parlement felt called upon to criticize the management of the large estates held by king, church, and nobles. The judges, after all, were recommending the breakup of most of these great estates, and they even confessed to a temptation to urge passage of a law prohibiting the conversion of good farm lands into decorative but useless parks.[22] As though conscious that some of their own recommendations might appear to be contradictions of their general policy, the parlement introduced a qualification into their argument for laissez-faire. They were prepared to admit that, though it was wise to allow men to follow their own interests, a little education could be helpful both to the individual and to the state.

> However, let us set no limits to liberty and to the right of property. The abuses of luxury must be attacked at their source: they can be remedied more easily if there appears to be no intention of reforming them. The government should improve the men themselves and allow them to care for their property and cultivate their fields any way they please. Bureaus, wisely established, will be able to enlighten them concerning the best methods, and even encourage experiments; their interest will do the rest. The government must exert an influence only through protection.[23]

21 I, 387–388.
22 I, 388.
23 I, 390–391.

In order to understand what the parlement meant by "protection," it is necessary to examine their specific proposals for the improvement of French agriculture.

3. The Improvement of French Agriculture

For the improvement of agriculture the parlement proposed a few positive measures and a great many negative ones. They did not reject completely the remedy of positive government intervention in matters pertaining to agriculture, but the burden of their plea was that agricultural production be liberated from the shackles of a great many unwise regulations, taxes, and laws.

Attention has already been called to the parlement's desire for the breakup of large, poorly managed estates and for the prevention of floods caused by the careless felling of trees. Road building was another government action of which the parlement approved as an aid to agriculture. Using Provence as an example they pointed out that certain parts of the province could have a flourishing agriculture if they had roads on which to send their goods to market. The roads should be carefully planned, so that they would use as little good agricultural land as possible; where necessary, the existing roads should be straightened with the same end in view.[24]

It was to be expected that the magistrates would use examples from their own province, which was agriculturally poor and had need of every possible device for making the soil yield some kind of crop. In 1699 there had been an attempt, which the parlement mistakenly called the first of its kind, to encourage agriculture in Provence.[25] The king had proposed the

24 XI, 386–393, 401–403.

25 As early as the first decade of the seventeenth century the economist Barthélemy de Laffemas had recommended, and King Henry IV, through the Commission of Commerce, had ordered the execution of a project for establishing silk culture in France. Subsidies were given to merchants who in return supplied mulberry trees, mulberry seed, silkworm eggs, and instructions to those who were to undertake the culture, and guaranteed to buy all the silk produced. Provence was one of the places where mulberry trees and silkworms were distributed, and though the project was none too successful

establishment of nurseries of mulberry trees, and the province
had subsidized the project, which was evidently none too successful. From time to time during the eighteenth century the
province considered again the encouragement of mulberry tree
planting as a means of founding an industry for the manufacture of silk. Although several attempts to subsidize tree nurseries had small success, the parlement resented criticisms that
this form of agriculture was undesirable because it made use
of soil which might better be employed in raising more necessary provisions. Contending that all forms of work deserved
protection, they defended the tree nurseries and the people's
right to engage in this form of agriculture.[26] The parlement's
memorials do not make it entirely clear whether the authors approved of government subsidies to tree nurseries as a positive
action for the encouragement of agriculture, or whether their
main purpose was to defend the right of farmers to plant whatever they pleased. It is possible that they favored the subsidies
as a means of making France more self-sufficient; the memorials mention subsidies only rarely and in cases involving the
competition of foreign nations. There can be no doubt whatever about the parlement's dislike of restrictions on the right
of proprietors to plant what they pleased, for this opinion appears again and again in the memorials.

Tariff protection was a form of positive aid to agriculture
which the magistrates did not scorn. Although their attitude
toward most existing tariffs was one of hostility, the judges
were capable of demanding protection for some products, such
as vegetable oils, large quantities of which were produced in
Provence. The parlement suggested that an import duty be

in most parts of France, silk culture in Provence was stimulated to a considerable extent. See Charles Woolsey Cole, *Colbert and a Century of French
Mercantilism* (New York: Columbia University Press, 1939, 2 Vols.), I,
46–50. The memorials written by the Parlement of Provence seem to indicate that by the eighteenth century silk culture in the province was far from
satisfactory, despite repeated efforts at encouragement.

26 I, 554–559; X, 76, 487–505.

placed on all oils entering France from foreign lands.[27] Another positive measure advocated by the magistrates was the formation of an agricultural society in Provence, for like many of their contemporaries throughout France they believed that such a society would be useful in promoting agricultural improvements. The administrators of the province had requested that they be allowed to form a society of agriculture and commerce, and in 1765, while the memorials were being written, the government at Paris granted permission for the formation of a society of agriculture, but refused the request for a society of both agriculture and commerce. The parlement strongly resented the fact that half of the request had been refused. They contended that in the case of Provence the two activities were inseparable; because of poor soil the province was forced to import such necessary provisions as grain and cattle and to pay for them by the export of less important products such as olive oil and wine; thus commerce was inseparably bound to agriculture, and a society for the promotion of both was to be desired.[28]

These few positive measures indicate that the parlement was not averse to encouragement of agriculture by mild governmental action, but their memorials pay a great deal more attention to the need for what may be called negative measures, or the sweeping away of existing abuses. In their view, agriculture, and indeed all economic enterprises in France, were seriously handicapped by numerous unwise taxes and regulations. The great majority of the parlement's suggestions and complaints were concerned with legislation of which they disapproved, and their fourteen volumes of memorials, viewed as a whole, constitute a vast indictment of much of the old régime. It is quite possible that the elements of liberalism in the parlement's thought arose in good part as a protest against this mountain of legislation, which had accumulated for at least a century. In any case, the magistrates of Provence, having de-

27 II, 544–549.
28 X, 530–531.

cided that the best means of setting the nation's finances in order was to improve the national economy, went on to demand that France's economy be liberated from antiquated restrictions and destructive taxes. This way of thinking, which is crucial to an understanding of the Provence memorials, appears not only in the parlement's observations on agriculture, but also in their discussions of commerce and industry.

Examining the condition of French agriculture in the 1760's, the magistrates found it bad. They even went so far as to assert that the agriculturists were poorer in this decade than they had been back in 1683. It was possible that the harvests were poorer than those of the earlier date, but even assuming them to be the same, the cultivator of the soil in the 1760's received less money for his crops, considering the general increase in the amount of wealth since the seventeenth century.[29] To make matters worse, the agriculturist of the 1760's had to pay more taxes. The magistrates considered it entirely possible that their agricultural contemporaries produced less, and had to pay more for the satisfaction of some of their needs.[30] It was in seeking an explanation for what they claimed was a serious agricultural decline that the parlement found occasion to criticize so much old régime legislation. Though many of their examples, as might be expected, were taken from the experiences of Provence, they believed themselves to be stating general principles which applied to all of France.

There had, for example, been an attempt to restrict the planting of vines, a restriction which the magistrates considered absurd and contrary to the rights and liberty of proprietors.

[29] It is not surprising that the magistrates held such a view, for the prices of at least some important agricultural products were lower in the years between 1760 and 1765 than they had been in 1760. For example, grain prices in France dropped steadily from 1760 to 1763, and though they rose during the rest of the decade, they did not attain the level of 1760 until after 1765. In the years between 1765 and 1770, however, the prices of grain, other cereals, wines, and meats all rose to points considerably above their levels of 1760. See C.-E. Labrousse, *Esquisse du mouvement des prix et des revenus en France au XVIIIe siècle*, pp. 98, 155, 271, 296.

[30] V, 592–593.

Why, they asked, should the government prevent an activity which would increase productivity, give employment to the people, and help the population to multiply? The land around Marseilles, barren and full of rocks, had been useless until covered with vines. Did the government feel itself compelled to save landed proprietors from their own mistakes of judgment? Vine culture was an expensive enterprise, and the man who decided to undertake it did not do so without careful thought, for he could expect no return for several seasons. Moreover, if too many vines were planted the price of the product would decline, and planting would cease; thus there was an automatic check on men's enthusiasm, and no need for governmental regulation. The parlement considered it fortunate that the restrictions on vine planting had not been enforced, but demanded that they be revoked.[31]

Another restriction on planting concerned tobacco, the manufacture and sale of which had been made into a monopoly. The magistrates thought it ridiculous that tobacco culture should be prohibited in all but a few parts of France, with the result that tobacco had to be purchased from foreigners at high prices. With vigor, but in this case with faulty historical knowledge, they argued that such a restriction on production would never have been allowed by Colbert.[32] With Louisiana lost, there was no longer even the excuse that restriction was helping France's colonies.[33] Tobacco culture should not only be allowed, but should also be protected by tariffs. Optimistically, the parlement predicted that under such conditions tobacco planting would flourish in France, and that the product could even be exported.[34]

31 I, 377–380; X, 447.

32 It was Colbert who restricted tobacco culture in France and in Canada in order to encourage it in the French West Indies. See Charles Woolsey Cole, *Colbert and a Century of French Mercantilism,* II, 22.

33 The parlement apparently chose to ignore the West Indies as a tobacco growing area of any importance.

34 XIV, *Ferme de tabac* (no paging).

The judges also wanted agriculture to be liberated from harmful export duties which, by preventing the sale of products, kept down production. In their opinion it was unjust for the efforts of cultivators to be nullified by laws which diminished or prohibited the sale of their goods. It was true that for half a century France's export duties had been gradually lowered, but there were still many evils to be corrected, for the existing duties had not been planned with the good of agriculture in mind; too often the government's revenue had been the only consideration. Such mistakes in policy tended to thwart the real purpose of the duties and to keep down the national income.[35]

The parlement had some reason to be encouraged, however, for in the matter of the grain trade, at least, the government was moving in what they considered the right direction. In December, 1763, inter-provincial commerce in grains was provisionally allowed, and in July, 1764, commerce in grains was made free within the kingdom, and exports and imports were allowed, subject to a light duty.[36] Like so many other people in France, including many of the *philosophes,* the parlement approved of this step. In their opinion, its only flaw was that the reform was too mild. The magistrates believed that French agriculture would benefit greatly if grains were exempt from all duties. Thus existing import and export duties should be suppressed. Liberty for the grain trade should be fixed by unchangeable law, except for cases of extreme necessity; the parlement admitted that in such cases natural law allowed some tampering with free trade in grains. As good citizens of Provence, which could not raise all the grain it needed, they were anxious that the people of their province should be spared the payment of duties on grain imported either from the rest of France or from abroad.[37] But as Frenchmen, and perhaps as landowners, they also held the conviction that agriculture in the

35 VI, 508–511; X, 415–417.
36 Carré, *Le règne de Louis XV*, p. 367.
37 I, 83–89.

whole nation would benefit if the price of grain were kept at a decent level.

> The most essential encouragement for agriculture is to open the way for the sale of its goods by the free circulation and exportation of grains. This policy, by protecting the husbandman from losses, will increase the care with which he works, and thus it will prevent the extreme dearness which causes famines. This double advantage has been proved. . . .[38]

There was no need to fear that too much grain would be exported, for the very fact that it could be exported would keep it at a suitable price. If further precautions were necessary, officials could be stationed at the borders of France, prepared to stop exportations if a crisis demanded such action.[39]

Although Provence, having no surplus grains to sell, would not profit from legislation allowing free exportation, the parlement was anxious to apply the same principle to other commodities produced in their province. Thus they complained about export duties on wine,[40] and they also wished to apply the principle of free export to the oils made from the olives of Provence. Because of export duties, the sale of these oils had fallen off; even the Marseilles soap makers had taken to using foreign oils instead of those from their own province, because the oils from Provence had to pay an export duty when they were sent to Marseilles, which was a "free port."[41] The magistrates demanded that olive-growing and oil-making be encouraged by the removal of export duties.[42] Such duties, whether

38 I, 399 *bis*–400.

39 I, 401–403.

40 XIV, 289–291.

41 XIV, 291–292. Marseilles as a "free port" was allowed to carry on commerce with foreign nations without the hindrance of import and export duties; but in order to prevent fraudulent avoidance of payment of export duties on goods sent to Marseilles and then shipped abroad, such goods (going from the rest of France to Marseilles) had to pay export duties just as though they were being exported.

42 XIV, 291.

on wine or grain or oil, were oppressive. People, after all, had a right to sell their products, and the good of agriculture, to mention only one reason, demanded that they be allowed to do so. "There can be no hope for agriculture as long as exports are prevented by these oppressive tariffs." [43]

Restrictions on the production and sale of goods were not the only evils that needed combatting. The parlement also pictured agriculture as staggering under too great a load of taxes, and in discussing this subject they fell back upon their favorite theme: that the way to fill France's treasury was not to crush economic enterprise with taxes but to allow it to grow and swell the national income, thus making easy the solution of the nation's financial problems. Applied to agriculture, this principle automatically condemned any tax which hindered agricultural prosperity,[44] for excessive taxation made farmers both poor and hopeless and thus prevented improvements. "Excessive taxation, poverty, and pressing needs are the source of all faulty cultivation and of all bad management in agriculture." [45]

Among the taxes which the parlement considered deserving of special attention because of the harm they did to agriculture was that form of the *taille* which they chose to call the *taille arbitraire*.[46] They insisted that this tax, the amount of which

43 XIV, 290–291.

44 I, 51–52.

45 I, 387.

46 The *taille,* one of the most famous of old régime taxes, was levied on persons and real estate but never on such movable property as merchandise. Since originally the *taille* was collected as a kind of substitute for military service, the nobles and clergy were exempt, and only the common people had to pay. The *taille* was collected in two ways: on persons (*taille personnelle*), and on property (*taille réelle*). In general, but with a few exceptions, the *taille* was collected on property in provinces which still had their estates (*pays d'états*) and on persons in provinces in which the estates no longer met (*pays d'élections*).

The *taille personnelle* was the more arbitrary of the two forms, and it was evidently this tax which the parlement meant by the term *taille arbitraire*. After an amount for the whole of France had been fixed by the king's council and then split up into sums to be collected in the various fiscal divisions of the nation, the generalities, *élections,* and parishes, the collections depended on a collector's arbitrary estimate of an individual's ability to pay, was a terrible scourge to agriculture and should be abolished. The magistrates congratulated their own province, which by virtue of being a *pays d'états* was free from the worst aspects of the *taille*, on its good fortune in escaping such a terrible tax.[47] Although admitting that they knew the full burden of the arbitrary *taille* only through the experience of others, they lamented the delay in reforming this evil. Despite their outspoken demands for reform, however, the magistrates refused to see any good in the proposal that a general register of the property of individuals be made, and contended that it was an impossible remedy which tended by its very impracticability to keep alive the evil. It would be far better if each parish would make its own register at its own expense. Meanwhile the *taille* could be fixed at its present rate for each generality, parish, and individual. The rates might even be lowered. The essential point was that each individual should be assured that there would be no more arbitrary increases in the tax. Thus agriculture would be encouraged, for people would no longer have any fear that their improvements would lead to higher

of the tax were made in each parish by individual tax collectors. Naturally this system led to abuses, for the collectors were prejudiced against some people, afraid of others, and in any case likely to make mistakes. As a result of this arbitrariness the poor paid most heavily and people subject to the tax tended to neglect their property in order to appear as poor as possible. The Parlement of Provence was not alone in condemning this evil, which was criticized by a great many philosophers and reformers.

The *taille réelle,* which was in effect in Provence, was levied on real estate, chiefly land. Because there was something definite on which to assess this tax, it was superior to the *taille personnelle,* but it was far from perfect. The registers (*cadastres*) of property were often faulty. In the eighteenth century there was a movement for reform of the *taille personnelle* by collecting into registers all relevant information about the wealth of persons and assigning a definite rate of payment (*taille tarifée*) for each of the various groups on the scale of wealth. Despite its obvious merits the plan was unpopular, for many people persisted in their distrust of registers and opposed any reform which would force them to reveal the exact amount of their property. See Marcel Marion, *Dictionnaire des institutions de la France,* pp. 526–531.

47 I, 55, 76–77, 399.

taxes.[48] The advantages of this stability could be retained even after the registers had been drawn up by all the parishes. Everyone could be given one opportunity to complain of any unfairness in his assessment, and after all such appeals had been heard and judged there would be no injustice in forbidding further complaints for a number of years. Though deprived of all hope of revisions, the proprietors would have the advantage of knowing that their taxes could not be raised, and would therefore have no reason to postpone repairs and improvements. Industrious people could go ahead with their plans. Only the lazy would suffer.[49]

Indignant as they were about the effects of the *taille* on French agriculture in general, the magistrates of Provence were perhaps even more bitter about the *gabelle,* which in their opinion had struck a cruel blow at the agriculture of their native province. The word *gabelle,* which originally had applied to taxes on other commodities, such as wine, had by the eighteenth century come to mean only a tax on salt, the collection and sale of which in France was a monopoly sold by the government to a group of financiers.[50] In the opinion of the parlement this monopoly sinned against the cardinal principle in financial administration, for the tax on salt kept down production in France and thus handicapped the people in their attempts to make a living. Salt was a vital necessity to agriculture. Without it livestock could not be cared for properly, meat tended to become scarce, and the resulting lack of fertilizer led to a decrease in the productivity of the soil. These effects, which could be seen everywhere in France, were the fault of the *gabelle,* which made salt expensive and scarce. In the mountains of Daphiné there was, for example, a place called Toland (*sic*), which had an excellent salt spring; but instead of permitting the free use of the salt by the inhabitants, the financiers in control of the *gabelle* paid an annual sum of

48 I, 76–79.
49 I, 80–82.
50 Marion, *Dictionnaire,* pp. 247–250.

money to the seigneur, on condition that he would help maintain
the scarcity of salt by prohibiting the use of the salt water which
he owned. Thus nature's benefits were flouted and flocks and
harvests in that country suffered. In Provence the story was
the same. Back in the seventeenth century the nobles of
Provence had opposed the *gabelle* on the ground that the
province's natural abundance of salt was needed as an aid
to agriculture. Acceptance of the tax was forced upon the
province, however, and in the century which followed the
predictions of the nobles came true. The consumption of salt in
Provence declined, and with disastrous results: fewer cattle,
less meat, fewer hides, less fertilizer, poorer soil. Such were
the effects of the *gabelle* on French agriculture as seen by the
parlement. Instead of exporting a surplus of salted meat to her
colonies the nation had to buy it from other countries. Were
it not for the *gabelle* every household could nourish a pig; yet
in most of the kingdom the peasants had no pigs because the
price of salt was too high.[51]

Another tax harmful to agriculture was the *corvée,* which
forced men to give up their time and labor rather than their
money. Each year for a certain number of days, varying from
six to forty, country people had to work without pay on the
roads of the kingdom.[52] Provence, being a *pays d'états,* was not
troubled by this extremely unpopular requirement, and the
parlement found satisfaction in this fact, for they considered the
corvée a terrible handicap to the agriculture of France. Forced
labor on the roads meant not only that people had to work without pay but also that men, wagons, and farm animals were
taken away from the cultivation of the soil; while workers were
deprived of wages the land was deprived of care. To make
matters worse, many of the roads built by the *corvée* were
ornamental rather than useful. The magistrates, who believed in
public works by soldiers, did not neglect this opportunity to
point out that the Roman roads were built by soldiers and were

51 IV, 825–826, 843–845; X, 399–401.
52 See Marion, *Dictionnaire,* pp. 153–155.

thus a benefit rather than a burden to the provinces. Congratulating their own province upon its exemption from the *corvée,* they remarked that apparently natural law was understood only in the *pays d'états.*[53]

For better or worse, agriculture was influenced by almost every kind of legislation. One of the reasons for the parlement's opposition to large standing armies and to a conscripted militia was that these forces took too many men away from productive labor on the soil.[54] Frequent wars also harmed agriculture by increasing taxes and reducing the number of men and the amount of production.[55] General economic conditions inevitably influenced the conditions of agricultural production. Low interest rates, for example, meant that agriculture would be stimulated; on the other hand concentration of wealth in one place, such as Paris, or in the hands of a few men, such as the financiers, meant poor circulation of money, higher interest rates, and languishing agriculture in a great many parts of France.[56]

The parlement's numerous discussions of agriculture in their memorials about the French finances were justified by their basic principle that the best means of filling the public treasury was to make the nation rich. An essential step in the direction of economic prosperity was the encouragement of agriculture, and a backward glance at the parlement's actual recommendations will demonstrate that encouragement, for them, meant a few positive governmental actions and a great many negative ones.

> . . . The best distribution of the land that can be made is to place its ownership, as much as possible, in the hands of those who cultivate it, and if care is taken not to overburden it with taxes, not to deprive livestock of salt by excessive prices, to avoid above all arbitrary taxation, to reestablish the circula-

53 I, 398–399; XI, 859–860.
54 I, 462–463; XII, 859–860.
55 I, 244–246.
56 I, 15, 392–393.

tion of money in the rural areas, and to maintain the value of grain by allowing its export, there is no need to doubt that our harvests will become infinitely more abundant, that the population will increase, and that it in turn will lead to the greater flourishing of agriculture.[57]

Where agriculture was concerned the parlement believed that the government's policy should consist for the most part of the removal of existing evils, especially restrictions and taxes, which stood in the way of prosperity. Government action was required, to be sure, but much of this action was to be either indirect or negative in character. Further study of the parlement's suggestions for making France prosperous requires an examination of their remarks about the other forms of economic activity.

57 I, 422–423.

CHAPTER V

INDUSTRY

La prohibition de fabriquer est contre nature; il est injuste d'empecher les citoyens de travailler suivant leur goût, leur talent, et le genre de leur industrie.

Mémoires, I, 675.

THE Parlement of Provence believed that industry, like agriculture, was a valuable and productive form of economic activity. Unlike their contemporaries the physiocrats, they did not consider manufacturing sterile, but estimated that out of a national income of a little over 2,000,000,000 *livres* approximately 800,000,000 *livres* were produced by industry.[1] When judged by the amount of wealth produced, manufactures were thus far from equal to agriculture, but they were nevertheless of great importance, both because of their productivity and because of their influence on the other forms of economic activity. The magistrates believed that agriculture, industry, and commerce were all interdependent; each aided the others, and a decline in one meant a decline in all three. Along with agriculture and commerce, industry therefore deserved the best form of encouragement that the government could give.[2]

I. THE FORM OF ENCOURAGEMENT

Although the magistrates filled their memorials with requests for the encouragement of manufacturing, they recommended very few positive governmental actions toward that end. It is true that they wanted a definite tariff policy which would provide for protection against foreign products and at the same time encourage the export of French goods.

Import duties can be kept at high levels; this is sometimes necessary for the good of the kingdom. There is no such thing

1 IX, 341–343, 382–383.
2 I, 452–453, 553–554; X, 73–74. See also Chapter IV, Section I.

as export duties being too low for our manufactured products and especially for the sale of our provisions.[3]

Associated with this opinion about tariffs was the parlement's belief that the nation should work for self-sufficiency by manufacturing products which would otherwise have to be imported from abroad.[4]

It is also true that a few of the parlement's statements may have been meant as favoring the use of public funds for the encouragement of manufacturing in France. Attention has already been called to their defense of the various eighteenth century attempts to encourage silk-culture in Provence; in this case the magistrates were certainly defending the right of proprietors to plant what they pleased, but they may also have meant to express approval of a project in which subsidies were being granted in the hope of founding a silk industry in Provence.[5] In another part of their memorials, while discussing how Provence's tax money was spent, the judges wrote of the desirability of encouragement for manufactures, and it is possible to find in this passage approval of government subsidies to industry.[6] But the point remains very doubtful. The magistrates, after all, had fourteen thick volumes in which to express themselves; yet, often as they used the word encouragement, they made no definite proposals for a program of subsidies to industry, and there is not enough evidence to prove that they favored this form of encouragement.

The parlement did state that the government, year after year, had urged Provence to encourage manufactures, but they argued that the province had been unable to do so because there were always too many obstacles in the way.[7] In discussing this

3 X, 422.
4 I, 552–553.
5 On this point see Chapter IV, Section 3.
6 X, 73–74.
7 X, 540–541.

state of affairs, the judges gave most of their attention to these obstacles, which they wanted removed, rather than to recommendations of aid to industry in a positive sense. As a result, their treatment of manufacturing in France was similar to their treatment of agriculture: it consisted mainly of urging the removal of obstacles in the way of production and prosperity. As in the case of agriculture, the magistrates saw industry impeded by a mass of unnecessary and harmful legislation. They spoke often of encouragement, but if we are to judge their understanding of this word by their actual recommendations we must conclude that to them encouragement meant for the most part the liberation of industry from restrictions.

> Let us conclude, then, that all work merits protection, but let us never forget that the care and conservation of our national patrimony must be given preference, and that this national patrimony consists of our original and independent wealth [grain, livestock, and iron, according to another statement in the memorials] and of those simple manufactures the products of which are intended for our use and are within the reach of the great majority of consumers. Protection for these simple manufactures is easy: it is enough not to damage them by faulty operations.[8]

Several elements of the parlement's thought are apparent in the above quotation, but two of them are especially related to the question of what form of encouragement should be given to industry. The magistrates state clearly their preference for the production of essential consumers' goods and, indirectly, their desire for national self-sufficiency. They also exhibit a strong tendency toward laissez-faire, evident in their faith that France's most important manufactures need only to be left alone, and even to some extent suggested by their unwillingness to discriminate overmuch between the various forms of enterprise.

8 I, 558–559.

2. RESTRICTIONS AND MONOPOLIES

That the parlement opposed discrimination is clearly shown
in their opposition to restrictions on manufacturing. Although
their own preference was for the manufacture of simple, essential goods, especially those for which agriculture furnished the
raw materials, the magistrates nevertheless insisted that all
manufactures deserved encouragement. To the question of
whether the making of luxury goods should be prohibited, they
gave a negative answer. Such a prohibition would be useless.
Luxuries did not appear because some people wanted to manufacture them, but because of public demand. Prohibitive legislation would only whet the public's appetite for luxuries, and this
appetite would be satisfied, legally or illegally, by imports from
other countries. All manufactures, whatever their character,
stimulated agriculture. If consumption of goods in France declined because of luxury on the part of some people and misery
on the part of others, this condition could not be remedied by
attacks on luxury manufactures or by attempts to change
people's tastes. The wisest course was to refrain from restric-
tive legislation against luxuries and to use their manufacture
as a means of attracting money from foreign lands.[9]

In the great eighteenth century debate over *toiles peintes,* the
magistrates were also on the side of liberty. This lengthy quar-
rel, in which some of the best-known writers and economists
of France participated, concerned the import and manufacture
of printed calicos. Largely as a result of the influence brought
to bear by manufacturers of other kinds of cloth, such as silk,
both the import and the manufacture of printed calicos were
prohibited by the French government until 1759.[10] The legislation of that date, which allowed printed calico to be made in
France or brought in from the outside, was heartily approved by
the Parlement of Provence. The magistrates pointed out that

9 I, 450–455, 552–554.

10 Edgard Depitre, *La toile peinte en France au XVIIe et au XVIIIe
siècles* (Paris: Rivière et Cie., 1912), pp. i–vii. Henri Sée, *Histoire économique de la France,* pp. 350–351.

the restrictions against *toiles peintes* had forced French manufactures to stand still while their foreign competitors were making progress; once having fallen behind in their methods, the French manufacturers had feared competition and had upheld the very prohibitions which were the original cause of their inferiority. The French cloth makers could not be blamed for their fears; the real fault lay with those who had restricted the liberty to manufacture. Freedom to import and manufacture *toiles peintes* was the proper solution to the problem. French manufacturers could still be aided by protective tariffs, but the outright prohibition of foreign cloth was both useless and harmful. Although admitting that they did not know all the effects of the relaxation of the restrictions against *toiles peintes*, the magistrates were confident that the makers of other kinds of cloth had lost none of their customers.[11]

> Thus all the evils predicted by the manufacturers of Rouen, Tours, and Lyons were nothing but useless oratory. Prohibitive legislation is usually caused by false reports and fantastic fears.[12]

Prohibitions of manufactures such as that of printed calicos were to industry what the restrictions on vine planting were to agriculture: a mistaken policy.[13]

> The prohibition of manufacturing is against nature; it is unjust to keep citizens from working according to their tastes, their talents, and their trades.[14]

In the opinion of the magistrates, monopolies were even worse than restrictions. Lumping the terms industry and commerce together, as was the practice of many eighteenth century writers, they expressed disapproval of monopolies in both forms of enterprise.

11 I, 673–676.
12 I, 689–690.
13 I, 453.
14 I, 675.

Competition among the subjects for work is the basis of liberty of commerce. It has rightly been said that it consists of each of them having the right to busy himself in the manner which he believes will be the most profitable or the most pleasant, provided it is not harmful to society. Exclusive privileges violate this principle more than prohibitions. For prohibitions have as their motive the interest of the state, often very badly applied, to be sure. Exclusive privileges are granted only to favor individuals.[15]

A decrease in competition tended to have bad effects, both on production at home and on competition with foreign nations.

It has been rightly observed that a privileged person when freed from competition has less incentive to strive for perfection and that the citizens are prevented from improving upon imperfect inventions by new discoveries, while foreign imitators can progress; as a result, perfection of the craft and cheapness of the goods are both sacrificed. The entrepreneur has no trouble maintaining his control of the prices and even has an interest in obtaining an extension of his privilege by making it appear, at the time when the privilege expires, that the craft is still in its infancy.[16]

15 I, 737–738. The magistrates acknowledge in a marginal note that the ideas in this passage are taken from the book *Elemens du commerce*. The author of this anonymous work, published in 1754, was the economist Forbonnais. The following, taken from Vol. I, p. 92, is the passage to which the magistrates referred.

L'autre espece de concurrence intérieure est celle du travail entre les sujets: elle consiste à ce que chacun d'eux ait la faculté de s'occuper de la maniere qu'il croit la plus lucrative, ou qui lui plaît davantage, lorsqu'elle est utile a la societe. Elle est la base principale de la liberté de commerce; elle seule contribue plus qu'aucun autre moyen, à procurer à une nation cette concurrence extérieure qui l'enriche et la rend puissante.

16 I, 738–740. The magistrates, in a marginal note, again cite the book *Elemens du commerce*. Here are Forbonnais' words, taken from Vol. I, pp. 303–304.

Dans les tems de barbarie, sous prétexte de dédommager les entrepreneurs des manufactures nouvelles du risque de leurs avances, de leur assurer un profit, de récompenser leur zèle, on leur accordoit des privilèges exclusifs. C'étoit renoncer en faveur d'un petit nombre d'hommes,

The parlement was aware that some people justified monopolies by arguing that something was due the originator of a new process for his contribution, but they refused to agree with this reasoning.

> It is claimed that favors are granted out of justice to the originators of a manufacture, a machine, or a new preparation, as though there were not other ways of rewarding them, ways more appropriate and more useful to the state. All those who have written about commerce have already refuted these pretexts.[17]

Holding such views, the parlement was bound to complain about some of the monopolies which existed in eighteenth century France. One of these, and one especially resented in Provence, concerned the making of porcelain. In the 1760's the famous Sèvres porcelain industry, owned by the state, was making a determined effort to rival the fine porcelain produced in Germany; a decree of 1760 had given it the exclusive privilege for the manufacture of almost every kind of porcelain.[18] The Parlement of Provence complained that important manufactures had grown up in Marseilles which could be very prosperous if only their activities were not limited by the porcelain monopoly. There were in Marseilles workers with talent in designing and in the use of color; materials were plentiful, and everything was ready for a thriving business. Some pottery had been made, but because of the porcelain monopoly the manufacturers did not dare to make the clay transparent. Already the workers were becoming impatient and were threatening to go to other coun-

---

à la concurrence des matieres premieres, des ouvriers, des capitaux, enfin à la perfection de l'art, au bon marché des ouvrages qui ne peuvent être le fruit que de ces concurrences. . . . De quelque manière que les choses tournassent, comme il importoit aux entrepreneurs d'obtenir une prolongation, l'art étoit toûjours peu avancé à l'expiration du privilège.

17 I, 738. Again the influence of Forbonnais can be seen, if these remarks are compared with the quotation in note 16.

18 H. Havard and M. Vachon, *Les manufactures nationales: les Gobelins, la Savonnerie, Sèvres, Beauvais* (Paris: Decaux, 1889), pp. 390–391.

tries; there was danger that France might lose these valuable craftsmen and be forced to buy the products of their art from foreign merchants. For this condition the porcelain monopoly was to blame. It was absurd that the people of Marseilles, a free port into which foreign porcelain could enter duty free, should be prevented from manufacturing porcelain of their own. For the benefit of a few privileged persons France was being deprived of an industry capable of greatly increasing her exports.[19]

As a further example of the evils of monopoly, the parlement drew upon their province's experiences with the soapmaking industry, recalling the ill effects of an exclusive privilege which, happily, no longer existed. On that occasion, the date of which the magistrates did not mention, one man had been given a business worth over 12 million *livres*.[20] Despite protests from some of the officials of Provence that the amount of soap manufactured was declining and that less and less oil was being consumed by the soapmakers, the monopoly had lasted for some time. Persistent opposition by the parlement and by the province

19 I, 758–763. The magistrates, who apparently had a specific local interest in mind, were eager to compromise with the porcelain monopoly. They suggested that the Sèvres manufacturers be granted an indemnity for allowing the poorer grade of Marseilles porcelain to be sold.

20 The outstanding soap monopoly, both in Provence and in the rest of France as well, was that established by Colbert in 1665. Acting with characteristic energy, Colbert at that time attempted to remedy a decline in soap production. After sending men to study the successful soap-making methods used in Genoa, he gave two men, Jacques Beuf and Pierre Rigat, the exclusive right to sell soap anywhere in France. They were expected to make soap, to buy the whole output of soapmakers already in existence, and to supply the whole nation. Colbert expected that Toulon would become the outstanding soap producing center in Provence, because of the extensive supplies of oil produced nearby. While the monopoly was in effect, soapmaking in Marseilles declined fifty per cent. There were strenuous objections to the soap monopoly, in other parts of France as well as in Provence, where the *assemblée des communautés* protested continuously. The privilege was finally invalidated in 1669. After that, soapmaking in Provence increased gradually during the rest of the seventeenth and in the eighteenth century, especially at Marseilles. See Charles Woolsey Cole, *Colbert and a Century of French Mercantilism,* II, 350–353, and V.–L. Bourrilly's section *Histoire économique* in *Les bouches du Rhône,* III, 196–197, 238.

had finally triumphed, and the monopoly had been discontinued. Recalling this experience, the judges were inclined to believe that any abuse was possible when an industry was in the hands of one man.[21]

Despite their aversion to monopolies, the parlement tended to take a realistic attitude toward them, realizing that it was easier to describe their evils in general terms than to overcome them. Compared with their estimates of the harm done by monopolies, the magistrates' suggestions for reform were moderate. They gave their chief attention to the question of the legal forms granting special privileges, insisting that whenever any such privilege was granted its existence should be advertised in all places where it had the effect of restraining people from some activity. Thus those whose "natural liberty" was being abridged would be informed of this fact; lawsuits would be avoided and everyone would know when the monopoly could be expected to expire. To this moderate demand the magistrates added another which perhaps reveals the direction their thought was taking. Any privilege extending to all parts of France should be registered by all parlements, for no single court had jurisdiction throughout the kingdom. In order to make this policy effective there should be prepared an account of all existing privileges. This account should be sent to all the parlements for registration, and then forwarded to all the *baillages* and *sénéchaussées* of the kingdom. All of the courts would thus be able to defend the interests of the provinces under their jurisdiction against unfair privileges secured by influential people close to the throne, and monopolies could no longer be extended beyond the provinces to which they were intended to apply. Privileges remaining unused for a certain length of time should be revoked.[22] Despite the moderate and legalistic appearance of these demands, it can be seen that the Parlement of Provence was recommending measures which, if accepted, would have granted the parlements some of the veto power which they had been at-

21 X, 401–406, 541.
22 I, 740–749.

tempting to exercise for so long, and which, moreover, would have enabled a single court to reject any monopoly or privilege in any part of France.

3. Labor and Guilds

Besides attacking restrictions and monopolies, which handicapped enterepreneurs, the parlement contended that laborers had a right to engage in any occupations which pleased them. Competition, and not government, would regulate the professions.

> Pressed, so to speak, by each other, men will place themselves where they can find subsistence, and they will create new means of subsisting. It is not the duty of government to decide who shall be sailor, laborer, or artisan; none of these professions will lack members. There is no need to fear that one profession will encroach upon another unless the state causes this inequality by unequal treatment.[23]

The magistrates did not intend, however, that laborers should be free to be idle. They were not averse to indirect methods of increasing the amount of work done, such as decreasing the number of holidays.[24]

Concerning the subject of guilds, the parlement did not speak directly, but in their discussions of other matters there can be seen a critical, and perhaps hostile, attitude toward guilds, an attitude such as that implied in the quotation above. They were convinced, in the first place, of the value of home industries carried on by families who worked part of the time in agriculture and part of the time at manufacturing.[25] Such home industries were in general not regulated by guilds. In discussing the sale of *lettres de maitrise,* which created new masterships and dispensed with apprenticeship, journeymanship, and a masterpiece, the magistrates also approached, indirectly, the subject of

23 I, 443–444.
24 I, 444.
25 I, 418–420.

guilds. They opposed these sales, not because they wished to protect the exclusiveness of the corporations of artisans, but on financial grounds. The sale of *lettres de maitrise* was simply a device to get money from the corporations of artisans, who in order to prevent an increase in the number of master workmen would themselves purchase the *lettres* from the government. The parlement denounced this policy, which was nothing more than a sale of offices, and which tended to multiply beyond all reason the number of corporations of artisans.[26] They were extremely critical of the corporations themselves, which in their opinion slowed up commerce and industry. Created by the government so that it could tax them, the corporations had to assess their members so that they could pay their debts; the existence of these debts helped to keep interest rates and the price of labor high, and to inconvenience commerce; the corporations not only owed money to individuals but also loaned it to the king, thus adding further to the complicated and harmful debt structure of the kingdom. Their financial affairs were made even worse by the lawsuits in which they were constantly engaging.[27]

In seeking a remedy for the multiplicity of masterships, the parlement came to agree in theory with the proposals of the estates of 1614. The estates had suggested that all masterships erected since 1576 be abolished, and that the trades be thrown open to poor people whose work would be inspected by officials. The estates had also proposed that all edicts on arts and crafts, together with all *lettres de maitrise* formerly granted, be revoked, and that no more *lettres de maitrise* and no more edicts taxing artisans because of their crafts be issued. The parlement thought that these demands ought to be granted, but they recognized that some use might be made of *lettres de maitrise* now that the harmful policy of issuing them had taken firm root in France. These *lettres* should not, however, be distributed for the mere purpose of getting money for the treasury.[28] Master-

26 VII, 324, 329-335, 338-344.
27 VII, 345-347; VIII, 345.
28 VII, 347-351.

ships could continue to exist in the form of licenses which would enable more people to work at the trades. Apprenticeship and journeymanship could be abolished, but there was some good in requiring masterpieces and periodic inspections of manufactures.[29]

From such a limited set of opinions it is difficult to draw definite conclusions. The parlement's views on guilds are somewhat cloudy as a result of being mixed with a discussion of the sale of masterships. Apparently their concrete proposals were somewhat more moderate than their abstract ideas on the subject of freedom of the professions. It is clear, however, that the magistrates wished to increase the opportunities for men of skill to enter the trades, and that they wished to decrease the harm done to the production and exchange of goods by corporations of artisans acting as debtors and creditors.

4. Taxation and Manufacturing

The parlement devoted considerable space in their memorials, as well as a good deal of stern language, to the harm done to manufacturing by badly conceived and destructively collected taxes. Such taxes made life needlessly difficult for manufacturers, hemming them in with unnecessary regulations and sometimes destroying industries entirely. In the opinion of the magistrates, France's administrators were guilty of having attempted, at great expense, to encourage luxury manufactures such as tapestries and fine linens while at the same time their tax policies were destroying the nation's simple "national" manufactures. For this absurd practice the judges did not blame the tapestry and linen industries; as we have seen, they believed that all kinds of production should be encouraged and that attempts to discourage luxuries were futile. But they held the administrators responsible for following false principles.[30] In Provence, for example, it was unjust that manufacturers of

29 VII, 347, 352–355.
30 I, 559–560.

silk had been granted favors while the industries making cards
and processing hides were being taxed out of existence; the
latter commodities had been made the targets of taxation without consideration of what their fate would be.[31] In France as a
whole the results of such practices had been disastrous for
manufactures.

> If anyone today should make a record of all the national
> manufactures which have been destroyed within the past hun-
> dred years, he would be terrified by the prodigious number of
> corpses produced by the blows of finance, and it would be easy
> to see how much our ordinary daily consumption has been de-
> creased. All of which is a sure sign of decadence.
>
> Periods when taxes and constraints have destroyed impor-
> tant manufactures, and caused them to be transported to
> foreign lands, are well known, but those industries which
> have perished as a result of poverty are for the most part un-
> known or forgotten. The fact is ignored that a great multi-
> tude of trades have been abandoned because of decreased con-
> sumption proportional to the extent to which the people have
> been plunged into the most extreme want, in accordance with
> the detestable statecraft of old-fashioned finance.[32]

Although the destructive effects of unwise taxation were not
limited to any particular part of France,[33] the parlement chose
its most outstanding examples from Provence. One of the industries which the magistrates were anxious to rescue from
excessive taxation was card-making. There had been intermittent taxation of playing cards in France since Henry III in
1583 had placed a tax on playing cards and dice. That particular tax had never been collected in Provence, however, and apparently the province's card industry was not greatly molested
until the eighteenth century. In 1701 a tax was placed on each
deck of cards manufactured, except those marked for export.
With various rate changes, this tax lasted until 1719. It was

31 I, 649–650.
32 I, 561–563.
33 I, 573.

reestablished in 1745, and in the following year the exemption of cards manufactured for the export trade was discontinued. As the years passed the tax on cards manufactured and exported gradually increased in amount. The proceeds were earmarked for the support of a royal military school. Collection was placed under the supervision of the Secretary of State in charge of war.[34]

The Parlement of Provence could scarcely find words strong enough to express their condemnation of this tax on the cardmaking industry. They aimed their criticisms both at the numerous annoying regulations associated with the tax and at the amount of the tax itself. One rule, for example, required that the cardmakers purchase envelopes from the tax officials and that they seal up the cards in the envelopes as soon as they were made, a procedure which damaged the cards by bending them. When this order went into effect the manufacturers were forced to relinquish their envelope making tools, some of which had been expensive. The cardmakers were also forced to buy paper from the tax officials, who furnished them with an inferior product at a high price; this paper, the judges contended, was manufactured at a factory belonging to the official in charge of the tax. Moreover the tax of one *denier* per card was payable on delivery of the paper, or in other words before the cards were even manufactured. Though in practice the tax was seldom collected at this time, the existence of such a rule was a constant threat to the cardmakers, who could be jailed for debt if they failed to pay their bills on time. Master cardmakers were granted ten sheets of paper out of every hundred free of charge, as a discount to cover inevitable waste during the manufacturing process, but the parlement contended that this indemnity was insufficient and paid for but half of the paper wasted.[35] Once the cards were made, the master cardmakers were required to have them stamped with an official seal, and since the cards could not be delivered until this requirement had been

34 I, 509–518.
35 I, 519–525.

met, delays on the part of the official who did the sealing often resulted in loss of customers for the cardmakers. To make regulation of the industry easier the manufacture of cards was restricted to certain areas; in some generalities cardmaking was completely forbidden. The parlement considered this rule an unjust and unwise limitation of manufacturing.[36] Those who were allowed to make cards were not permitted to raise prices in order to pass the tax on to the consumer. According to the magistrates the tax was too high—almost double the value of the merchandise—and had forced the cardmakers to relinquish most of their profits in order to keep their domestic trade. The foreign trade in cards, which had been the chief source of income, was entirely gone. The limitation of cardmaking to certain areas had not been effective, and packs of cards made in foreign lands were smuggled into the generalities where the manufacture was forbidden. To make matters worse, French cardmakers were emigrating to Switzerland, Germany, Spain and parts of Italy. Instead of exporting packs of cards, the people of Provence were beginning to import them.[37]

According to the parlement, the decline in cardmaking was causing a slump in the other forms of enterprise in Provence. Hard-hit by the tax on cards, paper mills in the province had declined from 57 in 1745 to the low number of 18.[38] The export trade in paper had been lost, and about 400 papermakers had emigrated. There had been in Provence a pasteboard industry which made use of the scraps of paper left over by the cardmakers, but this industry had declined with the decline in cardmaking. The cloth industry now had to import pasteboard for the boxes in which their products were shipped. The people of Provence had also lost the trade of foreigners who had

36 I, 525–528.

37 I, 528–537.

38 V.-L. Bourrilly in the section *Histoire économique* in the encyclopedia *Les bouches du Rhône* (III, 246) states that there were in Provence 56 paper mills in 1727, 45 in 1738, and 56 in 1770. Not all of the mills listed were in operation, however.

formerly come to buy the cards made in the province. The magistrates estimated that on the whole the tax on cards had lost for the province the annual export of 3,840,000 packs of cards valued at 400,000 *livres*. These figures, of course, failed to show the loss from increased imports of cards and paper.[39] Of 60 manufacturers and 380 laborers in the card industry there remained since the tax only 22 manufacturers and 15 laborers.[40] In view of all the disadvantages of the tax on cards, the parlement could see but one remedy: the tax should be abolished. The military school to which the returns were devoted could be supported by some more just and less destructive means.[41]

Another vicious tax, that on hides, was viewed by the magistrates as a veritable model of destructiveness. They were especially opposed to this tax, not only because it lay heavily upon one of Provence's industries, but also because the tanning industry was one of the simple, "national" industries which they considered especially important. For the processing of hides was related to what the judges called the "independent riches" of a nation, that is, grain, livestock, and iron, which were essential to national self-sufficiency. The tanning industry stimulated livestock raising and helped to increase the value of the land. Yet this vital occupation was threatened with extinction by the tax on hides.[42]

The practice of taxing hides had appeared in France as early as the sixteenth century, when officials began to mark the hides, ostensibly as a means of regulating the industry. Provence had not suffered greatly from this early legislation, which was not always universally enforced. An edict of 1759 had placed an-

---

39 I, 537–546.

40 I, 548. Unfortunately the parlement did not see fit to state the year of the tax referred to in the text, but it is assumed that they meant the tax of 1745, which had been increased by the 1760's when the memorials were written.

41 I, 641–642.

42 I, 551, 564.

other tax on hides, and the judges contended that already the number of tanneries in Provence was greatly reduced.[43]

As a result of this tax, the processors of hides were forced to submit to all sorts of inconveniences and injustices, as though they were engaged in a business harmful to the state, instead of furnishing their fellow citizens with a necessary commodity. Although the preparation of hides involved several steps, the tax officials insisted on marking the hides after the first stage in the process; thus the manufacturer was forced to pay not only for the weight lost by the hides during the remaining stages, but for all the hides in which flaws were found after the original marking. Three months after the marking, moreover, the payment of the tax was demanded, its amount depending on the weight of the hides at the time when they were marked. Thus the tax was levied on the hides which the tanner had purchased rather than on his profits from the tanning process. If a tanner made no profits at all, or even sustained a loss, he was still forced to pay the tax. Even in cases where the tanner was able to make a normal profit there was great inconvenience in the fact that many factors could disturb the payment of the tanner by his customers, while his payment of the tax on hides was fixed and inevitable. All the risks were taken by the manufacturer, who in addition was subject to all sorts of formalities, inspections, and fines.[44]

> Inconveniences, formalities, inspections, injustice, inequality, excessive taxation, advance payment of the duty at the factory before any sales have been made and even on the defective hides for which not even the equivalent of the duty paid is recovered; all the horrors which can make a profession disgusting, cause work to be hated, and stifle industry are here accumulated.[45]

The parlement claimed to have reliable information about the harm which the tax on hides had done to the tanning industry

43 I, 564–565, 574.
44 I, 584–596.
45 I, 582–583.

in their province. Because of the tax the number of manufacturers and workers in the province's tanning industry had decreased from 405 manufacturers and 728 workers in 1759 to 262 manufacturers and 252 workers in 1764.[46] Many manufacturers and workers had emigrated and had thus been lost to France. Production in the tanning industry of Provence had declined in proportion to the decline in the number of workers, and by 1764 dropped to about a third of what it had been in 1759.[47] The parlement estimated that as a result of the tanning industry's decline the province was losing over 400,000 *livres* a year in profits and wages.[48] Many of the laborers still employed by the tanners worked only part of the time. The magistrates believed that the loss to the province would be much greater if an estimate could be made of the effects on other industries of the decline in tanning.[49]

All of this harm done to the province might have been justified if the returns from the tax on hides had been great enough. But the magistrates estimated that when all the expenses of collection were paid the returns from the tax amounted to only 111,076 *livres* a year. Here the parlement had a splendid illustration for the idea which had turned their discussion of the French finances into an attack on so much of the legislation of the old régime.

> Thus Provence is deprived of 500,000 *livres* a year, manufactures are destroyed and transported to foreign lands, unhappy families are forced to expatriate themselves, and all in order to collect 111,076 *livres* which the king shares with his agents. There you have the science of finance.[50]

46 I, 658–659. These totals are taken from a table in the memorials. Marseilles, which had redeemed the tax on hides by making a lump payment, has not been included.

47 I, 598–600, 614–615.

48 I, 615–618. Once more Marseilles is excluded. It is interesting to note that workers in the tanning industry were paid 20 *sols* per day and worked from four A.M. until sunset.

49 I, 618, 620.

50 I, 632.

Such a state of affairs should not be allowed to continue; the tax on hides should be abolished. In view of the critical condition of the nation's finances, however, and in keeping with a practice which they often followed, the judges divided their proposals into immediate and subsequent measures. There should be an announcement that the tax would be discontinued, and this promise should be carried out within a reasonable length of time. Meanwhile, as an evidence of good faith, the government should grant all tanners a ten percent reduction in the tax as an indemnity for their losses occasioned by defective hides. Provence should be allowed to redeem the tax on hides by making a lump payment to the treasury. Pending the complete abolition of the tax, the government should put an end to inconvenient inspections and official interference with the industry.[51]

The parlement wished to free manufacturing not only from direct taxes but also from tariff duties which kept down production and hampered the sale of manufactured goods. A slight increase in some export duty, for example, was often enough to deprive a French industry of its advantage over its competitors. In such cases rival manufactures sprang up in other lands, and when the evil was discovered and the duty lowered those rivals already had a firm foothold.[52] The city of Marseilles, whose position as a free port led to tariff complications, furnished the judges with several examples of the way in which industries could be harmed by unwise tariff measures. Silk manufacturing in Marseilles suffered because their silks, on entering France, were subject to import duties as high as those on foreign silks. In the case of Avignon silks (Avignon was then a papal city) the Marseilles products even had to pay a higher import duty than the foreign ones.[53] The sugar refining industry in Marseilles also suffered because of its location in a free port. Unlike the rest of France, Marseilles, as a free port, was

51 I, 58–59, 641–644.
52 VI, 508–510.
53 II, 245–248.

able to import raw sugar duty free; thus the sugar refiners of Marseilles would have had the advantage over those in the rest of the kingdom had not the government intervened. In order to place the refined sugar of Marseilles on an equal competitive basis with that of the rest of France, the sugar loaves from that city were made to pay an import duty when passing into the rest of the kingdom. The justice of this duty was not contested by the Parlement of Provence, the judges of which merely contended that it was too high. A further handicap to sugar refining in Marseilles was that this duty had to be paid when sugar was shipped overland, through France, to such places as Switzerland and Piedmont: sugar exported to these places from Bordeaux, La Rochelle, and Rouen was given a rebate equivalent to the import duty which had been paid for the raw sugar; but sugar refined at Marseilles was not given the favor of a rebate on the import duty it had to pay on being sent across parts of France. The parlement contended that it was in the interest of the state that equality be granted to the Marseilles product.[54]

Soapmaking was another industry which was victimized by an overcomplicated tariff policy. Soapmakers had set up their business in Provence because of the plentiful supply of oil, but as in the case of sugar refining the government had attempted to collect duties in such a way that the products made in the various parts of France would all be treated equally. The government tried to maintain equality between soapmakers who already had oil or who could import it duty free, and those who had to pay duties on the oil they used. Marseilles, as a free port, could import oil duty free; therefore soap made in Marseilles was taxed when it entered the rest of France, the duty being nothing more than an indirect way of taxing the oil which had gone into the making of the soap. In this way protection was given to soapmakers who had to import their oil. But what about soapmakers in the rest of Provence, who used oil produced in the province? These men, according to the parlement,

54 II, 380–388.

were being treated unfairly, for their industry was being ruined by duties. Soap made in Provence and with Provence's oil was taxed on leaving its place of manufacture, on the ground that the use of locally produced oil gave it an unfair advantage over the soap produced elsewhere in France. To the parlement, however, their own province appeared to be the victim of unfairness. Provence, they contended, had already paid an *abonnement* in order to avoid taxation of its oil; that is, the province had paid a lump sum of money to the crown as a substitute for payment of the duties. The magistrates were thus able to argue that Provence's oil was being taxed twice: once when the province, by the *abonnement,* had redeemed its oil from further taxation, and a second time when the oil, now become soap, was taxed on leaving its place of manufacture. These duties were ruining the soapmaking industry of Provence.[55]

Although they gave most of their attention to local industries, with which they were most familiar, the magistrates believed that the effects of unwise taxation of manfactures were everywhere the same. At various times in France's history taxes had destroyed manufactures of woolen cloth and had forced their workers to choose between starvation and emigration. Taxes of one kind or another had crippled or destroyed the manufactures of hats, pipes, paper, and whalebone. Such methods of filling the nation's treasury could not square with the parlement's ideas on the proper conduct of the finances. The magistrates were inclined to agree with the remark of Pierre de Boisguilbert, the author of *Le Détail de la France,* who wrote that such methods were like tearing down an expensive house in order to sell a few sticks of wood.[56] This condemnation of the kind of taxation which dried up its own sources of revenue was of course in keeping with the parlement's favorite theme that a solution to the financial problem would be easy once the economic system of the nation was freed from the shackles of unnecessary and unwise legislation. Beyond the statement of this general prin-

55 II, 354–361; XIV, 293–294.
56 I, 569–570, 573–574, 578–580.

ciple the magistrates could say little, for they had to recognize
that the government was in dire need of money. Thinking of
the future, they confessed that they were tempted to recommend that all taxes directly affecting factories be abolished,
but they were willing to postpone the application of this principle until times got better. For the present the king should carefully consider whether it was suitable to tax industry at all, and
if the answer was affirmative there should at least be equality
in the assessment of the taxes. It was unfair that some industries, such as tanning and cardmaking, should be loaded with
taxes, while others, like the silk industry, were allowed to escape. To tax a particular industry was equivalent to attempting
its destruction. If there had to be taxes on industry they should
at least be assessed with equality and moderation.[57]

The parlement did not oversimplify the problem of encouraging industry to the extent of believing that French manufactures
suffered only from taxes and economic regulation. Attention
has already been called to their conviction that agriculture, industry, and commerce were interdependent. The magistrates
also saw a relation between distribution of wealth and the success of industry; the growth of extremes of poverty and wealth,
a tendency for which they blamed the government's financial
policies, meant that ordinary manufactured goods were too
crude for the very rich and too expensive for the poor.[58] The
parlement also thought that industry was seriously handicapped
by the high rate of interest, which in its turn was maintained by
the presence of too much debt within the nation.[59] Another influence as harmful to industry as it was to agriculture and
population was the waste of too much manpower in the army
and in the militia.[60]

Seen in review, the parlement's concept of the kind of encouragement needed for French industry is essentially similar

57 I, 58–60, 652–653.
58 I, 560–562.
59 VIII, 345.
60 I, 463; XII, 874–876.

to what they hoped would be done for agriculture. In both cases government action is demanded, but it is to a large extent action designed to remove the evils of accumulated legislation rather than to grant positive aid by the passing of additional laws. The parlement's recommendations are by no means compounded of laissez-faire alone, though a study of their beliefs reveals a strong tendency in that direction.   But as we shall see, most of the parlement's mercantilist impulses were concerned with the relation of France's economy to the economies of other nations. This tendency is only slightly evident in the parlement's views on agriculture and industry, but it can be seen to a far greater extent in their recommendations concerning commerce, discussed in the next chapter.

CHAPTER VI

COMMERCE

Malgré les dettes énormes dont l'état est surchargé, nous osons presque dire avec assurance que ce beau royaume ne peut succomber, si avec l'exportation libre des grains, la suppression des douanes et un tarif patriotique d'entrée et de sortie laissent un champ libre à l'industrie des françois.

Mémoires, II, 468–469.

BECAUSE the agriculture of Provence was poor, many of her citizens depended for their living on commerce.[1] It is therefore not surprising that the Parlement of Provence was anxious to express opinions on this subject. Commerce, in their view, was a vital part of the national economy, and as such was closely related to agriculture, industry, and population. Commercial prosperity was essential if the government's finances were to be set in order.[2] Merchants deserved this prosperity, for there were no fortunes more useful to society than commercial fortunes, and the nation would profit from an increase in the number of merchants.[3] The fact that France was in debt made it all the more important that her patrimony, a part of which was commerce, should be increased in value.[4]

It is true that the magistrates did not believe that existing commerce added more than a trifling amount to the national income of France. According to their estimates, foreign trade added little to the national income, the bulk of which was furnished by industry and agriculture. Trade within France, useful as it was, was incapable of adding to the national income, since the goods involved merely passed from one Frenchman to another.[5] For an understanding of their views about commerce, it is important to keep in mind a distinction between national

1 I, 373.
2 I, 241–242, 553–554; X, 439–440.
3 I, 444–445, 178–179.
4 I, 48–49.
5 IX, 341–343, 374–376, 382–383. It will be remembered that the parlement placed the national income at about 2,000,000,000 *livres,* of which 1,300,000,000

income and productivity. The magistrates discussed the question of the productivity of the various forms of economic activity only indirectly, in connection with the question of national income, but it can be seen that they considered internal commerce, which added nothing to the national income, as unproductive; and foreign trade, though capable of adding to the national income, was not productive in the same sense as agriculture and industry.[6]

But it is futile to linger very long over such theoretical questions as the productivity of commerce. It is safe to say that the magistrates themselves were not primarily concerned over such matters, but were interested in the practical problem of how to make France rich so that debts and taxes could be paid. Moreover, their conclusion that commerce was not at the moment adding much to the national income represented their opinion rather than their desire. To them, commerce was a vital form of enterprise which deserved extension and protection. Perhaps they had learned the lesson of the Seven Years War.

> Experience has demonstrated that our expenditures and our sorrows have been caused only by the inadequacy of the fleet: it would be a deadly illusion to exhaust ourselves ceaselessly in preparation for the kind of war which will not come and which can decide nothing, and to neglect that which always determines the destiny of nations, and which has become more decisive than ever in a century whose statecraft knows almost no other interests than those of commerce.[7]

or 1,400,000,000 *livres* were furnished by agriculture, and the rest by manufacturing. In view of statements which will be quoted below (see the last quotation in Section 1 of this chapter) the judges appear to contradict themselves on the subject of internal commerce: after stating that trade within France does not add to the national income, they go on to urge that "if commerce is fruitful the people will be rich." It must be remembered, however, that foreign commerce was able to swell the national income. As for internal commerce, the judges probably would have argued that it was capable of increasing the national income indirectly, since agriculture, industry, and commerce were interdependent.

6 See Chapter IV, Section 1.

7 I, 123–125.

1. Tariffs and Foreign Trade

Many of the parlement's opinions about foreign trade sprang from their conviction that the nation should be self-sufficient. France should never seek elsewhere what her own territory could produce: such was the ideal, to be approached as closely as possible. If France, failing to produce everything she needed, was forced to pay tribute to foreigners, she should at least make an intelligent choice of the foreigners. Rival powers should in no case be strengthened, and France's unavoidable imports should be obtained from nations which could become markets for French goods.[8]

Self-sufficiency should be accompanied by a favorable balance of trade.[9] The magistrates were eager to keep money flowing into rather than out of France.

> Every tax, every financial operation which deprives the nation of money must be rejected. If we believed that we could possibly be contradicted concerning this so obvious point, the pen would fall from our hands, for we would then be convinced that there was no desire to yield even to self-evident truth.[10]

It was serious enough for legislation to take money from the people and give it to the king: such an operation altered the distribution of wealth within France, at least until the king spent the money, but it made the nation as a whole no poorer. It was far more serious for legislation to drive money out of France entirely, or prevent its entry into the kingdom, for such operations made the nation as a whole poorer.[11] The magistrates were prepared to be realistic in their enforcement of this mercantilist doctrine. They did not believe that money could be kept in France simply by forbidding its export, and considered leg-

8 XIV, *Ferme de tabac*, n.p.
9 I, 75.
10 VII, 628.
11 VII, 629–631.

islation of this kind a relic of barbarism. The way to prevent the loss of money was to increase the nation's commerce. If there was an unfavorable balance of trade, the resulting debts should be paid as quickly as possible and an attempt made to overcome the commercial disadvantages which were at the root of the difficulty.[12]

As usual, the parlement had no trouble finding legislation in conflict with their principles. One of the reasons for their dislike of the tobacco monopoly, which they condemned for its restrictions on agricultural production in France, was its effect on foreign trade. The monopoly prevented tobacco growing in France, thereby making the nation less self-sufficient, and also led to the purchase of tobacco from other nations. Legal imports of foreign tobacco were supplemented by smuggling, a venture made profitable by the high price which the tobacco monopoly charged for its wares. The judges estimated that because of the tobacco trade more than 5,000,000 *livres* left France each year. This great blow to the French balance of trade was accompanied by positive aid to the foreign trade, shipping, and colonies of the nation's bitterest rival, for much of the tobacco imported by the tobacco monopoly was purchased from the British colonies in America. The parlement insisted that France could grow enough tobacco for her own needs; but even if foreign tobacco had to be purchased, they saw no need for helping England. It would be far better to buy tobacco from Brazil and from Russia, places which might be induced to import French goods in return. Perhaps Brazilian tobacco was, as some had contended, rather strong. It would be better to buy it and throw it into the sea if by so doing the French trade with Portugal could be increased and the commerce of the British weakened.[13]

France's notorious salt tax, the *gabelle,* was also blamed as an interference with the nation's balance of trade. Living by the Mediterranean, the people of Provence were no doubt par-

12 VII, 172–173.
13 XIV, *Ferme de tabac,* n.p.

ticularly conscious of the great amount of salt which France could produce if freed from the monopoly of the production and sale of that commodity. The parlement believed that France could easily have a flourishing trade in the export of salt to less fortunate nations. Every year they saw Dutch, Swedish, and Danish vessels arriving in French ports, unloading their cargoes, and sailing away empty to take on loads of salt from foreign lands. These same ships could depart loaded down with French salt, which could pay for goods imported into France. Only the existing salt monopoly stood in the way. As it was, the Dutch, Swedish, and other ship captains carried away French money, and paid it to other foreigners for salt.[14]

The parlement also regretted that France every year imported copper, iron, cinnebar, lead, and cobalt from other lands. They believed that mining in France should be encouraged as much as possible, so that these imports might cease. Even if the French mines produced barely enough to pay for their exploitation, the state would benefit from their full use, for imports of metals would be less and the money spent on the mines would, after all, remain in the kingdom.[15] Still another example of the parlement's belief in economic self-sufficiency and a favorable balance of trade concerns the law called the *droit d'aubaine*. According to this law the property of foreigners who died in France was confiscated by the crown, provided the property was located in France and the foreigners left no children born within the boundaries of the kingdom; even if the heirs were children born in France, however, they had to stay there in order to keep their inheritances. This law was a hardship for foreigners living in France, for it meant that they could not make wills or dispose of their property as they pleased. The parlement attacked the law on the ground that it was poor policy to treat harshly people who come to France to spend their money. Such measures as the *aubaine* were permissible only as means of retaliation when French nationals were mistreated in foreign lands. A wise

14 IV, 871–874.
15 VII, 428–430.

policy would attract foreigners, instead of threatening their property.[16]

Inevitably related to the questions of economic self-sufficiency, balance of trade, and flow of money was the subject of tariffs. Here the parlement found a splendid opportunity for attacking antiquated legislation. Like free-traders, but also like good mercantilists in the great tradition of Colbert, they demanded the annihilation of numerous tariffs and tolls which still hampered freedom of trade and economic unity within France. At the borders of the nation, however, they called a halt, and after taking stock of the situation decided against complete international free trade. The magistrates believed in freedom, but they believed even more in economic self-sufficiency. Thus in speaking of France's tariff system as a whole, the parlement could not find words harsh enough to describe the viciousness and unreason which in their opinion characterized that ancient mass of legislation. Their worst blasts of criticism were directed not at tariffs on the borders of France but at restrictions on trade within the kingdom.[17] But though less objectionable than the internal tolls and tariffs with which they were perhaps inextricably associated, the import and export duties of France were far from perfect. The parlement did not hesitate to demand a reform which they alleged had been recommended by most educated people for a long time. The internal barriers to trade should be abolished completely and there should remain only a single set of export and import duties for the whole of France.[18]

In arriving at this conclusion the magistrates had to resist the attractive absolutism of the doctrine of complete free trade. Admitting that the question whether a nation might or might not be better off with no tariffs at all was a debatable one, they summed up the arguments on both sides. The defenders of free trade contended that all tariffs were bad because over-

16 III, 89–90, 96–103, 116–117.
17 II, 2–4.
18 I, 67, 72–73.

charging was inevitable; the variations in commerce were so constant that it was impossible to maintain a reasonable set of tariff rates. They argued further that there was no sense in attempting to have every sort of industry in a nation, or in trying to prevent the entry of all cheap foreign products of good quality; for foreigners who came to sell might also be expected to buy. The Parlement of Provence considered these arguments and found them wanting. Face to face with the promise of an increased commerce, they recoiled before the possibility that the balance of trade might not be in France's favor. They feared, moreover, that in a free exchange of goods with foreign nations some of France's manufactures might suffer. They preferred the argument of those who contended that some export and import duties were necessary as an assurance that their nation's industries would have raw materials and protection from too much competition.[19] In the last analysis, they concluded, the burden of proof rested on the proponents of free trade.

> It would be useless to pursue this question further at this time, for the opponents of tariffs must, in order to abolish them, assume the existence of three conditions difficult of fulfillment:
>
> 1—that foreigners agree with us concerning reciprocal liberty;
> 2—that we be able to maintain by means of encouragements those industries unable to compete with foreigners and whose fall would cause too much money to leave the kingdom;
> 3—that our shipping at least approach equality with that of the maritime powers.[20]

Such conditions being out of the question, at least for the immediate future, the parlement preferred the more certain advantages of a uniform set of export and import duties for all of France.

19 I, 67–71.
20 I, 71–72.

There remained only the agreeable task of specifying what sort of export and import duties should be planned. The parlement did not believe that many changes would be necessary in the export duties designed to keep vital raw materials from leaving France.[21] Having accepted the principle of export duties, they were chiefly concerned that these duties should not be made too high, and they offered as a general rule that most export duties should be kept low at all times: for when French goods did not have an advantage over foreign goods it was necessary to lower the export duties; and when French goods did have an advantage they could best keep it if the duties were maintained at a low level.[22] Above all there should be no careless tampering with the right of citizens to sell their products.

> . . . There is a primitive justice which does not allow the subjects' right to sell their products to be taken from them. This law is inviolable. No attention must be paid to all insinuations to the contrary on the part of the financiers. The prince has a right to collect taxes in order to meet the public needs; the subjects certainly have a right to sell their provisions and the products of their toil. . . .[23]

Import duties, on the other hand, could be high. The magistrates accepted the principle of a protective tariff and were especially anxious that some of Provence's products, such as oil and wine, should receive protection. There was an automatic limit to protective tariffs, however, for if the rates were too high smuggling would begin. Thus the parlement's general tariff policy was to have import duties raised as much as possible without encouraging smuggling, and to have export duties lowered so that French agricultural and manufactured products would have outlets to world trade.[24] There should be free trade within the nation and uniform duties around its borders. The

21 II, 460–461.
22 XIV, 21.
23 XIV, 22–23.
24 X, 422; XIV, 232–234.

magistrates favored the principle behind Colbert's tariff of 1667, a protective tariff which had made foreign goods pay high duties but had then allowed them exemption from local duties within France. They believed that the tariff of 1667 had also attempted to favor the import of necessary raw materials and the export of French products. All of these characteristics, in the opinion of the parlement, were excellent bases for the uniform export and import tariff which they desired. They could not, to be sure, approve of many of the actual rates of Colbert's tariff, for they contended that these rates had been set so high that people, instead of paying them, bought smuggled goods. Since 1667, moreover, there had been so many regulations and interpretations concerning the tariff that it had become impossible to keep track of them. In most cases the officials themselves had only sketchy notes, and merchants, being in total ignorance, had no other alternative than to pay blindly what was asked of them.[25]

The makers of tariffs should never forget that the real purpose of their labors was to make the balance of trade as advantageous as possible for France. It would be a serious mistake to use the tariffs as a means of increasing the king's income, for such action would inevitably lead to failure. Indeed, it was to be expected that when a desirable tariff system, that is, one designed to favor France's balance of trade, was erected there would be for a time an actual decrease in the king's revenues from the tariff. But there should be no worrying on that score, for in the long run a tariff system designed to regulate trade would be far more profitable than one which aimed at revenue.[26]

If we sell more we shall buy proportionally, and, considering tariffs alone, the import duties and the export duties on goods which are reexported will indemnify His Majesty abundantly. If an increase in the revenue from tariffs is desired, let the export duties be lowered; but what does it matter after all whether the *Ferme des traites* collects more or

25 II, 270–276.

26 I, 74–76.

less? The real essential is that commerce enrich the people; if commerce is fruitful the people will be rich, and if the people are rich we would have to be very stupid indeed in order not to be able to procure revenues for the king.[27]

This passage has a familiar ring, for in it the parlement returns once more to its favorite theme.

2. SHIPPING AND COLONIES

Two other instruments of great importance to economic self-sufficiency and the balance of trade were shipping and colonies. The magistrates were anxious for France to make the most of her natural advantages, and to this end it was essential that fishing and shipping be encouraged and that the maritime population be well treated.[28] Vital as merchant shipping was, however, there was no use encouraging it unless it could be protected by a powerful fleet in time of war. Fully realizing that much of the warfare of their century was over commerce, and possessed of the belief that sea power would decide the "destiny of Europe," the parlement was convinced that French military policy had been wrong. Great expenditures had been made for land warfare which decided nothing, while the fleet had been neglected and control of the sea allowed to slip into other hands. This mistake should not be repeated. In a guarded reference which appears to suggest that England was in their thoughts, the magistrates expressed the opinion that the only war probable in the near future would take place on the sea. France should make ready a powerful fleet capable of protecting her shipping and colonies. There was no need to worry about the cost, for such a fleet would save money by preventing the loss of many precious men and ships; but in any case a powerful navy was essential regardless of expense. France must have it, or her glory would be eclipsed and her days of greatness ended.[29]

27 XIV, 70–71.
28 I, 424–425, 468–470.
29 I, 123–125, 198–199, 468–470; II, 391–393.

Besides being adequately protected from possible enemies, French shipping should be freed from cumbersome and harmful taxation. The tax called the *droit de cottimo,* for example, should be abolished. This tax was collected on vessels arriving from the Levant. The amount paid was determined by the kind of ship, with the result that people disfigured their vessels in order to avoid heavy taxation. The *cottimo* had the further disadvantage of being so inflexible that it was much too high for a cargo that was bulky and cheap, and much too low for one which consisted of small but expensive goods. Another tax harmful to French shipping was the *droit du consulat,* so-called because the king had allowed the Chamber of Commerce of Marseilles to collect it in return for supporting all consulates in the various ports of the Levant. The *cottimo,* the *consulat,* and similar taxes had the bad effect of increasing French freight rates and reducing the carrying trade in French ships. The parlement complained that high freight rates had already caused the loss, to French shippers, of their nation's own coastwise shipping, and also of most of its reexport trade. To make matters worse, Italians sailing under English and Dutch flags were beginning to compete with the French in the commerce with the Levant. Taxes which in any way aided such tendencies should be abolished.[30]

That the parlement did not wish the indiscriminate abolition of all taxes on shipping, but approved of duties which favored French shipping against that of foreign nations, is indicated by their opinion of the *fret.* The *fret* owed its name to its origin in an old rule that ships could not enter the ports of France unless officials were allowed to bind up (*fretter*) the merchandise on board. In time the *fret* had become a tax on foreign ships entering French ports. The provisions of the law were favorable to French shipbuilding as well as to shipping, for ships not made in France, even when owned by Frenchmen, had to pay the tax, unless the owners were granted exemption. The magistrates did not approve of exemptions to the *fret,* and

30 I, 51-52; II, 529-539.

regretted that the king had begun to grant them to British, Dutch, and Danish ships. They regretted also the fact that the *fret* was not conscientiously enforced, for they believed that this tax was founded on sound principles which deserved a rigid application. French shipping and shipbuilding should be granted additional favors in order that they might experience a quick recovery from the disasters of the Seven Years War.[31]

The subject of colonies also attracted the attention of the parlement. The magistrates were hardly colonial enthusiasts, but they considered colonies useful, though secondary in importance to the economy of the mother country. Thus while making every effort to increase the value of the colonies in the new world, Frenchmen should never forget that the most important conquest was to be made at home by means of better agriculture.[32] As an aid to the economy of France proper, however, colonies could be of great importance. The judges had heard some of their contemporaries argue that the French colonies cost the crown more than they were worth, since the returns from their taxes were less than the military and administrative expenses of keeping them. In the opinion of the parlement such a view was short-sighted and mistaken. Dealings with the colonies immensely stimulated the economy of France; their loss would mean less consumption, a smaller national income, and decreased returns from taxes within the mother country.[33] The magistrates also rejected the view, held by some, that colonies decreased population by taking away people from the mother country. The opposite was true, for by encouraging agriculture and commerce at home colonies were a stimulus to population and more than made up for the number of people who emigrated.[34]

31 II, 474–485.

32 I, 249–251.

33 XIV, 161–163.

34 I, 470–472. It is interesting to find this same argument used by Edward Gibbon Wakefield (1796–1862), one of England's ardent defenders of colonies in the nineteenth century, at a time when "Little Englanders" were being heard with respect.

In their memorials about the finances the parlement did not outline a detailed program for the exploitation of the colonies. Judging by their statements about Louisiana, which had been lost shortly before the memorials were written, they held the traditional view that colonies should be part of a closed system, furnishing the mother country with goods she could not produce at home and serving as a market for her products. This at least was the parlement's idea of what should have been done with Louisiana, and of what should still be done with the remaining French colonies. If, for example, tobacco planting had been encouraged in Louisiana, that colony would have grown strong and would have returned immense sums of money to France by consuming a great many of her products. The same policy could still be applied to France's remaining colonies by decreasing the consumption of tobacco grown by France's rivals.[35] It is impossible to state whether the parlement would have regulated what was produced in the colonies; the only evidence on this point, an expression of doubt whether the colonists should be allowed to refine their own sugar, appears to indicate that the parlement's statements about freedom of the professions were intended to apply only to the mother country.[36] The magistrates evidently did not wish to grant the colonies entire freedom of trade with the mother country, but they believed that commerce would benefit from a simplification of the taxes on colonial goods. They objected, for example, to the double taxation which resulted from the collection of both export duties on goods leaving the French West Indies and import duties on the same goods when they reached France.[37]

3. INTERNAL COMMERCE

From their statements about foreign trade it is clear that the parlement favored a considerable amount of government intervention for the maintenance of economic self-sufficiency

35 XIV, *Ferme de tabac*, n.p.
36 II, 374–375.
37 II, 388–391.

and a favorable balance of trade. Concerning internal commerce the judges were not so definite. As in the case of agriculture and industry they often used the word "encouragement," but there remains the problem of examining their interpretation of this term.

The magistrates drew a distinction between their own views about the encouragement of commerce, and those of their forefathers, who had considered it sufficient to work hard at agriculture and leave commerce free. Now that harmful legislation, engineered by the financiers for their own benefit, had undermined commerce, it was perhaps necessary to offset this evil by a policy of encouragement.[38] For a long time the administrators of Provence had wished to encourage commerce, as well as agriculture, but two obstacles had constantly stood in the way. Provence's poverty and the ever present fear of taxes had forestalled projects for aiding commerce, and the ignorance of the province's chief administrators had prevented useful actions and had sometimes led to unwise ones. In a sense these two obstacles sprang from the same fundamental cause. For the past hundred years those in charge of Provence's administration had been so busy protecting their province from tax collectors that they had had little time or money to spend on positive improvements in commerce and agriculture.[39]

Although favoring encouragement in principle, the parlement had little to suggest in the way of positive aid to commerce. It is true that they wanted their province to have a carefully planned and systematically maintained system of roads, designed to meet all the needs of commerce. Such a network of roads required a general study of the commercial needs of all parts of the province, some of which were poor only because of lack of communication with the outside world.[40] As an aid in making such a plan, and also as a means of improving administrative appreciation of some of the province's needs, the parle-

38 X, 397–398.
39 X, 538–540, 548.
40 XI, 386–393.

ment recommended the formation of the society of agriculture
and commerce already mentioned in connection with agriculture.
Believing as they did in the interdependence of the two forms
of economic enterprise, especially in Provence, the judges
could not understand why the crown, in a decree of 1765, had
sanctioned only an agricultural society.[41] Projects such as road-
building and the formation of economic societies, however,
can hardly be considered recommendations of strong governmental intervention for the promotion of commerce. They
amount to little when compared with the parlement's constant
attacks on the great mountain of legislation which they considered harmful to the internal commerce of France. It would
appear that the parlement's use of the term "encouragement"
for internal commerce was similar to their use of that same
term in their discussions of agriculture and manufacturing.
If such is the case, their concept of encouragement consisted
mainly of the freeing of commerce from unwise restrictions
and taxes. At any rate, the amount of legislation from which
the judges wished to free commerce is impressive.

The parlement's greatest condemnation of outdated and
destructive legislation was without doubt their memorial on the
subject of internal tariffs, tolls, and other obstructions in the
path of commerce. Mincing no words, they described first the
situation in Provence, as was their custom in dealing with
problems of taxation.

> In Provence duties are collected on goods entering by land
> or sea, whether they come from foreign lands or from the
> other provinces of the kingdom. Duties are likewise collected
> on goods leaving this province under the same circumstances;
> and stranger still, there are cases where these taxes are col-
> lected on goods produced in Provence and circulating within
> the province.
>
> The places from which goods and provisions come, their
> destinations, and the routes which they take, determine the
> duties which are due. The great number of these duties, their

41 X, 530–531; XI, 452–454.

variety, and uncertainty concerning the rates, are hindrances to commerce. It is as though an evil genius, hostile to France, had created this arrangement in order to deprive the state of prosperity and to keep from the people that well-being which brings happiness to them and wealth to kings.

All this is not the work of a single hand, for there is no one man, however evil his intentions, who could conceive of so complete a plan for destruction and ruin. The fault lies with a collection of injurious operations produced successively by the ignorance, barbarism, waste, or even violence and cupidity of certain individuals.[42]

In their memorial on tariffs of all kinds the parlement listed no less than twenty-two taxes on commerce which were in effect in Provence.[43] Some of these were export and import duties which, because of the great diversity in status among the provinces, managed to disrupt the internal trade of France. Best known of these export and import duties were the *traites,* which were collected on goods entering or leaving France or passing from certain provinces into others. Provence was one of those provinces, called *provinces réputées étrangères,* which had to pay export and import duties in their relations with each other and with the section of France called the *cinq grosses fermes.* These *cinq grosses fermes* consisted of a block of twelve provinces which traded freely among themselves; all of them were subject to Colbert's famous tariff of 1664 and had at their frontiers the same export and import duties. Provence was *réputée étrangère* because it was one of the provinces lying outside of this block of territory. Thus, unlike the provinces of the *cinq grosses fermes,* Provence did not belong to a free trade area, and had to pay duties on goods exported to or imported from other provinces.[44]

42 II, 1–3.

43 See II, *Quatrième suite du premier memoire.*

44 Marion, *Dictionnaire,* pp. 538–539. In addition to the *cinq grosses fermes* and the *provinces réputées étrangères* there were a few provinces called "effectively foreign" (*de l'étranger effectif*), which had been recently added to France and which had kept free communication with foreigners but were separated from France by tariffs.

One of the many taxes which Provence had to pay because of her position was called the *traite foraine*. The Parlement of Provence resented the existence of this tax, which was an export duty supposed to be collected at certain offices throughout the kingdom. Provinces which had consented to the establishment of the offices collected the *foraine* on goods going abroad or into provinces which had refused to establish the offices. But although Provence had established the offices for the *foraine,* the tax was still collected both on goods entering and on goods leaving the province.[45] In the opinion of the judges this situation represented the height of injustice, for Provence, in the interest of greater economic unity for France, had given up her right to export goods without paying the *foraine* and had gained nothing in return. Goods still paid the *foraine* on entering Provence from the rest of France. Even timber cut in Provence and then floated to other parts of the province by way of the Rhône had to pay the tax, because of a theory that the timber was being sent from Languedoc to Provence. The parlement also contended that Provence ought to be allowed to send her products freely into the older parts of France. Since Provence had accepted the offices for collection of the *foraine,* and since export and import duties were now collected at Provence's borders, there was no longer any reason for considering that the province had privileges harmful to the rest of the monarchy. Justice demanded that the barriers between Provence and the older parts of France be abolished.[46]

Another of the tariff barriers which had great influence on the commerce of Provence, and indeed of most of France, was the *douane de Lyon*. Although essentially an import duty, the *douane de Lyon* also acted as an export duty in some cases. This tariff had to be paid on most goods going from Languedoc, Provence, and Dauphiné to the city of Lyons to be consumed or exported to places such as Piedmont, Savoy, Switzerland, and Germany. There were other rules as well; for example

45 II, 8–16, 34–36.
46 II, 70–79.

goods entering France from Italy or Spain had to pass by way
of Lyons, paying the duties as they went. Thus this tariff at
Lyons stood as a great barrier to commerce between the south-
eastern provinces and the rest of France, and also to commerce
between France and foreign lands.[47] In the old régime such
tariffs were often piled one upon the other. Another tariff
which managed to reach much of the commerce within France,
as well as a good deal of foreign trade, was the *douane de
Valence*. Similar to the *douane de Lyon* in its general characteristics, this tariff had to be paid on all goods crossing or going
up or down a certain section of the Rhône, no matter what their
destination.[48]

Some of the many taxes on commerce were based on a sort of
compulsory service. There was, for example, the *poids et casse
de Marseille,* which had to be paid on all transactions in goods
by weight at Marseilles. It was compulsory for the seller and
the buyer in all such transactions to have the product weighed
by officials to whom they paid the tax, and who kept records of
sales.[49] Some of the taxes were river tolls such as the one called
the *denier de Saint André*. Originally established in order to
raise money for the fortification of Saint André castle, this tax
had to be paid on all goods ascending, descending, or crossing
a certain section of the Rhône. The Parlement of Provence regretted that France's natural gifts were made useless by such
taxes, of which there were many. The city of Arles, for example, profited very little from its position on the Rhône, for
the many taxes forced people to send their goods by land instead
of along the river.[50] But at Arles itself there were taxes such
as the *deux pour cent d'Arles,* which was levied on all merchandise passing the town either by land or by way of the river.
There was even a tax of uncertain origin called the *liard du
baron* (or *albaron*) which for some reason was collected along

47 II, 171–172, 187–189.
48 II, 285–286.
49 II, 393–397.
50 II, 412–414, 422–425.

with the *deux pour cent d'Arles* and which the Parlement of
Provence contended was an outright invention of the tax
officials.[51]

Although the parlement gave special attention to the taxes
which harmed the commerce of their own province, they did not
seek a solution which would apply to Provence alone. The
situation was everywhere essentially the same.

> The sad details which we have been outlining call for little
> reflection. They tell their own story. The description varies
> from one province to another only in the names and rates of
> the duties; and this diversity manages to make the confusion
> worse. When travelling through the kingdom one finds at
> every step bureaus and guards. It is as though all the provinces
> were armed for the purpose of stopping communication. In
> this kind of war, which finance has declared on commerce,
> the Frenchman travelling or trading within his fatherland ad-
> vances as though he were in enemy country: he must be
> armed with permits and passports, and must constantly un-
> dergo questionings and tedious verifications. Pitiless agents
> located at various points despoil those who have neglected to
> take the necessary precautions, and seek to victimize them for
> their ignorance or omission of these irksome formalities.[52]

This disorderly condition within the nation, caused by internal
tariffs, river tolls, and other such duties, made foodstuffs and
raw materials expensive, handicapped industry, and decreased
consumption. For these reasons and as a result of innumerable
formalities commerce tended to decline. The duties themselves,
besides being harmful to the economy, were expensive to collect. Their variety and complexity forced the various provinces
to work against each other, so that the improvement of one
often meant the decline of another. This clash of interests was
harmful to the state.[53] The Estates General of 1614 had been

51 II, 428–433, 444–447.
52 II, 448–449.
53 I, 66–67; II, 450–452.

right in demanding that that the barriers to internal trade from province to province be removed and that all duties be collected at the borders of the kingdom. France should have a uniform tariff at her borders and free trade within.[54] Now that there was no longer any Estates General, the Parlement of Provence presumed to speak in the name of the nation.

> We entreat his majesty to order that all his subjects enjoy the same liberty and immunities, and that they therefore be able, as fellow citizens of the same state, to trade freely and carry French merchandise wherever they please. It is the nation that makes this request. We are merely speaking in her name.[55]

The parlement expected that there would be objections to such a great proposal of reform, and they were prepared to answer them. Opponents would probably argue that certain provinces would hold back, and that the decrease in the public revenues would be too great. It was quite possible that some French ministers had already seen the need for internal free trade but had feared popular prejudices concerning provincial privileges and the traditional conduct of the nation's finances. If so, the ministers in question had feared France's prejudices more than her ruin.[56] The judges insisted that there was no longer reason to anticipate opposition from the so-called *provinces réputées étrangères,* since they would benefit from the increased export of goods which would result from the proposed unified tariff. That tariff would of course take into account the legitimate interests of each province, and if necessary these would even be protected by some form of reservation or compensation. Provence, for example, would retain her inviolable privileges, but would recognize certain obligations resulting from her union with the rest of France. Once its legitimate interests were safeguarded, no province should be allowed to impede arrangements

54 I, 72–73; II, 5.
55 II, 6–7.
56 VI, 535–537.

necessary to the common good. Instead of considering themselves isolated societies, the provinces should realize that they
had more to gain as members of the French monarchy.[57] These
are surprising words, coming from the magistrates of one of
France's most fiercely independent provinces, but it must be remembered that the Parlement of Provence expected or at least
hoped to have a virtual veto power over all future legislation
emanating from Versailles.

The parlement refused to recognize that an anticipated decline
in the government's income was an adequate reason for postponing internal free trade. Ever since the partial steps taken toward
a unified tariff in 1667 the income from the interior tariffs had
been declining. The decline had now reached a point where the
income was scarcely worth the expenses of collection, not to
mention the harm done to commerce by interior tariffs and
tolls. Abolition of these taxes would be balanced by increased
returns from the unified tariff which would be placed along the
frontiers. The example of England, which had no interior
tariffs, was proof enough that such a reform would be effective.
But above all the people of France would profit from the absence of annoyances, from internal free trade, and from the
greater sale of their products abroad. The resulting flush of
prosperity would before long be reflected in a growing stream
of wealth flowing into the coffers of the king.[58]

Internal tariffs and tolls were not the only forms of taxation
harmful to French commerce. The magistrates were also bitterly opposed to the *aides*, which were duties on the consumption
of certain products, chiefly wines.[59] By diminishing the consumption of these commodities, the *aides* not only hurt commerce but also decreased agricultural and industrial production
as well. The parlement even asserted that if the *aides* were
abolished the national income would rise by at least 100,000,000

57 II, 454–457; VI, 532–535.
58 II, 457–467; XIV, 241.
59 V, 23–27.

livres. Besides raising prices and decreasing consumption these taxes handicapped commerce by means of all sorts of petty vexations and inequalities in their collection. Because some provinces were subject to the *aides* and others were not, the wines of such a place as Provence might remain unsold while a neighboring province was reduced to the unhappy expedient of drinking plain water. Where the *aides* were high, merchants had to choose between closing their shops or evading the tax and running the risk of severe punishments.[60]

Still other taxes harmful to commerce were opposed by the judges on the ground that they were monopolies. Attention has already been called both to the parlement's dislike of monopolies in general and to the specific monopolies which they attacked in their memorials.[61] These opinions are also related to the subject of commerce. Believers in competition, the magistrates were convinced that France would be more prosperous if there were a greater number of merchants, even though the profits of each individual merchant were less.[62] They criticized the tobacco monopoly not only because of its harmful effects on the balance of trade but also because the monopolists were able to exercise a tyranny over consumers by limiting the quantity of tobacco sold and keeping its price too high.[63] Likewise the *gabelle,* already mentioned as a monopoly harmful to agriculture and foreign trade, was productive of high prices and diminished commerce at home.[64]

Commerce, and indeed all sorts of enterprises, could also be troubled by regulations which interfered with what the judges called "freedom of contract." There was, for example, the *contrôle,* a tax which had been established for the purpose of giving contracts the added security of a formal registration. All

60 V, 581–582, 598–599.

61 See the chapters on agriculture and industry.

62 I, 444–445, 737–738.

63 XIV, *Ferme de tabac,* n.p.

64 IV, 825–826, 828–831, 842–843.

contracts and legal actions had to be submitted in abstract to the proper officials, and a fee paid. The trouble was that the law was too complicated; there were too many fees, and the average citizen was often cheated by the collectors, with the result that people deliberately neglected to register contracts and ran the risk of being duped or involved in lawsuits. Such annoyances as the *contrôle,* though indirect, had a harmful effect on commerce.[65] A similar legal formality was the *insinuation,* the requirement that legal documents in which the public might have an interest, such as wills, be registered.[66] Ostensibly these legal formalities had been ordered for the public good, but in the parlement's opinion they were merely camouflage designed to hide additional taxes. There was a genuine need for the *contrôle,* though its regulations could be considerably simplified. Other formalities such as the *insinuation* were merely repetitions which destroyed men's faith in the notaries and therefore undermined the "freedom of contact." [67]

Like agriculture and industry, commerce was stimulated by low interest rates. Conversely, the debts of provinces, cities, and corporations of artisans raised interest rates and tended to diminish commerce by leading to taxes which increased the prices of goods.[68] Commerce, like agriculture and industry, was important to the solution of France's financial problems, for though not in itself productive it was dependent on agriculture and industry, as they were on it, and all three, together with population, had to be improved if the government's debts were to be paid. As with agriculture and industry, the way to make commerce thrive was to attack the mountain of old legislation which was holding it back. This meant that commerce should be given a great deal more freedom, but it did not mean that commerce should be completely free. Believing in national self-

65 I, 62–63; II, 560–561.

66 II, 561–562.

67 II, 567–572, 581–583.

68 I, 15, 644; II, 550–552; VII, 345–347.

sufficiency and a favorable balance of trade, the parlement sought the attainment of these ends by means of careful regulation of foreign commerce. To a large degree internal trade was to be free. The conclusion is inescapable that the parlement's opinions about commerce were essentially mercantilist in their main outlines, since they aimed at the economic unification of the nation and at the strengthening of the national economy with an eye to economic self-sufficiency and competition with other states. Related to these opinions are the parlement's views on wealth, which will be considered next.

CHAPTER VII
THE ROLE OF MONEY

Le laboureur anglois est vétu, il mange de la viande qui est un aliment qui donne des forces, il prend même son thé avant que d'aller au travail. Plus une nation consomme et plus elle est riche.

Mémoires, I, 572–573.

L'esprit d'interet et de venalité qui perdit autrefois le peuple le plus celebre de la terre et qui se repand dans la nation, forme contre l'economie des finances une conspiration presque générale qu'il faut étouffer.

Mémoires, I, 166–167.

THE Parlement of Provence did not assign to money a place at the top of their scale of values. The measure of a nation's wealth was not the amount of money it had but its consumption.[1] True wealth consisted mainly of the necessary commodities which nations and people wanted.

> Grain, livestock, and iron are the true riches, which are called independent, since their possessor can be self-sufficient, and since those who lack them cannot do without them. If a nation, in addition to these foremost gifts of nature, has large supplies of wine, salt, and hemp; if the land which it inhabits is surrounded by seas alive with fish; if it enjoys a pleasant and temperate climate, it has everything reason recognizes as genuine blessings; it need desire nothing more.[2]

Money had none of these agreeable qualities, but was simply "a portion of metal to which the prince gives a form, a name, and a stamp to certify the weight and the denomination the exchange which can be made for anything which men wish to trade." [3] Money was thus a useful medium of exchange, but it had value as well, and it is interesting to note that like many of their contemporaries the judges had no single rule for determining value. In their view, the value of money was complicated by

1 I, 573.
2 I, 551–552.
3 VII, 178.

several factors: there was a legal value arbitrarily set by the government, an intrinsic value which depended on the weight and purity of the metals, and an "accidental value" which depended on the commercial circumstances of the moment.[4]

The parlement was concerned lest money be regarded in an improper light and its importance overestimated. In their opinion money might be considered a means of getting necessities for the individual and for the state, an instrument of pleasure, and a source of esteem and power. Only the first of these views was legitimate. To seek money as a means of providing necessities was not to worship it for its own sake. But on the other hand, money as a source of pleasure was a corrupting influence, and money as a stepping stone to fame and power was even worse. Once let money usurp the place of true honor and all the nation's values would be undermined; all forms of genuine merit would be overlooked in a disgusting scramble for the accumulation of fortunes.[5] The public would begin to honor the wealthy, attaching to them attributes of virtue and power. Everything would become venal. The government itself would be in danger of sharing the popular illusions and would add to them by openly respecting the amassers of money.[6]

In making these statements the parlement was not anticipating future dangers but was expressing convictions concerning the actual state of society in France. The magistrates were by no means entirely devoted to the *status quo;* in some respects, as has been shown, they favored the forces of change, while in others they tended to look backward rather fondly into the feudal past. In the case of money they shared the prejudice of most of their fellow parlements and entertained a violent dis-

4 VII, 176–177. Elsewhere (VII, 71–76) the judges declared that the value of money was composed of the price of the material, which depended on abundance or scarcity, and of the expenses of manufacture and the fee which the king placed on money.

5 I, 170–173.

6 I, 173–176.

like of wealthy capitalists and financiers; this feeling appears again and again in the Provence memorials. If money was becoming the supreme good in France, the government was in large measure to blame. Lacking funds, the administrators of the kingdom had thought all the more highly of those who were well-to-do, and had allowed financiers to build great fortunes while the nation was going bankrupt. The parlement wished to call a halt to such tendencies, which they evidently felt were a threat to the position of the traditional nobility. At any rate, they wanted the nobles to maintain their places of honor in the state, and suggested that the sale of titles be discontinued and that the nobles take over administration of the finances.[7]

1. Maxims about Money

It was not enough, however, to maintain a proper attitude toward money. Money was the source of complicated problems which had to be handled carefully if the national economy was to remain on an even keel. As was their custom, the magistrates discussed the relation of these problems to the economy of France, emphasizing those maxims which they considered most suitable and most true.

One of their convictions was that the cheapening of money by so many French kings had been a terrible mistake. Depreciation of money was ruinous to the whole economy, and especially to the king, who as first among the rich was bound to suffer from such an operation.[8] Fortunately, in the view of the parlement, a declaration in June, 1726, had put an end to the constant fluctuations in the value of French coins. (Their metallic content had at that time been fixed at proportions which were to last until 1785.) [9] The magistrates of Provence expressed their hearty approval of this reform, and were quick to flatter their sovereign by pointing to the glory which stabilization of the

7 I, 164–166, 211–212, 177–178.

8 VII, 27–28.

9 Carré, *Le règne de Louis XV*, p. 95.

money had won him.[10] The parlement believed that increases in the value of money were just as harmful to the economy as a cheapened coinage, for a rise in the value of French money meant heavier taxes, hardships for laborers and debtors, and a decline in exports.[11] The medium of exchange should be kept constant in value, so that people entering into engagements could do so without fear of hardships or expectations of too easy profits.[12]

A problem related to the aim of keeping money constant in value was what to do about fluctuations in the commercial value of gold, silver, and copper, the metals of which coins were made. From observation and from their reading of economic works, the judges had learned what is today known as Gresham's law: that under certain conditions coins are driven out of circulation. They reported, for example, that a rise in the commercial value of copper in the southern provinces had made profitable the melting down and sale of small copper coins, with the result that commerce in those provinces was suffering from a scarcity of small change.[13] The judges had found in their reading another possibility of fluctuation in the supply of money. According to the economist Dutot there should be the same percentage of purity in the gold and silver used for the making of coins, so that coins of one metal would never be preferred to those of the other metal. This view was supported by Forbonnais in his *Elémens du commerce,* with the added warning that it would be wise to coin metals of the same degree of purity as those of neighboring nations, lest cheaper foreign coins be substituted for their betters.[14] The parlement was also

10 VII, 28–29.

11 VII, 140–141.

12 VII, 144–145. On this point the parlement was in complete agreement with the economic writer Dutot, who believed that the money should be left alone and neither increased nor decreased in value. Concerning Dutot, see Chapter I, Section 2.

13 VII, 90–91.

14 VII, 185–186. Concerning Forbonnais, see Chapter I, Section 2.

familiar with Richard Cantillon's *Essai sur la nature du commerce en général,* at least to the extent of having noticed some of his remarks on the ratio of silver to gold. Cantillon had asserted that only expenses and risks of transportation allowed the existence of different ratios of silver to gold in different nations. A state whose ratio of silver to gold took too little account of the commercial value of those metals was in danger of losing coins of the metal which had been undervalued.[15] Without claiming any originality for their views, the parlement therefore concluded that if harmful fluctuations in the money were to be avoided there should always be a ratio between silver and gold which was the same as the ratio between the commercial values of those metals.[16]

But how was such a ratio to be maintained when the commercial values of gold and silver were constantly fluctuating? For the answer to this troublesome question the parlement was willing to accept the judgment of two writers on economic subjects, Forbonnais and Dupré de Saint-Maur. In the opinion of Forbonnais it was sufficient that the state set a legal value to silver and allow commerce to fix the value of gold.[17] The view that silver and gold, the values of which were bound to fluctuate, could not both serve as a measure of value in commerce was likewise supported by Dupré de Saint-Maur in his *Essai sur les monnoies, ou réflections sur le rapport entre l'argent et les*

15 VII, 97–99.

16 VII, 79–81, 91–93.

17 VI, 158. Forbonnais wrote as follows. "Ce qu'on vient de voir sur la proportion des monnoyes d'or & d'argent confirme le sentiment de Mr. Law, que les Etats ne doivent point fixer la proportion entre les metaux, parce qu'elle varie sans cesse, & ce changement occasionne dans l'intervalle des transports ruineux, ou nuit à certains commerces. Il suffit que le prix du marc d'argent soit fixé; le commerce fixera suivant ses besoins le prix du marc d'or."—*Recherches et considérations sur les finances de France depuis l'année 1595 jusqu'à l'année 1721* (Basle, 1758), I. 53. The parlement used this work constantly as a source of information; they refer to it more than to any other book. This does not mean that they accepted the author's opinions on every subject, for they did not; but they took a great deal of factual information out of the book, and in some cases—of which the above is an example—they paraphrased its words.

denrées. This writer argued that two such metals could not serve as a measure because the very essence of a measure was that it should be the same in all its parts. He also agreed that only silver need be given a legal value by the government.[18]

Content to accept these opinions, the parlement concluded that it would be best not to fix the proportion between silver and gold, since such action would necessitate constant government interference with the money, a policy of which they did not approve. Like Forbonnais, the magistrates believed that it was enough to fix the legal value of silver and to allow the value of gold to be fixed by commerce. If this plan should prove impossible, the next best policy would be to make certain that the proportion between silver and gold was kept reasonably accurate with relation to the market values of those metals. Unfortunately such a policy had not been followed in France, for in the judges' opinion the ratio of silver to gold, which in 1641 had been the highest in Europe, had become dangerously low by the 1760's.[19]

As already indicated by their views on commerce, the parlement attached considerable importance to the problem of keeping an adequate supply of money in France. Besides urging the necessity for a favorable balance of trade, the magistrates gave some attention to other matters related to the supply of money. For a long time there had been in France regulations limiting the amounts of gold and silver used by goldsmiths, and sometimes the work of these makers of luxury products

18 VII, 94–96. Dupré de Saint-Maur's *Essai sur les monnoies* appeared in 1746. The passage to which the parlement refers reads as follows. "Deux métaux différens, comme l'Or & l'Argent, ne peuvent pas être ensemble la Mesure du Commerce d'un Pays, parce qu'une Mesure doit être invariable, & doit avoir les mêmes rapports dans toutes ses parties, au lieu que la proportion entre l'Or et l'Argent change quelquefois; c'est pourquoi il faut regarder l'Argent seul comme l'unique Mesure du Commerce."—*Essai sur les monnoies* (Paris: Méquignon, 1746), p. 10. The author, who was a follower of Locke, acknowledges Locke's *Some Considerations of the Consequences of the Lowering of Interest and Raising the value of Money* and his *Further Considerations Concerning Raising the Value of Money* as the sources for the above quotation.

19 VII, 158, 161.

had been suspended entirely. The parlement did not believe in such methods. If the aim was to guarantee an adequate supply of specie it would be better to remove some of the restrictions on commerce. If the aim was to discourage the making of luxury goods such prohibitions were futile; luxury should be attacked at its source, which was unequal distribution of wealth.[20] There were, indeed, occasions when the making of luxury products was a positive service to the state, for a nation might conceivably have too great a quantity of precious metals, and it was even safe to say that France would have been corrupted and depopulated if she had been unfortunate enough to possess great mines of silver and gold. The parlement believed that whenever a nation had attained such prosperity that there was on hand too much silver and gold, it was beneficial to the general well-being if the rich used these metals for expensive decorations instead of allowing them to swell the amount of coin to a dangerous extent.[21] The judges did not mean to imply that France in the 1760's had too great a supply of money; nor did they wish to complain that specie was lacking in the nation. According to their estimates the existing supply of specie amounted to about 1,200,000,000 *livres*, an amount which they apparently believed adequate for France's needs.[22]

France was not suffering from lack of specie but from certain evils which prevented its circulation throughout the kingdom. Not the total amount of money, but its circulation was of vital importance to the solution of France's financial difficulties, especially after a long war in which commerce had been interrupted and taxation had been heavy.[23] If circulation was not reestablished with the coming of peace, economic recovery would be delayed and the next war would find the nation exhausted.[24]

20 VII, 232–236, 238–239.

21 VII, 237, 432.

22 VII, 151–153, 237. Expressed in terms of weight, the amount of specie came to 24,000,000 *marcs*, there being at that time 50 *livres* per *marc*.

23 VII, 237–238.

24 I, 49–51; X, 329–340.

Taxation, even in peace time, had to be watched carefully lest it interfere with the circulation of money. Any kind of taxation which drove money from the kingdom, or prevented its entry, was of course unforgivable, for money lost to France was lost to circulation within France. Ordinary taxation, however, could not do so much damage. Money taken from the pockets of the people and placed in the coffers of the king was not lost to France, and there was still a good chance that the king would spend it for the needs of the state and thus put it into circulation again. But here lurked a serious danger. If taxation was too heavy, so that it interfered with the economy, circulation of money in the nation was bound to suffer; and if the taxes were collected and spent in an improper fashion the result would be a concentration of wealth in the capital and in the hands of a few men; the rest of the nation would not get the money it needed and would be in debt to the capital, which would come to resemble the head of a giant set grotesquely on the body of a midget.[25] This was a condition which the parlement professed to see developing in France, and which they hated.

2. The Danger of Great Fortunes

To the Parlement of Provence the growth of great fortunes was an alarming development, full of danger for the economy of France. They saw this danger on every side: it threatened the growth of population; it slowed up the circulation of wealth; it lay behind monopolies and some of the most offensive taxes; it crept into the very ministries of the king and headed off projects for reform. While the national income and the people's consumption of goods were declining, the distribution of wealth in France was growing more and more unequal and vicious. Against the background of poverty in the nation could be seen the glitter of great fortunes and unbridled luxury.[26]

The Parlement of Provence complained that the rich were the

25 VII, 627–630.
26 V, 595.

most favored people in France, but their remarks about the distribution of wealth, scattered through their memorials, lead one to believe that they were not so much concerned about the rich as about a certain kind of riches. Almost all of the parlement's complaints about the distribution of wealth were directed at a certain kind of wealth in the hands of a certain group of men, the financiers. The magistrates saw France being devoured by a multitude of financiers and their agents. These men, who should have been working at more useful professions, had fastened themselves like leeches upon the nation. It had become a commonplace matter in France to see people who performed functions of little importance receiving great rewards, while better men carried on important work for inadequate pay. It was almost as if society had been planned so that everyone having some connection with finance would become wealthy. And yet the contribution of financiers to society was not great. A first-rate merchant deserved more honor for his services than a financier. Fortunes accumulated in the management and collection of public funds deserved neither recognition nor praise.[27]

The parlement's memorials on the finances make it clear enough what kind of property the judges favored and what kind they distrusted. Indeed, they stated categorically that the most important kind of property was real property (*immeubles réels*).[28] Despite this fact, financial fortunes were the ones which received all the favors. Just as most of the financial legislation of the kingdom favored the rich at the expense of the poor, so that same legislation had the serious defect of favoring the possessors of cash and annuities at the expense of the landowners.[29] In the opinion of the parlement this preference for financiers and their money was far from accidental. The government, wasteful and continually hard-pressed for funds, had been forced to look for aid to the financiers. Because of the lack of money, its importance had been overemphasized by the king's

27 I, 180–181, 184, 456.
28 II, 613–614.
29 II, 611; VII, 458–459.

administrators; they had allowed the financiers excessive returns for their services, and the more the government had
needed money the greater had become the privileges and power
of those who furnished it.[30] This malady had developed to a
serious degree.

> As long as finance continues to exist, the ministry will be its
> plaything or its slave; the resolutions most harmful to com-
> merce and to the nation will be artfully inspired or com-
> manded by necessity; the wisest resolutions will be eluded
> and made useless.[31]

Proof of the high position occupied by the financiers was
the way they managed to increase their fortunes by securing from the government fruitful privileges and monopolies. In
addition to the privileges already mentioned, such as the *gabelle*
and the *Ferme de tabac,* there was the powder and saltpetre
monopoly, which in the opinion of the parlement was making a
few financiers rich in a manner thoroughly harmful to the state.
The manufacture and sale of gunpowder and saltpetre had been
farmed out to a company of financiers who agreed, on their
part, to fill the king's powder magazines at a low price and to
sell gunpowder and saltpetre to the public at fixed prices. As
a means of furthering their work, the members and employees
of the company were given certain privileges. No one was
allowed to collect saltpetre without permission of the company.[32]
Searchers for saltpetre had the right to enter houses or cellars,
except in religious institutions. Exemptions, moreover, diminished the amount of certain taxes which they had to pay, and
they were excused from service in the much-hated militia.[33]

In the opinion of the judges this powder monopoly was a
splendid illustration of the multitude of abuses which could
accumulate in an enterprise conducted by financiers. They

30 I, 183–184.
31 XIV, *Ferme de tabac,* n.p.
32 VII, 491–492.
33 VII, 502–514.

condemned the monopoly for many reasons. Its employees sold powder at weights less than those stipulated in the contract with the king; thus the public was cheated from the start, and if they cared to examine the powder purchased they would find it inferior in quality to that made in foreign lands. Searchers for saltpetre, commissioned by the monopoly, annoyed people by entering their cellars, tearing them up, and not repairing the damage, as they were required by law to do.[34] But these were minor inconveniences compared with the disastrous effects of the monopoly on domestic production of saltpetre, and on foreign trade. In their greed the monopolists offered low prices for the saltpetre collected, with the result that their agents became discouraged and collected amounts of saltpetre inadequate for France's needs. Saltpetre had to be imported, thus weighing against France in the balance of trade. To make matters worse, the company, through its political influence, managed to set the price of gunpowder so high that foreign powder was smuggled into France and good French money flowed out of the nation.[35] This sorry state of affairs was by no means justified by the low price which the king paid for gunpowder, for the powder which he received was dangerously poor in quality and less in quantity than he had bargained for. The king's gains were so slight that they could not begin to balance the harm done to the nation and the scandalous profits of the financiers.

The Parlement of Provence had examined the company's reports on the administration of its monopoly for the years 1762 and 1763. If these accounts were to be believed, the financiers operating the monopoly had been victimized by their own zeal to serve the state, and had actually lost 267,000 *livres* in those two years. But the judges were not inclined to accept the figures presented by the monopolists, and expressed the conviction that the figures were false beyond the shadow of a doubt.[36] Their comment on this form of fraud was a condemnation of the

34 VII, 534–541, 604–607.
35 VII, 547–549, 631–632.
36 VII, 577–578, 622–624.

profits of financiers not only in the powder monopoly but in all enterprises in which finance profited from government favors.

> Everyone knows that the *Fermes générales,* the postal service, powder and saltpetre, provisions and clothing for the troops, military hospitals, and excise offices are mines which enrich all those who can get their hands on them; and, to limit ourselves to the powder contract, most of the interested parties have had a hand in it for more than thirty years; almost the same persons are involved every time the agreement is made; it is merely a customary and unnecessary formality when the new contractor takes possession; a favored few use all their influence to perpetuate themselves and their families in an enterprise the conditions of which they are able to dictate; from long experience they know how to calculate.[37]

The judges had their own estimate of the profits from the powder and saltpetre monopoly. Having studied the amounts of powder and saltpetre produced and sold, the prices charged, and the wages of employees, they believed the average yearly profits of the company to be over 1,000,000 *livres,* and the financiers' profit on their contract with the king to be about 175 per cent.[38] Thus the management of this monopoly by the financiers was beneficial only to themselves and to the foreigners who sold them saltpetre or smuggled gunpowder into France. For the king's meagre gains the public paid many times over. While French money to the extent of 1,000,000 *livres* a year went abroad, the nation was failing to produce an adequate supply of the gunpowder vital to its own defense. Conditions could not be worse.[39]

The judges, in this case as in some others, were not so extreme in their proposals for reform as might be expected in view of their general principles. They wished, nevertheless, to strike a blow at the financiers in charge of the saltpetre and gun-

37 VII, 578–579.
38 VII, 603, 620–622.
39 VII, 632–633, 648–649.

powder monopoly. Perhaps with an eye to the expediency of their proposal, they were willing that in this particular case the monopoly should continue to exist, partly because it was already in operation and partly because of the importance of gunpowder to the defense of the state.[40] But the business of manufacturing and selling powder and saltpetre should be taken out of the hands of its present managers, for it was absurd that financiers should be entrusted with an enterprise which was the rightful province of merchants; for some reason the parlement believed that merchants could be trusted to manage the monopoly honestly where financiers could not. After a public announcement of the conditions of the enterprise—for secrecy was to go, along with the financiers—there should be bidding by merchants for the gunpowder monopoly. Competition would thus, in some measure, be obtained.[41] With secrecy and the influence of the financiers eliminated it would be easy to arrange a proper form of contract. France would have an adequate supply of nationally produced saltpetre if the price offered to the collectors of that commodity were raised; there was no need to stimulate the collectors by offering them privileges. By lowering the price of gunpowder the evil of smuggling could be stopped. Only foreigners and financiers would regret these reforms.[42]

Other privileges besides the gunpowder monopoly encouraged the financial fortunes so distasteful to the parlement. The judges found these fortunes flourishing wherever the government had granted monopolies and special privileges, and this condition was especially bad in the case of the *Ferme générale*. This *Ferme générale* consisted, at the time when the Provence memorials were written, of a group of sixty financiers who had advanced money to the government and in return were allowed to collect a good many of the nation's taxes, among them the *gabelle, aides, traites, domaines,* and *tabac.* The collection of

40 VII, 635.
41 VII, 624–626.
42 VII, 626–627, 636–639, 646–649.

these various taxes had formerly been "farmed out" to several groups of financiers, instead of one, but from the time of Colbert there had been a tendency to join the "farms" together, as a means of reducing the number of officials and of increasing efficiency. By the mid-eighteenth century it had become customary for the king, every six years, to grant to some individuals a contract for the collection of the taxes which were to be farmed out. The person securing the contract was aided by a group of financiers who served as bondsmen. These men, known as Farmers General (*fermiers généraux*), were paid interest on the money advanced, and usually managed to collect enough from the taxes to assure themselves a comfortable profit. Their position as tax collectors and creditors of the state was reasonably secure, for though the name of the individual contracting with the king changed often, the group of financiers could hardly be ousted, since the government was never able to repay them in full and counted on future advances from them. The Farmers General were extremely unpopular in the 1760's, and not the least of their critics were the parlements.[43]

The Parlement of Provence, in discussing the taxes collected in France, lamented over and over again the fact that tax farmers were able to accumulate great fortunes. Attention has already been called to their criticisms of the *Ferme de tabac* for restricting production, charging too much for tobacco, and favoring foreign merchants and colonies. All of these activities of the tobacco farm were also contributing to the growth of great financial fortunes in France and to the decline in the circulation of money which was vital to a healthy economy; money concentrated in the hands of a few financiers could not circulate through the provinces, and money sent abroad to pay for foreign tobacco was lost to the nation entirely.[44] The financiers of the *Ferme générale* also made tremendous profits from the collection of the *gabelle,* the tax on salt. Although the parlement did not trust the accounts of the farmers, which

43 Marion, *Dictionnaire,* pp. 232–235.
44 XIV, *Ferme de tabac,* n.p.

they considered to be full of falsifications and evasions,[45] they
were willing to use these accounts as a basis for their own cal-
culations, and by this method they estimated the profit from the
Ferme des grandes gabelles for 1765 at 5,822,000 *livres*.[46] The
story was the same for the *domaine*, which included numerous
taxes collected by the Farmers General.[47] Once again using the
accounts of the collectors themselves, the judges estimated that
the yearly profits from the *Ferme des domaines* in Provence
alone amounted to approximately 790,000 *livres*.[48] The profits
from the *aides* were also considerable. For the year beginning
October 1, 1759, one of the worst years of the Seven Years
War, the profit of the *Ferme des aides* had been 4,000,000
livres, according to the farmers' own accounts. The parlement
suspected that the profit had been still greater. They estimated
that since the coming of peace the farmers' profit from the
aides must have risen to over 6,000,000 *livres* per year.[49]
In their examination of the tariffs (*traites*) the judges found
the same evidence of untrustworthiness in the accounts and the
same large profits for the *Ferme générale*. In this case they
believed the profits for the year 1765 to be a little over 6,000,-
000 *livres*.[50]

45 IV, 464–465.

46 IV, 452–453. Diversity in the various parts of France was an outstanding characteristic of the arrangements for collection of the *gabelle*. For this
purpose there were six different parts of France, in each of which the tax
was collected differently. The *Ferme des grandes gabelles* was the largest of
these parts and consisted of twelve provinces. It received its name in the days
before the various farms were unified, when it was the biggest single farm.
The *gabelle* was heavy in these twelve provinces, and the consumption of a
minimum amount of salt per person was compulsory. See Marion, *Dictionnaire*, pp. 247–250.

47 The *domaine* included everything to which the king had property rights
whether real property (*domaine corporel*) or duties owed to the king because of his position as sovereign (*domaine incorporel*). Originally the
king's entire income had come from the *domaine*, just as any feudal lord's
income came from his lands and the dues owed him, but as time passed and
the needs of the state increased other taxes had to be levied. See Marion,
Dictionnaire, pp. 181–182.

48 III, 600–601.

49 V, 553–554, 559, 579–580.

50 VI, 499–500.

In the opinion of the parlement great fortunes came into being as a result of privileges granted by government; then, in a kind of vicious circle, the holders were able to use their financial power to get still more privileges. The judges believed that most of the great fortunes were concentrated in the region of Paris. They had the age-old distrust of the countryman for the city, and evidences of this distrust, paralleling their dislike of the financiers, are scattered throughout their memorials. Paris was the metropolis which swallowed the population and money of the provinces. France was suffering from excess of taxes and the growth of huge fortunes, and the money from both taxes and fortunes tended to be spent and to remain near the throne. Thus concentrated, the money was wasted on luxury instead of circulating through the provinces where it belonged. Paris, city of luxury and finance, was making the provinces pay tribute. Churchmen and nobles and people from all walks of life were attracted to the capital, and the money they spent there, if circulated through the kingdom, could have revived whole districts which were in want.[51]

If France was to prosper it was necessary to break up these personal and geographical concentrations of wealth and restore circulation to the kingdom. All parts of the state should be kept in equilibrium. If people who had no business in Paris were made to go home, the metropolis would still have a large enough population. Bishops, for example, should not be allowed to get their hands on such a large proportion of the ecclesiastical revenues; they would then be forced to return to the country and look after their flocks.[52] The government should make money flow back into the provinces, where it was so badly needed. Whenever possible, public money should be spent in the provinces; soldiers should be busied with useful public works, and the state should purchase tools and raw materials in the localities where they were stationed. As much as possible the taxes collected in a province should be spent there instead of

51 I, 206–208, 392–395.
52 I, 395–397.

being sent to Paris and back again when supplies were needed; circulation would be improved if the government's purchases were made at once, before the money escaped to the metropolis.[53]

The parlement also believed that an attack should be made on the great fortunes, especially the financial fortunes. Great fortunes should never be allowed to form in the first place, but if they did form they should be divided up, for the monarchy would be healthier politically and economically without great aggregates of wealth. Great fortunes as well as poor circulation of money were the cause of luxury and waste. The population increase would be greater if there were no very rich or very poor people. For these reasons the great fortunes should be divided, but this did not mean that the people should be made to hate riches; though great riches were harmful to the state, there was nothing wrong with an honest profit; men should still be encouraged to seek money by means of hard work.[54]

As a first means of dividing fortunes, the parlement recommended that the government cease to give monetary rewards for services to the state. Special merit should be rewarded, not by money, but by honors. The regular servants of the state should of course be paid money, but they should receive fixed salaries which were neither too high nor too low; the parlement believed that salaries too large or too small would stimulate greed and dishonesty.[55] Unfortunately the practice of granting favors reached even into the church, for there were many commendatory abbés enjoying life in Paris on money scraped together by the poor.[56] The parlement's main attack, however, was directed at the financiers. In their opinion finance and financiers simply were not necessary in a monarchy where honor was preferred to money.[57] The judges believed that it would be a simple matter to find honest men capable of collecting the

53 I, 234–236.
54 I, 168–170, 175–178, 428–431.
55 I, 177, 179–180.
56 I, 394–395.
57 VII, 624–625.

taxes and willing to do the job for a few thousand *livres* a year. Since it was fitting that all men become accustomed to modest rewards for their labor, this solution was the proper one. Financial officials were no exception to the rule, and should be paid fixed salaries that were adequate but not excessive.[58] As for the holders of large amounts of cash and annuities, their property should be taxed at least as severely as real estate, which was the most important form of wealth.[59] With fortunes divided and the immense profits of the financiers eliminated the circulation of money would be restored and the provinces of France would flourish.[60]

3. The Danger of Debts

Not only concentration of wealth but also the accumulation of debts was a threat to the circulation of money and to the proper working of the economy. The Parlement of Provence was firmly committed to the view that the nation's debts should be paid as quickly as possible. Let others argue that it was wise not to pay the state's debts, that high interest rates were beneficial to commerce, and that if interest rates fell an increase in the price of labor would result. Let others argue that the state should owe, so that individuals would be able to loan it money. The parlement could not accept such views. They regarded the state's debts as a sickness to be cured. When the state was heavily in debt even the meeting of interest charges necessitated weighty taxes; thus the people paid over and over again in the form of interest the amount of the original debt.[61] A state in debt became, moreover, a little less its own master, for under pressure of need for money such a state found it difficult to act as it saw fit in all cases. Debtor states usually had to pay an annual tribute to foreign capitalists who had loaned them money, with the result that the exchange rates were influenced

58 I, 181–182; III, 615–618.
59 II, 613–615.
60 I, 394.
61 I, 6–8.

against their currency. There were still other disadvantages to a public debt. When people with money found a ready place for it in loans to the government, land values tended to fall. Moreover, instead of investing in productive agricultural, industrial, or commercial enterprises, people tended to place their capital in safe but sterile loans to the government. And as though this were not harm enough to the economy, the government, pressed by its debts, was forced to lay the shackles of taxation upon the various forms of enterprise.[62]

The parlement believed that this sad perspective would become a happy one as soon as the debts of the state were paid. The money which would otherwise have been loaned to the government would be used for the improvement of agriculture and other forms of production. Interest rates, which had been kept high by the government's demands for money, would automatically drop. It would become easy for men to go into business, and the number of enterprises would be greatly multiplied.

Some people, to be sure, argued that the increased amount of available money would raise the cost of labor, but the parlement considered this argument absurd, as though the same people were objecting to the entry of gold and silver into the kingdom. The judges, moreover, did not believe that the cost of labor would rise as a result of a change in the uses to which money was put within France; they argued that only an increase in the total amount of money in France would raise labor costs, and they doubted that labor costs would, even then, rise sharply or in proportion to the increased quantity of money. But the best argument of all, in their opinion, was that low interest rates would keep down labor costs by increasing the means of subsistence, encouraging population growth, and leading to competition among a greater number of workers. If, on the other hand, the national debt was allowed to remain, increased taxes on consumption would be necessary and the cost of labor would rise.[63]

62 I, 9–11; 550–552.
63 I, 11–16.

In their insistence that the national debt should be paid as quickly as possible, the parlement touched upon the dilemma which was inherent in their analysis of France's financial problems. The debt, like so many of the taxes and so much of the outworn legislation of their day, was an obstacle in the way of improving the economy and making the nation rich, for by diverting capital from useful investments it was helping to dry up the sources of the nation's wealth. For the good of the economy it was essential that this obstacle be removed; but unfortunately, according to the view which the parlement had deliberately chosen, the best way to remove the debt was first to make the nation rich. The manner in which the judges turned away from this dilemma and throughout most of their memorials placed their emphasis on the removal of legislation harmful to the economy rather than on the immediate payment of the debt has already been described. This approach did not, however, change their view that the debt was harmful to the economy and should be paid.

The whole question of debt was further complicated by the fact that the parlement did not consider the government's debt to be the only one harmful to France. In their opinion it was a mistake to consider as the debts of the state only the sums owed by the king. There were also debts owed by the clergy, by the *pays d'états,* by towns, and by corporations of workmen; payment of all such debts should be part of a general system of reform designed to lower interest rates, increase the circulation of money, and stimulate the national economy.[64]

The financial condition of the clergy will serve as an illustration of the parlement's opinions concerning the debts of all the various corporations. The judges considered the growth of the clergy's debts an alarming condition which should be checked at once. They believed that the amount of money owed by the clergy had increased from approximately 17,000,000 *livres* in 1740 to over 100,000,000 *livres* in the 1760's. Not only did this growing debt keep interest rates in France at a

64 VIII, I, 337–338.

high level, but it also worked in opposition to the principle which the judges considered essential to the solution of the nation's financial problem: by attracting the money of capitalists, who naturally preferred the church finances to more risky investments, the clergy's continual borrowing diverted the flow of capital from productive enterprises; thus the all-important sources of wealth from which the government in its hour of need had a right to expect aid were being slowly dried up.[65]

The parlement believed, moreover, that the financial operations of the clergy, the provinces, the cities, and the corporations of artisans all had the effect of virtually alienating some of the taxes which belonged to the state. Because of the interest due on money borrowed by these corporate bodies there was a constant flow of annuities and payments of one kind or another to a class of *rentiers*. In order to make these payments, the clergy, towns, and other corporate bodies had to collect taxes from their members; thus these taxes were in effect collected for the benefit of the *rentiers* instead of for the benefit of the state. As the parlement observed, the great landed seigneurs of former times had enjoyed the collection of some of the public taxes, but this condition was apparently giving way to a new tendency whereby a portion of the state's revenues were being purchased by the *rentiers*. It was as though the state had alienated a part of itself.[66] Needless to say, the parlement was eager to see the debts of the state and of the various corporations within the state paid, and an end put to the incomes of these *rentiers*. Such a reform would drive some of the financiers out of Paris and back to the provinces where they belonged. This blow at the financial fortunes would also have the effect of reducing the consumption of luxury goods to a point more in keeping with the true condition of the national wealth.[67]

65 VIII, 1–2, 337–338.
66 VIII, 338, 343–344.
67 VIII, 346–347.

Another reason for paying the debts of the state and of the various corporate bodies was that such a reform would release great amounts of money and enable individuals to borrow. The parlement, although opposing loans to corporate bodies, believed firmly in borrowing by individuals. Borrowing by corporations always slowed up the circulation of money and harmed the state, but borrowing by individuals always animated circulation and strengthened the state. When an individual secured a loan he increased the value of his property and the effectiveness of his industry. Even when an individual wasted the money borrowed there was no loss to the state, for the funds soon passed to someone with more ability. As long as the state, the church, and such bodies as provinces and towns were eager to borrow, money would flow their way, because of the greater safety of such investments. Interest rates would remain high and individuals would be unable to obtain sufficient capital for their needs as long as the debts of corporate bodies remained unpaid. The parlement believed that this condition should be ended, for it was desolating the French countryside. Low interest rates and an abundance of money were necessary if agriculture, commerce, and industry were to flourish and the population was to grow.[68]

Thus, in summary, it may be said that the parlement thoroughly appreciated the role of money as capital and was concerned that money should be invested in places where it would do the nation the most good. Money should be seen for what it was, a useful instrument, and should not be worshipped. Money should be kept sound, without dangerous variations in its value, and should be kept circulating, so that there would be enough of it for the needs of all parts of the nation. Unfortunately, there were several obstacles in the way of the proper use of money in France. The growth of great fortunes and the concentration of the nation's wealth in or near Paris were decreasing the circulation of money throughout the rest of France. The parlement especially disliked the operations of the fi-

68 VIII, 344-346.

nanciers, who in their opinion had taken advantage of the government's needs to seek favors for themselves and to accumulate great fortunes. The parlement was also opposed to the existence of large debts owed by the state and by corporate bodies within the state, for such debts tied up money which should have been invested in productive enterprises and made necessary taxation which further handicapped production. The judges were anxious for the debts of the state and of corporate bodies to be paid, so that individual citizens could improve the national economy by borrowing money at reasonable rates of interests. They viewed extinction of the government's debt as both a cause and a result of prosperity, but their actual recommendations leave the reader with an unmistakable conviction that prosperity was to be attained first and at all costs. What the parlement was willing to do about paying the national debt can best be understood by examining their statements about taxation.

CHAPTER VIII

TOWARD A NEW FINANCIAL SYSTEM

L'impôt qui détruit la source de l'impôt est le délire de la finance.
Mémoires, I, 55.

Ce n'est point une servitude, c'est un devoir et un interêt commun à tous les citoyens de contribuer en proportion de leurs facultes aux besoins de la patrie, l'important est de contribuer de la manière la moins onereuse, et qui entraine le moins de fraix d'exaction qui sont en pure perte pour les peuples et pour l'état.
Mémoires, IX, 240–241.

IT has been seen in previous chapters that the bulk of the Provence memorials consisted of an evaluation of old régime economic legislation, and that much of this legislation consisted of taxes. Thus far we have considered only the parlement's opinions concerning the influence of these taxes on the economic system of France, for the judges refused to limit their discussions to the problem of improving the finances, and insisted upon dealing with larger issues of political economy. The parlement's twofold analysis of the government's financial problem must not be forgotten, however. In the opinion of the judges it was important not only that all economic legislation be brought up to date, so that France might become prosperous, but also that the tax structure be modernized, so that the nation's wealth might be efficiently tapped and the government furnished with an adequate income. It is therefore fitting that the parlement's opinions of the taxes *as taxes* should be considered.

1. MAXIMS ABOUT TAXATION

Concerning this subject of taxation the parlement made numerous general pronouncements in the form of maxims, and by collecting these together it is possible to form some idea of the principles of taxation in which the judges believed. Their most important maxim about taxation was the one, already mentioned, which defined the proper relation of taxation to the economy as a whole. It should never be forgotten that the finances depended on the economy and that taxes harming population, agriculture, industry, or commerce were inexcusable.[1] There could be no justification for taxes which destroyed the very sources of future revenue:[2] even the complete exhaustion of the treasury could not serve as a valid excuse for taxes which crippled the national economy.[3]

Another frequently mentioned rule about taxation dealt with the question of who should pay taxes and what should be the share of each. The judges contended that the state had a right to tax the whole people in order to meet its needs. The days when the king was expected to rely on his *domaine* as the chief source of revenue were clearly gone.[4] Thus all citizens stood in a similar relation to the state in matters of taxation, but all should not pay the same amount, for it would be terribly unjust for the poor to pay the same as the rich.[5] Taxation was a duty to be performed by every citizen according to his ability to pay.

> It is not slavery but a duty and a common interest of all citizens to contribute to the needs of the *patrie* in proportion to their ability to pay; the important point is that they contribute in the least burdensome manner, and in a way which will occasion the least possible expenses of collection, which are pure loss for the people and for the state.[6]

1 I, 51–52, 241–242.

2 I, 55–56.

3 IV, 847.

4 III, 543–544.

5 V, 595–596.

6 IX, 240–241. The idea that all citizens ought to contribute to the needs of the state according to their abilities was of course no novelty by the 1760's. The magistrates of Provence could have been influenced by a number of writers. They were familiar with the work of Vauban, who in his *Dime royale* (1707) said that since all subjects of a state needed its protection, all should contribute to the needs of the state, and that there was ". . . une obligation naturelle aux sujets de toutes conditions, de contribuer à proportion de leur revenue ou de leur industrie, sans qu'aucun d'eux s'en

In the opinion of the parlement the existing taxes favored the rich over the poor and, more annoying still, the *rentiers* and possessors of personal property over the landowners.[7] There were other inequalities. Townspeople were favored over country people in the payment of certain taxes, notably the *aides*,[8] and Provence, a small and agriculturally poor province, was harder hit by taxes on vegetable oils than larger and richer provinces.[9] With respect to the clergy, the magistrates carried their maxim concerning the universal duty of paying taxes to its logical conclusion. They rejected the theory that the clergy were exempt from taxation, and condemned this doctrine as scarcely worthy of the most ignorant nations, to say nothing of enlightened eighteenth-century France.[10]

Moreover, all mystery and obscurity should be abandoned and the government's financial condition and plans for taxation should be given full publicity. The judges insisted that the people of France were so enlightened that there was no need to fear their response to an equitable tax program. Mystery in such matters was a great evil and extremely harmful to the state.[11] There existed in France certain taxes, such as the *insinuation*,[12] which were officially justified as necessary to the well-being of the state, but which actually had no other purpose than to increase the king's revenues. Such taxes did not really

puisse raisonnablement dispenser . . ." Vauban concluded that all exemptions were unjust. See Vauban, *Dime royale,* reprinted in E. Daire (ed.), *Economistes financiers du XVIIIe siècle* (Paris: Guillaumin, 1851), p. 48. The magistrates of Provence were also familiar with the writings of Boisguilbert, whose *Le détail de la France* (1697) recommended that the *taille* be assessed with justice, ". . . c'est à dire que les riches payent comme riches, et les pauvres comme pauvres . . ." See Boisguilbert, *Le détail de la France,* reprinted in E. Daire (ed.), *Economistes financiers du XVIIIe siècle,* pp. 208–209.

7 II, 611.

8 V, 603–604.

9 XIV, 232.

10 VIII, 2.

11 VI, 537–539.

12 See Chapter VI, Section 2.

succeed in fooling the people; on the contrary, they weakened confidence in the government. The needs of the state were reason enough for collecting taxes, and there was no necessity for misleading the people concerning the real purposes of the various taxes.[13] Nor was there any excuse for the common practice of attempting to hide the weight of taxes by varying their names, a practice which burdened the pocketbooks of the citizens with needless expenses of collection in a futile effort to spare the public mind.[14] If the nation's finances were to be put in order an actual increase in knowledge was needed: knowledge by the government concerning the true condition of the people, and knowledge by the people concerning the government's affairs. Mystery served only to hide abuses and to make the people suspicious. Whoever counseled that the citizens be kept in the dark had given bad advice, for with adequate publicity the people could be taught to serve as the king's watchdog in financial matters.[15]

If the people were to understand and watch over the finances, the existing tax structure would have to be greatly simplified. Simplicity was an ideal which the parlement mentioned fondly and often in their memorials. The nation's taxes, they asserted, and indeed all matters pertaining to the finances, should be given a clear, simple, methodical arrangement.[16] A complicated system of taxation such as that existing in France inevitably meant great expenses of collection and odious formalities for the people. The parlement believed that a wise rule to follow would be that the best taxes were those the collection of which was least troublesome and expensive. Conversely, any tax which cost too much to collect stood condemned as vicious either in itself or in its form of collection.[17] This rule of simplicity was

13 II, 567–569.
14 IX, 433–435.
15 I, 35–36; VII, 8–11.
16 I, 187.
17 II, 790–791; V, 583.

violated in France by the existence side by side of the *taille,* *capitation, aides,* and *gabelle,* for though four taxes might appear at first glance to guarantee four times as much income, this naïve expectation was not justified by the facts. Variety and overlapping in the taxes led to increased expenses of collection and administration. The various taxes, moreover, tended to steal from each other; a rigorous tax on consumption, such as the *aides,* left the people with less money and more determination to resist payment of the remaining taxes; thus the government was unable to obtain the sums anticipated from such taxes as the *taille* without an increased use of force which multiplied costs of collection and left the countryside desolate.[18] Again and again in their memorials the judges repeated the maxim that an excessive number of taxes would always yield diminishing returns.[19] A similar rule applied to excessive demands made in the name of any one tax, for if rates were too high or methods of collection too severe, smuggling and other forms of disobedience would invariably result.[20]

Uniformity in matters of taxation and finance was another maxim constantly advocated by the parlement. Just as all rules should be simple and familiar to the people, so should the rules be uniform in all parts of the kingdom. Variety in taxes or in any kind of legislation meant inequality among individuals and provinces.[21] If rules were everywhere the same there would be fewer abuses and less arbitrariness in their enforcement.[22] The parlement's intention, already mentioned,[23] of devoting an entire memorial to the planning of a uniform financial administration for France testifies to the importance which they attached to this maxim.

18 V, 595–596.
19 I, 51–52; II, 582–583.
20 I, 679–680.
21 I, 450–452.
22 VI, 638–640.
23 See Chapter II, Section 2.

2. France's Main Taxes

The Parlement of Provence found the tax structure of France sadly wanting when measured by the standard of their maxims on taxation. The government's main source of revenue in the decade following the Seven Years War consisted of direct taxes (*taille, capitation, vingtièmes,* and *corvée*) and indirect taxes (*gabelle, aides, octrois, traites, tabac,* and *domaine*). The direct taxes, except the *corvée,* were collected by government officials. In the decade following the Seven Years War all of the indirect taxes listed above were included in the *Ferme générale* and were thus administered by the company of financiers known as the Farmers General. In addition to the income from direct and indirect taxes the government received sums of money from the privileged clergy and *pays d'états.*[24] The parlement's investigation of this tax structure, like

24 This outline of the tax structure of the old régime is taken from several sources: Marcel Marion's *Histoire financière de la France,* I, 2–40, a section which describes the tax structure in 1715; Marion's *Dictionnaire des institutions de la France aux XVIIe et XVIIIe siècles,* in which various articles (*vingtièmes* etc.) describe the taxes added in the eighteenth century; Charles Gomel, *Les causes financières de la révolution française,* I, 7–8; and Raoul Busquet, *Histoire des institutions de la Provence de 1482 à 1790,* Chapter VI.

The question of how much revenue the treasury received from the *pays d'états* is a difficult one. It is true that these provinces were often allowed to substitute flat money payments for the collection of some of the general taxes of the kingdom; but because the bookkeeping of the old régime was complicated and confusing, it is difficult to know just how much should be added to the income from the general taxes because of these payments. There is no such doubt about the contributions made by the clergy to the crown. The clergy, to be sure, insisted that their property was exempt by divine right from all temporal taxes. They thus disagreed with the monarchical theory that the royal right to tax could not be limited in any such way. Between these two theories, however, there was in practice a compromise; the clergy paid, but contended that they paid freely; the government, eager to receive these sums, which were called free gifts (*dons gratuits*), was willing to allow the disagreement concerning theory to remain, and even on occasion recognized, for a price, the clergy's claim to immunity. Thus, although the clergy retained autonomy in the collection of their taxes, called *decimes,* and continued to insist that the sums granted by

their examination of economic legislation in general, led them to recommend the reform of some and the rejection of many of the existing practices.

The magistrates considered the *taille,* as it was collected in most of France, a very badly assessed tax and a scourge to agriculture.[25] Fortunately Provence, a *pays de taille reélle* and one of the privileged *pays d'états* which were allowed to collect the *taille* in their own way, had escaped the worst features of this tax. Most of France, however, was subject to the *taille personnelle,* which the judges chose to condemn for its arbitrariness. This form of assessment left property owners in constant dread of sudden increases in their taxes, with the result that people failed to repair or improve their property. The parlement's proposal of a rigid assessment of the *taille,* based on a survey of property conducted by the parishes, has already been described in connection with their opinions about agriculture.[26] The judges, however, meant this suggestion merely as a temporary measure for the immediate relief of the taxpayers. With the possible exception of their proposal that the parishes collect registers of information about the property of those subject to the tax, they made no proposals for the permanent reform of the *taille.*

The tax with which the parlement found the least fault, and for which it had the greatest hopes, was the *capitation.*[27] Al-

their assemblies to the crown were free gifts, they did actually pay money to the state. The free gifts were paid every five years and sometimes oftener, and averaged for the years 1715–1788, about 3,000,000 *livres* a year. See Marion's *Histoire financière,* I, 37, and his *Dictionnaire,* pp. 105–106.

25 The *taille,* one of the best known taxes of the old régime, was levied on persons or on landed property. For a more detailed description of this tax, see Chapter IV, Note 46. We have already had occasion to discuss the parlement's opinions of the *taille* in connection with their views on agriculture, and it will therefore be necessary only to summarize those opinions here.

26 See Chapter IV, Section 3.

27 The *capitation* was a boldy conceived tax which, had its original principles been respected, might have gone far toward setting a precedent for the payment of taxes by everyone. Established in 1695, suppressed in 1698, and then reestablished in 1701, the *capitation* was supposed to tax all families

though the judges came to no final decision concerning the question of whether a single tax would be the best means of obtaining revenue for the king, there is evidence that they considered such a plan and that they thought the *capitation* a possible substitute for most of the other taxes.[28] The parlement believed that the principle of the *capitation* was good, though the name of the tax was inaccurate. They pointed out that the *capitation* was actually not a tax by head but a tax on each household or family; it was assessed according to the ability of the head of each household or family to pay, that ability originating in the person's income from either property or labor; the poor were exempt.[29] As it stood, the *capitation* was far from perfect. The parlement objected to the fact that in Provence it was subject to arbitrary increases without registration by the parlement or consent of the province. The judges suspected, moreover, that Provence had to pay more than her share of the *capitation,* and believed that the tax was unfairly distributed among all the various parts of France. The returns, moreover, were not as great as they could be, because the *capitation* had to compete with too many other taxes; a landholder, for example, had to pay the *capitation* on the income from his land, when he had already paid the *taille.* The clergy had redeemed the *capitation* by a money payment, and were thus exempt.[30]

or households except the very poor, regardless of their station. During the first three years of its existence it was even collected according to twenty-two classes of citizens, those in the wealthier classes paying more, but in the eighteenth century this system was abandoned in favor of a method similar to that used for collection of the *taille* in the *pays d'élections*. For most people, in fact, the *capitation* became little more than a supplement to the *taille*. Its original principles of equality were sacrificed to expediency. The clergy were allowed to redeem payment by granting the government a fixed sum, and the nobles, in actual practice, paid less than their share.—Forbonnais, *Recherches et considérations sur les finances de France*, II, 82–84, 101, 122; Marion, *Dictionnaire*, pp. 67–91; Busquet, *Histoire des institutions de la Provence*, pp. 281–283.

28 IX, 259–263.

29 IX, 241–246.

30 IX, 183–189, 194–196, 234–238, 259–261.

These characteristics, to be sure, made the *capitation* appear at first glance to be a poor tax. The judges even went so far as to say that if this tax, as some people claimed, could be proved incurably arbitrary and harsh for the poor it would have to be abolished. On the whole, however, they were inclined to believe that the evils of the *capitation* could be eliminated. They pointed out that the expenses of collection were not heavy, at least in Provence, and that the returns would increase tremendously when the *capitation* no longer had to compete with other taxes. Careful planning could bring about an equitable distribution of the burdens of the tax on the various provinces of France. The clergy could, and should, be made to pay their share. Some people, it was true, insisted on calling the *capitation* a "servile" tax, but this criticism was unjustified; the Romans had made use of such a tax and had not considered it servile; the poor, moreover, were exempt; and all persons able to pay taxes for the support of the state should not consider it a servile act to do so. On the whole the parlement considered the *capitation* a good tax if properly assessed. Without committing themselves to specific proposals, which they promised to make in their final memorial,[31] the magistrates made it clear that they were considering the *capitation* as the possible basis for a new and simplified system of finances, to take the place of the existing system, much of which should be suppressed.[32]

The parlement's stand on the question of the *vingtièmes*[33]

---

31 It will be remembered that they probably did not write this memorial; or at least, if they did write it, the present writer has no knowledge of that fact.

32 IX, 232–234, 236–246, 259–263.

33 One of the most disputed taxes of the eighteenth century was the *vingtième,* a form of income tax which, like the *capitation* was supposed in theory to reach everyone regardless of station. The *vingtième,* as its name suggests, was planned as a tax of one-twentieth of all incomes without exception, but time and the government's willingness to compromise altered its character until it was little more than a tax on incomes from landed property. There were many exemptions, and the tax became little more than a supplement to the *taille.* See Chapter I, Note 5.

was somewhat inconclusive. In view of the struggle over the continuation of the extraordinary taxes at the close of the Seven Years War, a struggle which was in part responsible for the writing of the parlement's memorials on the finances, one would expect the judges to have definite and perhaps even violent opinions on the subject of the *vingtièmes*. Such was not the case, however. The magistrates took the trouble to write a detailed history of the *dixième* and *vingtièmes*, but their opinions concerning these taxes were evidently mild. Concerning the *dixième* their attitude was neither friendly nor hostile. They were inclined to believe, with Forbonnais, that the main trouble with the *dixième* was that it was begun too late in a war which had exhausted the nation.[34] As for the *vingtième*, they did little more than ask for a collection of all the facts concerning this tax. The *vingtième* should be studied province by province for the purpose of finding out exactly what its product and expenses of collection were for each part of France. Indeed, this kind of study should be made for all existing taxes, as the basis for a simpler and more equitable plan of collection.[35]

As a contribution to the question of land taxes, the parlement attempted to estimate the income from landed property in France. They set the yearly gross product of agriculture at about 1,800,000,000 *livres*. When essentials such as seeds and the cost of nourishment for the agricultural population were deducted, there remained a net product of about 600,000,000 *livres*. This net product, the judges believed, was large enough to furnish an income for the king of 30,000,000 *livres* a year from each *vingtième*, provided this tax did not have to compete with other taxes on land. As matters stood, the king's yearly income from each *vingtième*, even including the *vingtième* collected on the profits of industry and commerce, was only 22,-000,000 *livres*.[36]

34 IX, 269–272; Forbonnais, *Recherches et considérations sur les finances*, II, 221–222.

35 IX, 310.

36 IX, 316–318.

Thus the parlement made clear their desire that there should be only one tax on the income from land, and demonstrated that the *vingtième* could serve as that tax. But they expressed no preference for the *vingtième,* as they had for the *capitation;* and it must be remembered that they did not entirely reject the *taille.* One can only guess what their final solution to the problem of a tax on land would have been. On the basis of the somewhat meagre evidence available, it would appear that they preferred the *capitation,* but were not yet prepared to offer a complete plan of any kind. It is clear from the parlement's treatment of the direct taxes that they favored a greatly simplified form of assessment which would do away with the phenomenon of taxes competing with each other, and there is some reason to believe that they favored a single tax, perhaps the *capitation.*[37]

The magistrates applied this same desire for simplification to their evaluation of the indirect taxes, most of which they believed to be harmful and unnecessary. It has already been stated that they considered the *gabelle* harmful to agriculture and commerce and therefore a violation of the fundamental principle that no tax should be allowed to diminish the production of wealth. The *gabelle* did just that, for by reducing the production and consumption of salt it undermined foreign commerce, the health of the French people, livestock raising, the supply of fertilizer, and the quality of the soil.[38] But the *gabelle* was also unfair and inefficient. For one thing, there were so many rules concerning it that to master them required almost a lifetime of study.[39] Record-keeping and enforcement

37 The *corvée,* a direct tax in the sense that it required men to labor for the government, could not, of course, enter into a discussion of the best means of securing income for the treasury. We have seen that the parlement opposed the *corvée* as harmful to agricultural production.

38 IV, 824–825, 828–829. For a more detailed explanation, see the chapters on agriculture and commerce.

39 IV, 1–2.

required the services of a vast army of officials, men who might better have been engaged in some more productive occupation.[40] All the efforts of these officials, however, did not prevent fraud and lawbreaking. The agents themselves cheated the people by selling them damp (and therefore heavy) salt. There was much smuggling; and such practices not only undermined respect for law but also led to the need for still more enforcement officers, all of them taken from more productive work, and for a host of severe punishments, which also deprived France of citizens who might otherwise have been of some use to the state. All of this police work had to be paid for by the people.[41]

As though these defects were not enough, the *gabelle* also stood condemned of favoring the rich and of being especially hard on the poor. Consumption of salt was about the same for rich and poor, but the rich could afford the high prices, while the poor could not; in many cases, moreover, the rich were able by means of privileges to obtain salt at prices lower than those paid by the poor.[42]

For the reform of the *gabelle* the parlement, as was often the case with them, had what might be called a first and a second choice. It is clear that the judges thought it best to have the *gabelle* abolished entirely; but realizing that such a drastic step would not be welcomed, they were ready with alternative proposals. They knew, moreover, that they would be called upon to demonstrate how the government could get along without the 35,000,000 *livres* per year income from the *gabelle*. Despite their own convictions that the tax did not really produce a sum that large and that no tax which hurt the national economy was justified, the judges were prepared to show how the *gabelle* could be reformed without a loss to the treasury.[43]

40 IV, 821–822.
41 IV, 820–821, 832.
42 IV, 823–825.
43 IV, 845–847.

Without committing themselves definitely to any single plan, the parlement made clear their sympathy for the proposal that the *gabelle* be made into a *capitation,* arguing that the *gabelle* was already nothing more than a defective *capitation* which placed the main burden on the poor.[44] There were several ways by which the treasury could be compensated for any loss of income which might result. One plan would be for the provinces to continue paying the sums which the government had received from them for the *gabelle,* but to pay them not to the farmers but to the government's amortization fund until the debts of the state were extinguished. A similar plan would be for the provinces to accept and undertake to pay an equivalent portion of the nation's debt. If abolition of the *gabelle* should be unacceptable to the king the tax ought at least to be lowered and made uniform throughout the kingdom.[45] If the more conservative proposal of keeping the *gabelle* but abolishing its abuses should be accepted, the judges believed that there could still be a plan for dividing the state's debts among the provinces: the *gabelle* would be everywhere the same, but provinces would be allowed, if they so desired, to increase the weight of the tax on their own people as a means of paying the portion of the nation's debt which they had accepted.[46]

The magistrates professed to be withholding judgment of these various plans until their last memorial.[47] It is probably safe to say, however, that in theory they preferred the conversion of the *gabelle* into a *capitation* but that they recognized

44 IV, 862–866. The judges acknowledged that the point about the *gabelle* being merely a disguised *capitation* had been made in a manuscript work on public law by a certain Fleuri. They may have meant Claude Fleury (1640–1723), an *abbé,* confessor to Louis XV, and a prolific writer, especially on ecclesiastical history. One of Fleury's works, *Droit public de la France,* was not published until 1769, and therefore must have existed in manuscript form for a long time after the author's death.

45 IV, 866–867.

46 IV, 860–870.

47 IV, 870.

that a proposal for retention and reform of the *gabelle* was more likely to be accepted by the government. It is interesting, in any case, to note the parlement's preference in both plans for at least some provincial autonomy either in the collection of the tax or in the payment of a part of the nation's debts, a point of view which may be interpreted either as a genuine desire for local self-government or as a devious plan for the avoidance of taxation. Despite their suspension of judgment concerning the fate of the *gabelle*, the parlement did not hesitate to outline certain reforms which may be termed their minimum requirements for the reform of that tax. If the *gabelle* continued to exist at all, the tax should be a mild one, no longer out of proportion to the true value of the salt. There should be an end to the great variety in rules and regulations in the different parts of France. There should be no restrictions on the export of salt once France's domestic needs were supplied.[48]

Another form of indirect taxation, the *aides*,[49] violated almost all of the parlement's maxims, and especially that which denied any tax the right to harm the national economy.

It is not going too far to suppose that the people's income would increase by more than 100,000,000 in the provinces sub-

48 IV, 870–873.

49 The *aides* were duties on the sale of certain merchandises, chiefly beverages, but also a few other commodities such as playing cards, oil, and soap. Because of complete or partial redemption of these duties in some of the provinces, there was greater diversity in France with regard to the *aides* than for even such confusing taxes as the *gabelle* and the *traites*. The *octrois* were very similar to the *aides* in that they were taxes on merchandise and similar to the *traites* in that they were a form of tariff. They consisted of taxes on such products as wine, livestock, and building materials and were usually collected on these goods when they were taken into the towns. The *octrois* had been granted (*octroyés*) to the towns, but not all of their proceeds remained in town treasuries, for the state usually managed to claim half of the money collected. Largest and most important were of course the *octrois* of Paris. By the order of July 12, 1681, the *octrois* were included in the *Ferme générale des aides,* which was to collect the duties, turning over to king and towns their respective shares.—Marion, *Dictionnaire,* pp. 402–404; Forbonnais, *Recherches et considérations sur les finances,* I, 311–313, 499.

ject to the *aides* if those provinces were freed from them, and, as a result, that the harm done them by this tax amounts to 100,000,000, not counting what they pay for the *aides* themselves, which we estimate at 48,000,000.[50]

Besides diminishing consumption and reducing the national income,[51] the *aides* actually cost the people several million *livres* more than the gross product received by the tax farmers, since cheating by officials together with fines and lawsuits caused by the *aides* cost the people another 6,000,000 *livres* each year. The parlement estimated that the people of France had to pay at least 54,000,000 *livres* a year because of the *aides,* and hinted that a figure of 60,000,000 *livres* would probably not be an excessive estimate.[52]

Not content with resting their argument on their own estimates, the judges mustered an array of authorities to prove that the *Ferme des aides* was a veritable nest of abuses. They pointed to Boisguilbert's *Détail de la France,* which deplored the fraud, harsh punishments, and tyranny associated with the *aides.*[53] In the writings of the economist Vauban they found support for their contention that the officials who collected the *aides* were guilty of cheating the public.[54] As though conscious that the testimony of these somewhat out of date authorities might not be considered valuable in the 1760's, they also cited the more recent *Recherches et considérations sur les finances de France* of Véron de Forbonnais. This author, whose writings were so often consulted by the magistrates, had assembled a formidable list of abuses in the collection of the *aides,* condemning them for their diversity, the privileges of the urban

50 V, 582.

51 V, 581.

52 V, 582–583.

53 V, 598–599; Boisguilbert, *Le détail de la France,* reprinted in E. Daire (ed.), *Economistes financiers du XVIIIe siècle* (Paris: Guillaumin, 1851), pp. 186–188.

54 V, 600; Vauban, *Projet d'une dixme royale* (1707), pp. 31, 62.

bourgeoisie, the equality of duties on foreign and domestic wines, and the equal taxation of wines which varied in quality. Although admitting that some of Forbonnais' statements were debatable, the judges expressed agreement with most of his arguments against the *aides,* especially his contention that these taxes yielded the crown only a fraction of what they cost the people of France.[55]

The parlement was aware, of course, that the Farmers General and their sympathizers defended the *aides* as a valuable part of the nation's tax program. The judges agreed with the farmers' argument that high administrative expenses were essential to a tax of this kind, but they turned the argument against its authors by implying that the existence of such expenses automatically condemned the tax.[56] They rejected entirely the statement of the *Financier citoyen,* a pamphlet favorable to the tax farmers, that the progressive increase in the product of the *aides* was proof either that the nation's consumption of goods was increasing or that the tax was well assessed. The magistrates preferred to choose their own authorities: Boisguilbert's *Détail de la France,* which contended that the increase in the product of the *aides* was made at the expense of other taxes such as the *taille;* and Forbonnais' *Recherches et considérations sur les finances,* which asserted that the consumption of goods by the French people had fallen off since the seventeenth century.[57] Nor could the judges agree with the argument that taxes on consumption were an easy way of filling the king's coffers without entailing hardships for the people. They insisted that taxes on consumption, unless assessed with extreme care, made the poor pay as much as the rich, and were therefore unfair. They repeated again and again that the *aides,* though appearing to yield a large revenue, were really little

55 V, 603–608; Forbonnais, *Recherches et considérations sur les finances,* I, 504–507.

56 V, 585.

57 V, 585–595; Boisguilbert, *op. cit.,* pp. 185–186; Forbonnais, *op. cit.,* I, 298.

more than a means of substituting a partially hidden tax for the more obvious ones, the products of which were declining as that of the *aides* rose. Added to the numerous other taxes, the *aides* enlarged expenses of administration and increased, rather than decreased, the hardships of the people.[58]

Without advancing it as a final solution, the parlement offered a sketch of what might be done to reform the *aides*. Their reform amounted to abolition of everything except the *octrois*, or entrance duties to the towns, which had been joined to the *Ferme des aides* in 1681. The judges proposed both to increase the income from the *Ferme des aides*, the king's share of which then stood at about 33,980,000 *livres* a year and to relieve the people of most of the weight of the *aides*. They estimated that by careful planning most of the *aides* could be abolished, and a yearly income of 40,000,000 *livres* still obtained. This somewhat breath-taking operation was to be accomplished by abolishing all the duties collected by the *Ferme des aides* except the taxes on goods taken into Paris, and similar duties for the other cities. The parlement was willing to tolerate entrance duties in cities (*octrois*), provided these were not harmful ones such as duties impairing the free circulation of grain.[59] To make up the sum of 40,000,000 *livres* which they proposed to get for the king, another 20,000,000 *livres* would be necessary, and the judges recommended that this amount be furnished by the generalities where the *aides* were in effect. These provinces should redeem—in other words abolish—the *aides* by assuming no less than 500,000,000 *livres* of France's public debt, and by paying a sum of 20,000,000 *livres* to the government each year. As though conscious that their readers might wonder where the provinces would get this money, the judges promised to devote

58 V, 595–596.

59 I, 83–84. It appears strange at first glance that the judges, who disliked internal tariffs and tolls, should allow these to remain. It should be remembered, however, that the *octrois* were not unpopular in the eighteenth century, and that the Parlement of Provence was anxious for townspeople and possessors of non-landed wealth to pay their share of the taxes.

Colbert's tariff of 1667 there had been numerous edicts, the so-called *droits uniformes,* granting free transit across France to certain products once they had paid import duties. Income from internal tariffs had thus tended to decline, a fact which made total abolition of these barriers to commerce a less drastic proposal.[67] This reform, together with a uniform set of import and export duties at the borders of the kingdom, would so encourage commerce that the relatively few remaining tariffs would actually yield a larger income than their predecessors. As proof of this point the parlement cited the example of England's internal free trade and substantial revenue from tariffs.[68] In keeping with their oft-repeated contention that the best remedy for financial ills lay in making the nation as a whole rich, they argued that the tariff reform which they proposed would raise France's general level of prosperity and increase the returns from other taxes.[69] This reform, the judges had no doubt, would in the long run more than balance any temporary losses to the treasury, but if the king should feel that a temporary decline in the state's revenues, even in so good a cause, was impossible, they were ready with suggestions for making this decline unnecessary. They believed that their tariff reform was so valuable that it would even justify transfer to the receipts of the treasury of part of the amortization fund for the payment of the nation's debts. If necessary, the *capitation* could be increased in such a way that rich people would have to pay more. The rich should not oppose this temporary sacrifice, which by paying for an improved tariff system would eventually increase their wealth.[70] Thus once again the parlement insisted that the treasury's needs were no excuse for postponing essential reforms.

67 II, 460–461. It should be added that after 1664 there had been a tendency to keep internal tariffs much lower than the tariffs at the borders of the kingdom.

68 II, 461; XIV, 240–241.

69 II, 457–460.

70 II, 467–472.

The *Ferme de tabac*,[71] another of the king's important means of indirect taxation, was condemned by the parlement both for its effects on the national economy and as a form of taxation. The judges' opinions on monopolies in general and on many of the evils of the tobacco monopoly have already been given, but the case of the *Ferme de tabac* is so typical of the parlement's approach to financial problems that it will perhaps be appropriate to collect together all of their opinions on this tax farm. The judges estimated that the people of France paid about 60,-000,000 *livres* a year for their tobacco. Of this tremendous sum the king received approximately one third; the rest was consumed by profits for the farm, warehouse keepers and retailers, officials who cheated the people by selling them damp tobacco, and foreigners whose tobacco was either purchased by the farm or smuggled into France. In return for their money, the French people received little satisfaction and much harm. They had to pay high prices for their tobacco. Men who might have been engaged in productive labor were kept busy working for the tobacco farm, hunting and punishing smugglers, or themselves smuggling tobacco into France. The tobacco farm took money out of circulation and placed it in the hands of a small number of rich men, and contributed to the inequality of wealth by helping Paris and the financiers at the expense of the provinces. In the field of foreign trade the tobacco farm, by limiting French production except for a few privileged places and by purchasing foreign tobacco, undermined France's balance of trade and sent money out of the country. Worse still, the tobacco monopolists chose to make purchases from France's enemy, England, and thus favored English shipping and colonies. In short, the monopoly of the tobacco farmers had succeeded in triumphing over almost all Frenchmen: sailors, colonists, merchants, cultivators, and consumers. They were thus guilty of violating the fundamental principle that taxes

71 The tobacco farm, as already explained, was a state monopoly of the import, manufacture, and sale of tobacco. Prices were fixed, and no tobacco growing was allowed in France except in a few privileged provinces.

should never be allowed to harm the national economy, which was the source of the revenues of both king and people.[72]

Recognizing with complete seriousness that the use of tobacco had come to stay, the parlement sought immediate reform of the tobacco farm. As was their custom, the judges offered both an ideal solution and a set of minimum requirements. Their ideal solution looked to the entire abolition of the tobacco farm, accompanied by one or two possible substitutions. If the tax on tobacco were abolished entirely, an increase in the *capitation* might make up for the loss in revenue. The tobacco tax, on the other hand, might be retained, and administration by government officials substituted for the farm. In either case the limitations on tobacco culture in France should be abolished, and foreign tobacco should be made to pay a heavy import duty. The parlement recognized, however, that partisans of the tobacco monopoly might be able to postpone for some time any fundamental reform. They therefore offered certain minimum requirements in the hope that these, at least, would be acceptable to the crown. If tobacco continued to be purchased from foreigners it should be purchased from those places, such as Brazil and Russia, to which French products could be sent in return; there should be no unnecessary strengthening of France's enemies; and French ships and sailors should be used in the tobacco trade.[73]

Concerning that most ancient of the sources of the king's income, the *domaine*,[74] the parlement was anxious that the proper

72 XIV, *Ferme de tabac* (no paging).

73 IV, 862-866; XIV, *Ferme de tabac*, n.p.

74 The *domaine* included everything in which the king or the nation had property rights. There were many definitions and distinctions with regard to the *domaine* in the old régime, but the one most useful in tracing its development as a source of income for the crown was that which distinguished the *domaine corporel* from the *domaine incorporel*. The *domaine corporel* consisted of real property, while the *domaine incorporel* was composed of duties which the crown collected because of sovereignty. In the Middle Ages the *domaine*, and especially the *domaine corporel*, had been the chief resource of the kings, just as the chief resource of any feudal seigneur was his land. As time passed, however, the needs of the state increased, and be-

attitude be taken. It was important that the *domaine* be viewed, not through the smoked glasses of ancient prejudice, but in the full light of rational principles of taxation. The *domaine,* to be sure, had once been the only resource of the kings, but it held that position no longer. The principle that the state had a right to tax the people in order to satisfy its legitimate needs was now well established. It should be recognized, moreover, that the real *domaine* of the king was the prosperity of his people. Recognition of this principle would pave the way for reform of the *domaine,* many of the duties of which were harmful to the economy of France. Abolition of such duties would of course mean some loss to the king as feudal chief of France, but it should never be forgotten that he was also the political chief, and that any reform which improved the economy meant greatly increased returns from the regular taxes.[75] The parlement wished emphasis to be placed, not on the outmoded duties of the *domaine* or on the king's position as feudal seigneur, but rather on the need for an up-to-date system of taxes which would provide for the king's needs as political head of the nation. In the magistrates' opinion, moreover, most of the duties collected by the *Ferme des domaines* were not a part of the legitimate *domaine* at all, but merely additional taxes masquerading behind its ancient name.[76]

cause of various alienations and usurpations the income from the *domaine* tended to decline. By the mid-eighteenth century the *domaine corporel* had become a negligible factor in the state's income. The *domaine incorporel,* however, remained an important source of revenue. Consisting not of real property but of various taxes and duties owed the king, it also served as a pretext for the creation and sale of numerous offices. Despite opposition by some economists who contended that alienation of parts of the *domaine* would lead to greater improvements in the property, the theory persisted that the *domaine* was inalienable. Commissions, by making searches for unpaid duties, often as far back as thirty years, aroused considerable fear and opposition on the part of property owners.—Forbonnais, *Recherches et considérations sur les finances,* I, 78–79; Marion, *Dictionnaire,* pp. 181–183.

75 II, 426–428; III, 451–456.

76 XIV, 753–754.

It was the parlement's conviction that the *domaine,* as it then stood, was full of abuses, expensive to administer, and mediocre in its returns.[77] Some of the duties, such as river tolls, invited suppression because they interfered with the nation's prosperity.[78] Most of the duties, in the hands of the farmers, had become instruments of oppression, for the farmers were forever inventing new ways to squeeze money out of the people. Indeed, the *domaine* had become a source of suffering to the poor and a source of income to the rich.[79] Hundreds of offices, many of them requiring of their possessors few services or none at all, had been created and sold;[80] there were so many of these offices that no one knew their exact number.[81] Yet the sale of offices was a pitifully inadequate means of obtaining money for the *domaine,* since in return for small immediate payments the government had to undertake immense long-term obligations. The judges did not object to the practice of selling offices so much as to the government's habit of selling too many of them, though they considered both practices unwise.[82] Their solution to this particular problem was for the parlements to be given the task of making records of all existing offices, with the understanding that once the record was made a commission would be formed for the purpose of deciding whether offices falling vacant were useful enough to be sold again or should be abolished. The judges hoped that few new offices would be created, and that a great many old ones would be abolished.[83]

Among the offices to which the parlement objected were those connected with the *papier terrier,* the record of duties owed the king by virtue of the *domaine.* The magistrates accused the commissioners in charge of the *papier terrier* of attempting to make

77 III, 468.
78 II, 426–428.
79 XIV, 757–758.
80 III, 147–148, 335–336, 483–484.
81 VI, 555–558.
82 VI, 565–566, 587.
83 VI, 755–757, 763–764, 767.

their investigations of the king's claims eternal, so that their positions and salaries would enjoy the same everlasting life.[84] In the opinion of the parlement the returns from the *domaine* were far too small to justify the continued expenses of administration and all these searches for unpaid duties.[85] Provence's experience, they pointed out, had been that while the product of the *domaine* was inconsiderable the province was nevertheless continually forced to spend large sums in defending itself against the exaggerated claims of the farmers.[86] The parlement had also examined the accounts of the *Ferme des domaines* for the whole of France. They expressed astonishment at the meagreness of its returns in proportion to the terrific sums spent on administration and on searches for unpaid duties.[87] The history of the *domaine,* they concluded, was a story of annoyances and hardships for the people, large expenses of collection, and small returns for the king.

Clearly such a situation demanded some sort of change. The parlement believed that the *domaine* should be either reformed or abolished.[88] They admitted that it would be possible, by a great effort, to put the *domaine* in good working order so that it would yield a respectable return to the state. Such an effort, however, would be very hard on the people of France, for many families would be ruined by rigorous searches for unpaid taxes. Even the completion of such a program would not remove the possibility of future waste and carelessness, and high expenses for administration would remain.[89] The parlement therefore had no desire to see the *domaine* restored to its ancient position in the nation's finances, but believed that the best plan

84 III, 484–486.
85 III, 500–504.
86 III, 466–467.
87 XIV, 729–731.
88 XIV, 759–760.
89 XIV, 762–763.

would be to keep the *domaine*, recognizing that its income was small and that its days of predominance in the finances were gone. Its administration should be greatly simplified. Harmful duties, such as river tolls, should be abolished, and the remaining taxes consolidated; for example, the *contrôle, insinuation,* and *centième denier,* all of which dealt with the proper registration of legal deeds and contracts, should be made into a single tax. Reforms of this kind would mean fewer employees, fewer records, and less expense.[90]

But the greatest saving of all would be obtained by turning the collection of the duties over to salaried government officials instead of to the *Ferme des domaines.* The parlement wished to call attention to the fact that, as matters then stood, the money taken from the people for the *domaine* went to five places: some consisted of losses sustained by the people without profit for anyone, losses resulting from the duties interfering with commerce; a second portion went to dishonest officials whose illegal gains did not show up in the accounts of the farmers; a third consisted of the expenses of administration; a fourth was the farmers' profit; and the final portion was the money which at last managed to reach the treasury. The parlement was bold enough to assert that most of the drains on the king's income from the *domaine* could be eliminated along with the farmers. A simplified set of duties, collected by paid officials, would do away with corruption and handicaps to commerce, cost less to administer, and assure the king the profits formerly taken by the farmers.[91] The task of bringing about this state of affairs should be entrusted to France's parlements, and once they had investigated all existing duties a curtain should be drawn over the past and no more annoying searches and investigations made.[92]

90 III, 611.
91 III, 553–554, 602–604.
92 III, 575–576.

3. TOWARD A NEW TAX SYSTEM

In writing their *Mémoires sur les finances,* the Parlement of Provence intended, after reviewing the existing financial structure of France, to outline a plan either for the reform of the taxes or for a complete new system of taxation.[93] Throughout their memorials the judges refer continually to this project, which was to be the final outcome of all their labors, and it is unfortunate that this summing up of their thought on the subjects of the French economy and finances is either unavailable or does not exist at all.[94] From scattered remarks in the memorials which they did complete, however, it is possible to list some of the ideas which the judges were considering for use in their reformed system of taxation. These ideas are not sufficiently detailed to be pieced together into a complete picture of what the parlement intended; it is probable, indeed, that the judges themselves had not yet fully decided upon the nature of their proposed reform. But their occasional references to this project are interesting as hints of the direction their plans would have taken had the parlement been able to complete them.

It may of course be assumed that the parlement's reformed financial system would have followed the principles of taxation and political economy of which they spoke so often in their memorials. Certainly its very foundation would have been the principle which they admitted to be the key to all their thoughts concerning the finances: that taxation could not rightly be planned unless its relations to the economy as a whole were studied.[95] The judges also made clear their desire for completeness, for an over-all view of the parts of the financial structure, all of which should be made to fit together neatly; the arrange-

93 I, 23. As we have seen, the judges planned to write five memorials, the fifth of which would deal with assessment of taxes and payment of debts.

94 It appears most likely that the magistrates never finished their memorials. See Chapter II.

95 XIV, *Ferme de tabac.*

ments should include even the finances of such hitherto unco-
ordinated bodies as the clergy, municipalities, and *pays d'états*.[96]
With completeness should come uniformity, and these two together would aid in achieving the orderliness essential to a
good financial structure. Obscurity, that hiding place for abuses,
would vanish. Records of incoming and outgoing money would
be simple and clear, and the funds for various purposes such as
ordinary state expenses and the amortization of debts would be
kept carefully separate.[97] Since knowledge was essential to such
a rational system of finances there would have to be available
a great collection of facts concerning the population, production, and consumption of France. The national income would
have to be known as a basis for planning what the nation's
income from taxes could be.[98] The taxes themselves would
have to be analyzed one by one and a great table drawn up
showing the annual product and the expenses of collection of
each tax.[99]

Whatever other elements their unified plan of taxation might
contain, the parlement made it clear that there would be no
place in it for the practice of farming out taxes to syndicates of
financiers. They did not, it is true, make a frontal attack on the
Farmers General; in no one place did they sum up the case
against the farm and reject once and for all this method of
collecting taxes. Perhaps they recognized that such an outspoken
approach would be coldly received at Versailles, for in at least
one case, that of the tobacco farm, they admitted that the

96 I, 29–31; V, 603; VIII, 1.

97 I, 187–191. It may be recalled, however, that the parlement was willing
to use some of the amortization fund as a means of making up for losses
sustained by the treasury while the tariff system was being reformed. This
willingness to violate one of their own principles seems to indicate that the
reforms which the parlement was continually demanding as an aid to the
economy were more important in their eyes than the principles for a new
tax structure. Apparently the judges believed that it would be time enough
to follow these principles *after* the national economy had been reformed.

98 IX, 344, 379. For a detailed discussion of the information which the
parlement wanted collected, see Chapter III, Section I.

99 IX, 310.

farmers would probably have influence enough to postpone for some time a complete reform. But the judges left no doubt whatever concerning their opinions of the farmers and of the practice of farming out the taxes. Though not summed up in any one place, their scattered condemnations of the tax farmers appear on page after page of the memorials, and the reader of those repeated references can retain no shadow of doubt concerning the parlement's views. The judges took no pains to hide their distrust of financiers and non-landed wealth. Their attitude of prejudice, and perhaps even of hatred, toward financiers, financial fortunes, luxury and concentration of wealth, all of which they tended to lump together and associate with Paris, appears again and again in the memorials.[100] They complained openly about the influence of financiers on the policies of the government.[101] In their descriptions of all of the major indirect taxes collected by the *Ferme générale* the same picture constantly reappears: complicated regulations, faulty accounts, obscurity, numerous and corrupt officials, and immense profits for the farm.[102] Thus without entering into any single discussion of tax farming the parlement made clear by many scattered remarks that they strongly disapproved of this method of collecting taxes.[103]

But perhaps the best way to discover what the parlement wished to have done about the *Ferme générale* is to review their recommendations concerning the main taxes collected by that

100 For a more detailed description of the parlement's attitude toward financial fortunes, see Chapter VII, Section 2.

101 XIV, *Ferme de tabac,* n.p.

102 For example, the parlement pictured the *Ferme des domaines* as attempting to squeeze the last possible *sol* out of the suffering people, and the *Ferme des traites* as being based on such a complicated contract with the king that nobody could understand it, least of all the people, who were left to the mercy of the farmers. See II, 112–113, and III, 453–454. For further examples, see the various references to the *gabelle, aides,* and *tabac* in the present study.

103 See, for example, their remark, when discussing the *domaine,* that farming out taxes meant abandoning the practice of tempering rules with justice. III, 140–141.

organization. If such a review is limited to the reforms which the magistrates considered ideal rather than to the compromise proposals which appear to be their second choices, it will be seen that the judges wished to abolish the *Ferme générale* entirely. They did not, to be sure, propose this abolition in so many words; they merely left nothing for the *ferme* to do. If they had had their way, the *gabelle* would have been suppressed and its place taken by an enlarged *capitation* collected, not by the farm, but by salaried government officials. The *aides* and *octrois,* administered for so long by the *Ferme des aides,* would have been almost entirely abolished; the only remaining duties, those on goods entering the towns, would have been looked after by town officials and not by the farmers. Government officials would have replaced the farmers as collectors of the duties associated with both the *traites* and the *domaine,* and would have been put in charge of the tobacco farm, provided that monopoly had been spared the hasty execution which was clearly the desire of the parlement.[104] Thus if the parlement's ideals had been put into practice the *Ferme générale* would not have retained a single one of its lucrative contracts for the collection of the taxes.

The method of collection which the parlement wished to substitute for the *Ferme générale* was known in the eighteenth century as *la régie*. This "administration" was the opposite to the practice of tax farming, and was supported by most of the opponents of the Farmers General. A tax which was placed under *la régie* was collected by officers known as *régisseurs*. Its income remained the property of the state, which paid the *régisseurs* fixed salaries and sometimes additional sums based on a percentage of the total product of the tax. Public opinion in the eighteenth century generally favored the *régie* system and opposed the *Ferme générale,*[105] and this verdict was upheld by the Parlement of Provence, which declared that *la régie* was

104 More detailed references to all of the indirect taxes mentioned above may be found in the earlier pages of this chapter.

105 Marion, *Dictionnaire,* p. 477.

one of the pillars of their reformed system of finances. As might be expected, the judges defended this method by pointing to its simplicity.[106]

The parlement's liking for simplicity and uniformity apparently led them some distance in the direction of a single tax as the solution to the problem of meeting the treasury's needs. There is good reason to believe that, had they completed a plan for a detailed reform of French taxation, the judges might have made use of the *capitation* as the basis for this new system. There is no doubt that they considered the *capitation* for this role, and though admitting that this tax had its faults, two of which were arbitrariness and unfair distribution among the parts of the kingdom, they expressed the hope that these evils would be removed.[107] Of all the multitude of French taxes, the *capitation* was almost the only one which they took pains to defend against its critics, contending that its principle of taxing households according to their ability to pay was just.[108] They stated openly, moreover, that the *capitation*, stripped of its abuses and increased in amount, might take the place of other taxes whose flaws were so numerous that total abolition was the only remedy.[109] As already pointed out, the parlement believed that an improved and enlarged *capitation* might take the place of the *gabelle* and of the tobacco farm; the clergy, hitherto granted autonomy in matters of taxation, could be made to pay their share; and this reformed *capitation* could be looked to for the replacement of revenues which might be lost in the reform of France's tariff system.[110]

This evidence of the parlement's favorable attitude toward the *capitation* does not prove that the judges had definitely made up their minds to reform the finances by means of a single tax based on the *capitation*. It is clear from a reading of the

106 III, 584–585.
107 IX, 232–234.
108 IX, 241–246.
109 IX, 259–263.
110 IV, 862–866.

Provence memorials that their authors had not yet come to any final decision on this matter. Although lamenting the overlapping of the *taille, capitation,* and *vingtièmes,* all of which taxed the incomes of landowners, the magistrates did not propose the abolition of the *taille* or of the *vingtièmes.* Nor did they recommend that all indirect taxes be replaced by the *capitation,* although they came close to such a recommendation. The *aides,* or at least some of them, and the *domaine,* greatly reduced and simplified, were to remain; they were no longer to be in the hands of the farmers, but they were to exist. The *traites,* in greatly simplified form, were also to remain, but their main purpose was to be the regulation of commerce rather than the securing of revenue. The parlement, moreover, was evidently not contemplating a single tax when they spoke of permanent taxes, the weight of which should be determined by the ordinary needs of the state, and of extraordinary taxes for the purpose of paying the state's debts.[111]

Nevertheless, in their attempts to plan a simplified financial structure, the parlement appears to have looked with some favor upon the single tax, an idea which was extremely popular in their day. There is no doubt that they considered using the *capitation* as the most important single part of the state's revenues. No more than this can be said from the evidence furnished by the parlement's scattered comments in the memorials which they completed; for it is evident that at the time when the first fourteen volumes were written the judges were not yet ready to furnish a detailed and definitive plan of taxation.

4. Payment of France's Debts

Just as the parlement intended eventually to outline the plans for a reformed system of taxation, so they also intended to deal with the problem of paying France's debts.[112] We have seen that the judges did not complete their plan of taxation but that they

111 I, 190–191.
112 I, 23.

offered some clues to its general outlines. Their scattered remarks on the subject of paying the nation's debts are less
satisfactory still. The magistrates knew considerably less about
the nation's debts than about its taxes, for exact knowledge of
what the government owed had been kept from both parlements
and public. Thus handicapped, the judges could only offer general suggestions for reform and promise a detailed plan when
they were given the necessary information.

It must be remembered, moreover, that the existence of the
debt had presented the parlement with a dilemma, the solution to
which they made the central theme of their memorials. Payment
of the debt demanded a greater income from the taxes, but the
parlement argued that the existing taxes were crushing the life
out of the national economy. How could more money be obtained without harming the sources of future revenue?

The parlement's answer, as we have seen, was to urge that all
existing economic legislation be brought up to date so that the
economy would flourish.[113] They insisted, to be sure, that
France's debts should be paid as soon as possible, for debts,
too, were harmful to the economy,[114] but they refused to place
the payment of the debts at the top of the list of essential steps
to be taken by the government. The national income, they
argued, was not unlimited, and if a choice had to be made as to
how this money should be used it was necessary to put first
things first. Before any of the national income was taken for
other purposes, the subsistence of the citizens should be assured.
Second came the ordinary expenses necessary to keep the state
going, expenses which had to be met if the government was to
remain solvent. Third and last came the claims of the state's
creditors. These should be satisfied as soon as possible, but to
pay the state's creditors at the expense of the subsistence of the
people or of the everyday operations of the government would

113 For a complete description of the parlement's analysis of the financial
problems facing France, see Chapter II, Sections 2, 3, and 4.

114 I, 7–8.

be to kill the goose that laid the golden egg.[115] Thus the parlement, while arguing in principle that France's debts should be paid, insisted that payment should not interfere with the well-being of the economy; and since their program of reform was designed to improve the economy, this was equivalent to saying that payment of the debts should not interfere with their program of reform.[116]

The parlement did, however, make several suggestions concerning means of paying the nation's debts. One of their first moves was to lecture the king and his ministers on the need for an economical administration. They were careful to indicate that economy was more than the mere failure to spend money.

> Economy consists less of the refusal to spend money than of its wise use. There can be no economy without a great understanding of genuine needs and of the extent of those needs. He who is economical knows equally well how to spend and how to save appropriately; that embraces almost the whole of statesmanship. What has not the long and disastrous economy of the expenditures necessary for the upkeep of the fleet cost France?[117]

Economy, even in the broad sense of wise spending, was lacking in France. Unfortunately money had come to be worshipped entirely too much; great fortunes had grown up, accompanied by luxury, and the respect for these shown by government and people alike was lamentable. It was essential that those in power change their point of view, cease to show so much reverence for the money which the treasury did not possess, and set a good example for the nation by organizing a severely economical administration.[118]

115 I, 42–47.

116 This point of view may be compared with the parlement's repeated statements that decline in the government's income was not a good reason for failure to reform the tax structure.

117 I, 34–35.

118 I, 145–147, 164–165.

There was, for example, the traditional view that the king should pay more than anybody else for the goods which he purchased. This practice had developed until it had become absurd. A distinction should be made between "nobleness" and "profusion". Careless spending by the king tended to give the public the idea that the treasury was bottomless.[119] The judges were quick to insist that they would retain all expenditures at court, provided these really added to the grandeur of the throne. Not all expenditures could be seen in this light, however, and the parlement suggested the appointment of a commission to examine and revise the expenses of the king's household.[120]

There were also other ways of saving government money. The judges believed that a reorganization of France's courts and the writing of a proper criminal code for the purpose of preventing crime would diminish the cost of justice. They suggested, in diplomatic language to be sure, that if the king would realize that what was given away had to come from the people, there would be fewer gifts and pensions. In cases where government money was to be spent, it was better to pay cash and save interest payments. When materials were to be purchased, such as the provisions for the army, the best method was to award contracts to the lowest bidder at a public auction. This task of awarding contracts should not be undertaken by the ministers at Paris, who were too busy to see that it was done properly, but by officials in the provinces. The parlement, as we have seen, was anxious that government money be spent in the provinces so that circulation would be improved and concentration of wealth avoided.[121]

As might be expected, the parlement favored the use of a budget in keeping track of the king's revenues and expenditures. Exact knowledge of the public debt was absolutely necessary to such a budget, for the ministers would have to plan how much money would be needed for current expenses, debts,

119 I, 147–152.
120 I, 147–152.
121 I, 204–206, 220–224, 235–236.

and interest payments. The size of the debt, moreover, should be announced to the people. The amount of money needed for current expenses would determine the extent of the ordinary taxes, while the magnitude of the debt would determine the extraordinary taxes. There should be no transfers of funds from one section of the budget to another; the treasury and the amortization fund should be kept strictly separate. There should be a fund in reserve for unexpected expenses, such as war.[122]

The amortization plan, to be effective, would have to provide for payment of interest on the debt, as well as part of the debt itself. There should, in fact, be an arrangement which would gradually decrease the size of the interest payments due, so that as the debt became smaller the taxes for its payment would become less heavy.[123] But along with the amortization fund, the government should also plan to accumulate a fund to be used in case of war. Such a fund would spread the costs of war over a long period and would make it unnecessary to upset the economy with sudden wartime taxes such as the *vingtièmes*. There was no use promising to abolish the *vingtièmes* unless steps were taken to make such taxes unnecessary.[124]

These observations about economy, the use of a budget, and the need for an adequate amortization plan appear reasonable enough, but because of their general and elementary nature they cannot serve as evidence that the parlement had any definite or detailed plan for the payment of France's debts. There is, indeed, little reason to suppose that the parlement had any such plan. Aside from their general observations on the need for order in the finances, the judges made only one definite suggestion for the payment of the debts. Apparently they believed that the Royal Treasury should be freed from the task of financing the interest payments and debts, and that the money

122 I, 190–195.
123 I, 115–117.
124 I, 117–120.

for this purpose should be kept entirely separate from that used for current expenses. How, then, should the debts be paid? Early in their memorials, the judges suggested that the nation's debts be assumed by the people,[125] and it is probably safe to say that by "people" they meant "provinces". Again, when discussing the need for simplification of the indirect taxes, they proposed that the *gabelle* be abolished and that each province continue to pay a sum equal to the net product formerly furnished by this tax; the provinces should continue to pay these amounts into the government's amortization fund until the debts of the state had been extinguished. When discussing this plan, the judges repeated the suggestion that it might be desirable to divide all the debts of the state among the people by some such arrangement.[126] The same idea appears again in the parlement's discussion of the *aides;* most of these, the magistrates believed, could be redeemed by the provinces, which would charge themselves with the payment of 50,000,000 *livres* of the national debt.[127]

It is perhaps to be expected that a group of magistrates in a *pays d'états,* accustomed to the redemption of various taxes by money payments, should think of such a plan. But the Parlement of Provence, at least in the memorials which they completed, failed to do more than suggest the bare outlines of the project. They offered no answer to the troublesome question of how the provinces were going to get funds with which to pay the debts. They left no hint of the method by which such a plan could be kept from interfering with the unified and simplified tax program which they wanted adopted; if their solution, as is quite possible, lay in a decentralized administration of tax collections, the magistrates did not reveal this fact. It is evident that, as in the case of their idea that the *capitation* might be used as the basis for a new system of tax collections, the parlement was toying with a proposal the implications of which they

125 I, 116–117.
126 IV, 866–867, 869–870.
127 V, 606–609.

had not fully worked out. In the absence of their final memorial, in which they promised a full solution, it is impossible to discover what the full details of their amortization plan would have been.

The parlement's failure to work out detailed plans for the collection of France's taxes and the payment of her debt is scarcely surprising if we remember their interpretation of the problem faced by France at the close of the Seven Years War. By insisting that the way to solve the financial problem was to make the nation prosperous, they stepped from the realm of finance into that of political economy. Thereafter the problem which they faced was twofold: how to increase the production of wealth in France and how to satisfy the government's need for money without harming the economy and drying up the sources of future income.

In their quest for the solution to this twofold problem the parlement chose to weigh in the balance France's existing system of taxes and economic legislation; with considerable eagerness they embarked upon the task of judging this great mass of rules and practices, of evaluating its effect upon the economy, and of bringing it up to date. More specifically, the parlement aimed to free the economic system from unwise laws and at the same time to collect the information necessary for an eventual reform of all matters pertaining to taxation and finance. They planned their memorials with this purpose in mind. They would deal first with the abuses most urgently in need of reform, for the nation, like a sick man, should be allowed to regain its strength; if surgery in the form of a complete change in the fiscal system should prove necessary, the operation should take place after all the pertinent information had been collected; consequently the judges reserved for their final memorial the discussion of a completely new tax system and of a plan for the payment of France's debts.

In the two memorials, amounting to fourteen volumes, which they completed, the parlement went a long way toward achieving their goal. They planned to describe the worst abuses af-

fecting the economy of France and to list the taxes collected
in Provence, but in the actual writing of these fourteen volumes they managed to discuss all the main taxes for the whole
of France and to include numerous and significant observations on the subject of political economy. As a result these memorials are a vast storehouse of information and opinions concerning the economic legislation of their day. If the parlement
failed to do still more—to outline a complete system of taxation
and a plan for payment of France's debts—they at least laid
down the general principles of these final reforms. It is likely
that the subjects about which the judges chose to write reflect
their true interests; if so, it is safe to conclude that the parlement preferred the task of criticizing the mountain of existing
legislation to the more constructive one of planning a new
financial system. In any case, the two memorials which they
completed cannot be blamed for failing to do what they did not
set out to do. As it was, the parlement exceeded the king's instructions and left behind them an extremely significant criticism of the old régime.

CHAPTER IX

GOVERNMENT AND THE ECONOMIC SYSTEM: CONCLUSIONS

L'industrie du peuple francais opérera des prodiges si elle est encouragée par la liberté . . .

Mémoires, I, 51–52

Protegez l'agriculture, le commerce, et les arts; laissez un champ libre à l'industrie, à l'exception de celle qui voudroit tromper l'étranger. Les hommes sortiront des entrailles de la terre, et convertiront les pierres en or.

Mémoires, I, 454

HAVING reviewed the parlement's opinions of French economic and fiscal policies at the close of the Seven Years War, we may now summarize their views on the relation of government to the economic system.

1. THE ART OF GOVERNMENT

In writing their memorials on the finances, the Parlement of Provence had occasion to discuss the role of government only indirectly, in connection with such subjects as population and the various ways of increasing the nation's wealth. From these scattered remarks, together with some conclusions drawn from the parlement's remonstrances and decrees, a brief outline of the magistrates' political beliefs may be drawn up. One of their ideas was that the government ought to watch over and increase the welfare of the people. They lamented the fact that too often this obligation had been forgotten.

> Excessively arbitrary [financial] systems have caused the administration's obligation to devote all its activities to the public welfare to be forgotten; in opposition to the sovereign's intentions, a blind policy, tending toward despotism, has threatened to divide the ever common interest of prince and subjects; and since it has ceased to be the law of the land, the people have misunderstood the general interest.[1]

1 I, 163–164.

In the opinion of the judges, the public well-being was likewise the concern of provincial governments; thus the true aim
of Provence's administration was to do as much good as possible.[2] Public welfare as an aim of government was also implied
in the parlement's statements about population. Indeed, the art
of government, stated in terms of population, consisted of
increasing the number of people and making good use of them,
and since the judges themselves insisted that the population
would not increase unless the people were well-treated, it is
reasonable to conclude that public welfare was at least one of the
aims of government.[3]

But in the parlement's remarks about the art of government
there is another and perhaps equally important idea. A sovereign
would be more powerful if he fostered an increase in the
population and was careful to make good use of his subjects.
Obviously the parlement's words about population and the art
of government may be interpreted as meaning that the strength
of the state was just as much an aim of government as the
people's welfare. Others of their convictions, such as their desire
for economic self-sufficiency and a favorable balance of trade,
are likewise subject to this double interpretation: the belief in
economic self-sufficiency and a favorable balance of trade may
be viewed as evidence that the parlement wished above all to
strengthen the state, but these policies may also be viewed as
means of increasing national wealth and public well-being.
Thus despite the parlement's statement that administrators both
at Versailles and in the provinces should promote the public
welfare, there remains a reasonable doubt whether the magistrates of Provence considered the well-being of the people or the
strength of the state to be the primary aim of government.
One can only be certain that they considered both aims
important.

Whatever its primary aim, the government of France was certainly viewed by the parlement as a monarchy whose powers

2 X, 538–539.
3 I, 250–251. See Chapter III, Section 2.

were limited by the rights of its citizens, by natural law, and by the sacred privileges of at least some of the provinces. Property rights could not be tampered with,[4] and there was a certain "primitive justice", the parlement insisted, which did not permit the government to deprive its subjects of the right to sell their products.[5] The magistrates spoke of the French monarchy as a government under which it was possible to be at once faithful subjects and free men.[6] Like so many of their contemporaries, they felt the reality of natural laws, and used them as arguments against practices of which they disapproved. For example, they accused the militia system, which drafted men and punished deserters with death or the galleys, of being contrary to natural law.[7]

In keeping with these ideas on the limitations of government was the parlement's pride in the fact that Provence was a *pays d'états*. For the judges believed that the maxims of the *pays d'états,* provinces which were to a certain extent able to manage their own affairs, were closest to natural law and should be extended to the *pays d'élections*. They were thankful that Provence had its own rights and constitution, and boasted that in their province citizens were protected from inequality in taxation much more than in the *pays d'élections*. There were abuses in the *pays d'états,* to be sure, but they were less important, and the remedies were more easily obtained.[8] The parlement, as we have seen, was tireless in its efforts to defend the historic constitution of Provence, and the rights which the judges claimed to find in that constitution thus amounted to another limitation on the power of the monarchy.

Among the privileges which Provence retained when joined to France in 1481 was that by which her estates were allowed

4 XIV, *Ferme de tabac,* n.p.

5 XIV, 22–23.

6 I, 481–482.

7 XII, 861–862.

8 XI, 373–374, 379–382; Robert, *Les remontrances et arrêtés du Parlement de Provence au XVIII* siècle, p. 522.

to meet and give their consent to the collection of taxes.[9] But
in 1639 the estates of Provence met for the last time.[10] There
had been a decade of conflicts between the estates and the crown,
during which the estates had resisted more and more the crown's
demand for money. Richelieu's government, far from satisfied
with this condition, neglected to convoke the estates again,
and subsequent administrations saw no need for altering this
policy.[11] After 1639 another and less recalcitrant body was
called by the crown to sanction grants of money by Provence.
This was the *assemblée générale des communautés,* an institution born of the sixteenth century religious wars, when civil
strife in Provence had prevented the calling of the estates. These
general assemblies, attended mainly by members of the third
estate chosen in the towns, were more easily called together
than the estates and more nearly represented the real taxpayers, since only a token representation of the nobility and
clergy attended.[12]

Believers in a considerable amount of local autonomy, the
magistrates insisted that for the good of their province the
ancient estates of Provence should be restored. Suspension of
the estates, they argued, had been a violation of Provence's
constitution. The righting of this wrong would greatly improve
both the administration and the economy of the province. The
much-needed unified system of roads, for example, could only
be planned under the supervision of the estates.[13] Indeed, most
projects for improving the economy of Provence had been impossible because of lack of money; since taxes already weighed
heavily upon the landowners, there had been fear of increasing
them, and the tax burden could not be shifted without the consent of the estates. Moreover, instead of being examined by the

9 Busquet, *Histoire des institutions de la Provence de 1482 à 1790,* pp. 3,
176.

10 Until 1787, just before the revolution.

11 Busquet, *op. cit.,* pp. 201–202.

12 Busquet, *op. cit.,* pp. 203–207.

13 XI, 452–454; XIII, 564–568.

cour des comptes, the parlement's rival of long standing, Provence's accounts should be inspected periodically by the estates.[14]

The parlement's desire for the recall of the Provence estates was probably not unselfish. The suspension in the seventeenth century had for the most part been viewed with indifference by the members of the third estate in Provence, but the nobility of the province long continued to agitate for their return. The reason for this difference of opinion is obvious if it is remembered that the traditional organization of the estates gave the nobility and clergy two-thirds of the deputies, leaving the remaining third for the rest of the population. Toward the end of the old régime the nobility of Provence, hit harder and harder by such taxes as the *vingtième,* renewed their efforts to bring back the provincial estates, but as might be expected, the third estate was far from anxious for the return of a body in which the nobility and clergy were preponderant. Thus the Parlement of Provence, in demanding the recall of the estates, was furthering the aims of the nobility of their province, a class to which they themselves, as nobles of the robe, belonged.[15]

The parlement's statements about natural law and about the rights of citizens and provinces clearly indicate that they

14 X, 538–539; XIII, 237–238.

15 Busquet, *op. cit.,* pp. 252–254. As 1789 approached, the question of calling the various provincial estates was more and more widely discussed in France. Although the king hesitated to allow the taxpayers to hold discussions, the provincial estates appeared less dangerous than the Estates General. In 1787 estates were formed in the generalities which had never had them before. At the end of that year the estates of Provence were allowed to meet again. This trend toward decentralization and local self-government, which the Parlement of Provence helped to further, was later to effect seriously the course of the French revolution. The constitution of 1791 gave local self-government to the newly created departments and districts. Two years later, under the stress of foreign war and the Girondist revolt, the latter caused in part by conflicts between the central and local governments, the Jacobins had to revert to centralization and dictatorship in order to maintain their control and, as they claimed, to save the revolution,—Albert Mathiez, *The French Revolution,* Translated by Catherine Phillips (New York: Knopf, 1929), pp. 89–90, 93–94.

believed the French monarchy to be "limited" in certain respects. The magistrates insisted, however, that these precious limitations to the power of the crown were an inherent part of the traditional constitution of the monarchy. Above all they were careful to avoid any appearances of innovation or novelty in their political ideas. Not only the Provence memorials on the finances but also the many remonstrances and decrees issued by the parlement in the course of the eighteenth century bear witness to this fact. M. P. Albert Robert, a careful student of the parlement's remonstrances and decrees, concludes that the political views of the magistrates were essentially reactionary and that they turned to history rather than to the new political science for solutions to the problem of government. In the parlement's remonstrances M. Robert finds the judges demanding a return to the days when the king governed paternally, the Estates General deliberated concerning the affairs of the kingdom, the parlements guarded justice, and the provinces enjoyed their own independent administrations.[16] This picture of liberty without anarchy and legitimate authority without despotism is reenforced by the parlement's occasional observations on government in the Provence memorials.

But the statement that the Parlement of Provence was politically reactionary does not tell the whole story. Although M. Robert accepts the fact that the parlement misread the lessons of history, there remains the problem of indicating in what direction these errors in historical scholarship were leading. We have seen that by the close of the Seven Years War the Parlement of Provence had associated itself with the political activities of the league of sovereign courts led by the Parlement of Paris.[17] We have also seen that in the second half of the eighteenth century this parliamentary league, which claimed that all the parlements of France formed an indivisible body, advanced doctrines which if accepted would have altered dras-

16 Robert, *op. cit.,* pp. 658–659.

17 Busquet, *op. cit.,* pp. 110–113. For further details, see Chapter II, Section 1.

tically the traditional character of the French monarchy. By contending that the parlements of France, in the absence of the Estates General, were the rightful representatives of the nation, that registration of a law meant the consent of the nation to that law, that the parlements could refuse registration until the king took into account the changes they had proposed, and that the crown could not enforce registration, this judicial league was in effect dividing the sovereignty between king and nation and unwittingly paving the way for the French revolution.[18] If we may assume that the Parlement of Provence, in allying itself with the league of sovereign courts, shared their views, the conclusion is inescapable that despite their cloak of traditionalism the political opinions of the parlement were revolutionary in nature.[19]

2. Freedom versus Intervention

The parlement's beliefs concerning the proper relation of government to the economic system are somewhat confusing if attention is paid only to their general statements on the subject. The judges stated that the French people would accomplish wonders if given sufficient freedom for agriculture, industry, and commerce; yet they also referred many times to the need for protection and encouragement for the various forms of enterprise.[20] Protection, encouragement, and freedom are not, of course, mutually exclusive terms, and as we have seen in the case of tariffs, the parlement was capable of wanting both

18 Roger Bickart, *Les parlements et la notion de souveraineté nationale au XVIIIᵉ siècle*, pp. 266–269, 271–273, 275–278; Marion, *Dictionnaire*, pp. 422–424, 427–429. For further details, see Chapter I, Section 4.

19 The correctness of this assumption is to some extent supported by the parlement's attitude toward the Declaration of November 21, 1763, which led to the writing of the Provence memorials, and by the large part which the judges clearly intended the sovereign courts to play in the reform of taxation and economic legislation in France. Needless to say, the actual revolution toward the outbreak of which the ideas of the judges contributed would not have been to their liking.

20 I, 51–52, 454–455.

protection and freedom. But the problem remains: to what extent did the parlement want government intervention in economic matters? This question can best be answered not by pondering over a few scattered statements of a general nature, but by summarizing the measures actually advocated by the judges as means of improving the economic system of France.

Such a summary must include numerous instances where the parlement recommended greater liberty. Their conviction, already mentioned, that property rights and the right of citizens to sell their products were sacred, and their occasional use of the concept of natural law, furnish a philosophical justification for their attacks on economic restrictions. Moreover, in the field of agriculture, at least, the parlement subscribed to the now famous doctrine that the best interests of society would be served if each individual were allowed to seek his own well-being in his own way. Although forced by their dislike of large holdings to admit that some proprietors could benefit from education, the judges nevertheless clung to their belief that agriculturists knew their own best interests.[21]

The parlement also believed strongly in freedom for the professions. It was not for the government to determine what profession a man entered; each person should be allowed to do the kind of work which he considered most lucrative and pleasant, provided that work was not harmful to society. While admitting that there was some good in such guild regulations as the requirement of a masterpiece, the judges agreed in principle with the Estates General of 1614, which had wanted all trades thrown open to poor people.[22] There was no need to fear that some occupations would attract too many people, or that others would suffer; an overabundance of workers would make an occupation unprofitable, while a demand for labor would increase its price; thus an equilibrium would be maintained automatically, without intervention by the state.[23] Closely

21 See Chapter IV, Section 2.
22 See Chapter V, Section 2.
23 I, 454–456.

related to the parlement's belief in vocational freedom was their
faith in competition, which could be counted upon to keep prices
of goods and of labor at reasonable levels and to encourage the
discovery of new means of subsistence.[24] Conversely, monopolies
and special privileges were in most cases harmful to the economy, for they decreased competition, prevented necessary improvements, and kept prices high.[25] The judges also wished to
defend "freedom of contract" in the special sense noted above
against certain legal taxes such as the *insinuation*.[26]

The parlement's belief in certain forms of liberty was based
on a conviction of the futility of attacking some things or attempting to force the acceptance of others by means of legislation. This point is best illustrated by their views on luxury. For
the most part, the judges disapproved of luxury. Although useful on rare occasions as a check to the harm which might be
done by an overgreat supply of precious metals,[27] luxury in most
cases sprang from the concentration of wealth and was harmful
to the circulation of money so essential to the smooth func-
tioning of the economy.[28] Despite their opposition to luxury,
however, the judges had no faith in attempts to legislate it out
of existence. There was no use forbidding luxury manufactures,
which were simply the result of a demand; prohibitive legislation would actually increase the demand.[29] Luxury could only
be destroyed by attacking its source.

> All these rules are no more obeyed than other sumptuary
> laws made from time to time and which are badly suited to
> the monarchy. It is necessary to attack luxury at its source,

24 I, 15, 443–444; XIV, *Ferme de tabac,* n.p.

25 See Chapter V, Section 2. Examples of the monopolies and privileges
which the parlement most disliked have been given in Chapters IV, V, VI,
and VII.

26 See Chapter VI, Section 3.

27 VII, 237–238.

28 See Chapter VII, Section 2.

29 I, 552–553.

which is inequality of fortunes, and not to wish to stop the effects while the cause still exists.[30]

Other examples of the parlement's lack of faith in the force of direct legislation are furnished by their views on marriage and money. Although believing in a large population, the magistrates thought that laws to encourage marriage were useless, for if conditions in a nation were such that marriages declined, direct legislation on the subject would have little or no effect. Laws to prohibit the export of money from the country would likewise be useless as long as the balance of trade remained unfavorable.[31] Indeed, the parlement's most important maxim about money was that it should be let alone as much as possible.[32] These beliefs about money, marriage, and luxury, together with the parlement's trust in competition and freedom of the professions, indicate an awareness of economic forces working independently of the will of the government. The ideas on money, luxury, the professions, and competition are all related to the phenomenon of demand in a commodity or labor market. The idea about marriages parallels the parlement's belief that the best method of solving the government's financial difficulties was the indirect one of increasing the production of wealth.

One of the most important kinds of freedom demanded by the parlement was, as we have seen, freedom of trade within the kingdom. France was one nation and should behave as such. The provinces should realize that the best interests of all would be served by the abolition of internal tariffs and tolls.[33] And just as commerce should be freed from barriers within France, so should money be allowed to circulate unhindered by personal or geographical concentrations of wealth.[34]

30 VII, 238–239.

31 See Chapter III, Section 2, and Chapter VI, Section 1.

32 See Chapter VII, Section 1.

33 See Chapter VI, Section 3.

34 See Chapter VII, Sections 1 and 2. In the case of money, however, the parlement recommended a positive policy of government spending as a means

In the light of these opinions on economic freedom it is easy to understand the parlement's use of the term "encouragement" for agriculture, industry, and commerce. Judged by their actual demands, encouragement meant, to a large extent though not entirely, freeing the economy from the shackles of existing hindrances to production and distribution of wealth. These eighteenth century observers were confronted with a veritable mountain of legislation much of which ran counter to their beliefs concerning the needs of the economy. If the nation was to be made prosperous and the treasury filled, this mountain had somehow to be reduced. It is true, of course, that the process of reduction would require government action. False principles of taxation and economic regulation would have to be abandoned, the growth of great financial fortunes would have to be discouraged by the withdrawal of monopolies and special privileges, and the debts of the state and of corporate bodies within the state would have to be paid. But these actions, necessary as they were, were but a prelude to a greater freedom; they represented, not an increase in government intervention, but to a certain extent its removal from the economic system.

There is another side to this story, however, for in passing judgment on the economic legislation of their day the Parlement of Provence found several important instances in which government intervention in economic matters was justified, and in some cases even recommended further intervention. Their views on national defense and foreign policy, subjects related, in the minds of the magistrates, to the problems of political economy, have at first glance a distinctly liberal appearance, but may also serve as an example of the parlement's approval of government intervention when national interests were at stake. As we have seen, the parlement considered large standing armies, and even the conscripted militia, harmful to population, morality and production.[35] War itself they opposed, though they

of increasing circulation. As we have seen, the parlement was willing to extend freedom in the flow of commerce only to the borders of the kingdom.

35 See Chapter III, Section 2.

were not pacifists. Wars were fine theaters for the ambition of courtiers and people in favor with the government, but they brought only sorrow to most of the people.[36] Moreover, warfare did not pay.

> War has always been humanity's folly, and this is especially true now that the most important cause of war is not worth even a fourth of the cost of a single campaign; someone has rightly said that in modern warfare the gain is 1, the loss 1,000 the risk, 1,000,000.[37]

Looking around them at the condition of European nations, the judges concluded that preparations for war had become ruinous to all of them since the introduction of permanent standing armies. France, unfortunately, had set the example.[38]

Common sense demanded that these conditions be changed. Offensive warfare should be abandoned entirely. In case of attack, war for defense would still be necessary, of course, but there was no need to continue the harmful practice of maintaining large armies drawn from the productive portion of the population. Looking backward to the feudal horde and forward unknowingly to the armies of 1793, the parlement insisted that every citizen should be a soldier for the defense of the *patrie*.[39] France could easily abandon offensive warfare, for her territories were just the right size and there was no need for extending them. Large empires were likely to be weak.[40] Even if conquest were desirable, the jealousy of other powers would not permit such a policy. By being prepared to defend herself and by maintaining the respect of both allies and potential enemies, France could eliminate the danger of attack.

These opinions resemble the almost pacifist "liberalism" of the nineteenth century, but the parlement had other ideas as

36 See XII, 868–870.
37 XII, 861–862.
38 XII, 861–862.
39 I, 459–463.
40 I, 242–244.

well. Characteristically, they supplemented their liberal beliefs with recommendations for government action. As we have seen, the judges considered the immediate construction of a powerful fleet essential if France was not to be eclipsed as a great power. Commerce, they believed, had become the decisive factor in the wars of their century. Without mentioning England by name, they implied that the only war in which France was at all likely to be involved was a war on the sea.[41] An inadequate fleet would be more costly in the long run than an adequate one, for both warships and merchant ships would be lost unless superiority or at least equality in sea power were attained. The time had come to cease favoring land armies and fortifications at the expense of naval power.[42] French shipping, the parlement believed, should be encouraged not only by the removal of oppressive taxes but also by duties such as the *fret,* which penalized foreign competitors, and by additional favors which the judges supported in principle but did not name.[43]

The parlement's desire for a strong fleet and for the encouragement of shipping parallels their belief in positive government action for the maintenance of economic self-sufficiency and a favorable balance of trade. Aided by her colonies, France should produce the goods she needed, rather than buy them from foreign lands. Goods which could not be produced at home or in the colonies should at least be purchased from nations which were in turn buying French products. Thus a favorable balance of trade would be maintained, and money would flow into rather than out of the nation. As we have seen, the judges were quite willing to discuss the pros and cons of complete free trade until the discussion led to questions of self-sufficiency and trade balance; at that point they stopped short and recommended a "patriotic tariff" which was frankly protective. Further consideration of complete free trade was apparently impossible for

41 I, 124–125; XII, 888–889. See also Chapter VI, Section 2.

42 I, 196–199.

43 II, 474–485. See Chapter VI, Section 2.

them, since it would involve calling into question the economic self-sufficiency which was with them a major premise.[44]

The judges also favored a certain amount of government intervention in economic matters within France. They believed, for example, that the king should undertake a program of public works, and their discussions of the need for this program reveal a faith in government spending as a means of improving the national economy. It was axiomatic, they felt, that an expenditure useful to the state should never be regretted, provided it was made within the kingdom.[45] The king should apply this maxim to public works by setting aside each year a sum of 5,000,000 *livres* to be spent for necessary repairs and improvements within France.[46] Timid souls might be frightened at first by the thought of such spending, but they should remember that in the long run a policy of public works would more than pay for itself.

> Every proprietor who is careful of his inheritance employs an annual fund for repairs on his estates. Surveying his provinces, the king must do likewise, and it is suitable that the troops be used for this purpose. Bridges, dikes, rivers made navigable, and all kinds of works devoted to public utility will soon make of this kingdom the richest and most populous land in the universe.
>
> The chief aim of these public works must be the welfare of the people, but one may keep in mind the idea of finding in them some revenue for the treasury . . .[47]

It was true that there had been failures of public works projects in the past, but the reason had been that the projects had been too large for individuals to finance, and those who had attempted them had often ruined themselves and brought about the loss of public confidence in such enterprises. The expense

44 See Chapter VI, Section 1.

45 VII, 430–431.

46 XI, 492–493.

47 XI, 493–495.

of such works was not to be feared if the government would take a hand. The projects would no longer be turned over to companies of stockholders. Soldiers and criminals could be put to work on them.[48] The parlement even advanced the persuasive argument that public works could serve as a means of providing for princes of the royal house. As matters stood, the "joyous arrival" of a prince meant that he had to be provided for by withdrawing lands from commerce and from the ownership of individual families. A sum of 20,000,000 *livres* spent on public works at the birth of each new prince would remove this necessity. New values would be created, and the national wealth would increase to such a point that the prince in question could be given an income out of the increased revenues from the general taxes, or perhaps in part from fees connected with the improvements themselves.[49]

The parlement never doubted that public works would increase the wealth of the kingdom. A carefully planned system of dikes along a river, for example, would not only prevent floods but would also make possible the cultivation of much land never before used. As a matter of fact, the judges wanted such a system of dikes along the Durance River, in Provence, and estimated that in that case an expenditure of 8,000,000 *livres* would save about 12,000,000 *livres* worth of land from the water. Even the original outlay could not be considered a total loss, since the very spending of that money would stimulate circulation and benefit the economy.[50] The same rule applied to other public works. As already indicated, the parlement favored the construction of a unified system of roads in Provence. Bridges should also be built, and the judges were bold enough to assert that their construction should not be delayed out of consideration for the profits of seigneurs who owned ferry boats. Also, canals could be dug, and rivers made navigable.[51]

48 I, 423–424; VII, 430–431.
49 XI, 495–496.
50 XI, 461–465.
51 I, 423–424; XI, 471–475, 492.

Not all such projects demanded the attention of the crown, for the magistrates also believed in public works sponsored by their own province. Indeed, one of their arguments in demanding that both the provincial estates and a society of agriculture and commerce be allowed to meet in Provence was that these bodies were necessary for the planning and financing of public works.[52] The judges believed that a policy of positive actions for the good of the province was in order.

> The ancient estates [of the province] thought only in terms of defense and security. Now that more light has been shed upon commerce and upon its influence on the wealth and happiness of the people, our estates are beginning to become aware that they ought to do all the good which they can, and that it is a successful constitution which gives to each community the backing of the whole province for those works which can improve it.[53]

It would be a mistake to conclude from these words that the parlement had come to favor every possible kind of intervention by the province in economic matters, but it is clear that the judges favored a policy of public works, the subject which they were discussing in connection with the above statement.

In addition, the parlement in at least one case favored government regulation of the conditions of enterprise. This enterprise was mining, and the judges were concerned because the mines of France did not yield enough. Gold and silver did not matter, for a flourishing economy would attract precious metals from other countries, but though France had numerous mines and pits for copper, iron, and lead she nevertheless had to import these metals. Believing as they did in economic self-sufficiency, the judges were anxious to remedy this weakness by increasing

52 XI, 469–471.

53 XI, 465–466. It will be remembered that Provence's estates were no longer meeting in this period. In the passage just quoted the judges evidently meant either the *assemblée des communautés* or "estates" in the sense of the three orders of nobility, clergy, and third estate.

the productivity of French mines.[54] It was therefore essential that wasteful exploitation of France's mines be eliminated. Provence, for example, had abundant coal, and the judges were glad to report that within the past dozen years the province's soapmakers, dyers, and hatters had found it a cheaper fuel than wood and had been able to undersell their competitors. But there was danger that careless mining might make it impossible to get a good deal of the coal out of the ground.[55]

All this called for both encouragement and regulation of mining by the government. The parlement believed that there was in France sufficient capital and sufficient desire for profits, and that capital could be attracted to mining provided its owners had confidence that the managers of mines knew what they were doing. It was therefore desirable that young men be sent abroad and trained in the latest methods of mining. Criminals and even slaves could be used as a labor supply.[56] The problem of regulation lay in seeing that mining enterprises were neither too large nor too small, and that waste of natural resources was prevented. If men with too little capital were allowed to mine wherever they pleased there was danger that they would take from the earth only part of the product, leaving the parts most difficult to get at, which required more expensive equipment; thus it was possible for men with insufficient equipment to mine in such a way that the more inaccessible deposits of coal or iron ore could not be reached without danger of flooding or caving in the pits already dug. On the other hand, care should be taken that too great mining concessions were not given to any individual or company; too great concessions might lead to neglect of some of the property; they tended, moreover, to deprive other industries of necessary capital and to cause inefficiency by reducing competition.[57]

54 VII, 428–430.
55 VII, 412–413, 433–435.
56 VII, 429–431.
57 VII, 431–432.

It will be noted that the parlement's desire for regulation of mining may be related to their belief in self-sufficiency and a strong competitive position for France with relation to other nations. As a matter of fact, virtually all of those instances where the parlement asked for government intervention in the economic system are directly or indirectly related to self-sufficiency and foreign trade, and this appears to be more than an accident, since most of the judges' recommendations concerning the domestic economy of France were for greater freedom. Thus, as already indicated, the parlement's views on commerce amount for the most part to a plea for free trade within France and for protection and regulation at the borders of the kingdom. In agriculture the economic agents should be free to follow their own interests except for a few minor reservations such as, significantly enough, the conservation of timber for the fleet. We have seen that the judges offered virtually no plans for the regulation of industry. Although it is true that they stated on one occasion that inspections of manufactures were not harmful in principle, and although they expressed the mild opinion that there was some good in requiring masterpieces of skilled workers,[58] the great bulk of their recommendations consisted of demands for greater freedom. In their own words: "Leave industry a free field, except for those industries which wish to outwit foreigners." [59] We have seen that even in the fields of foreign policy and military affairs the parlement was eager to direct the national energies away from land armies, fortifications, and continental wars, and into greater efforts on the sea, where the commercial wars of their century were being fought.

To be sure, not all of the parlement's recommendations for government intervention in economic matters fit so neatly into the pattern of foreign competition and domestic freedom. Their belief in public works and government spending is not so easily classified, and perhaps offers an exception to the rule. As we have seen, the parlement also recommended the collection of

58 VII, 347, 352–355.

59 I, 454.

a great deal of information about population, production, and consumption in France, to serve as a kind of thermometer with which statesmen could test the health of French society.[60] The mere possession of all this information would not of course guarantee excessive government intervention in the domestic economy, for though the judges clearly intended that the information should be used for bettering the condition of the people, we have seen that their concept of betterment consisted, more often than not, of the removal of obstacles to freedom; still, the possibility of positive government actions resulting from the collected information cannot be entirely discounted. Finally, there is no doubt that the parlement approved of certain forms of indirect intervention in the domestic economy. They were anxious to check the flow of population to Paris, and they recommended that idleness and immorality be curtailed by a decrease in the number of holidays.

It would be a mistake, however, to view the parlement's memorials on the finances solely as the argument of a case for and against economic freedom. In justice to the writers of the memorials, their main purpose must be kept in mind. Their chief concern was not with abstract principles but with the problem of how France could be made more prosperous so that the treasury could be filled. This was a self-imposed task, as we have seen, and it may even be regarded as a task undertaken as a means of avoiding the more difficult and unpleasant problem of organizing an adequate and efficient system of finances. However that may be, the central and all-important fact about the Provence memorials is that the authors undertook to evaluate the great mountain of economic legislation which had accumulated during the old régime. Wittingly or unwittingly, in their attempts to indicate possible improvements in the nation's economy the judges set out to bring this mass of legislation up to date according to their lights. As their discussion advanced from regulation to regulation and from tax to tax, the parlement found occasion to deal with many specific in-

60 See Chapter III, Section 1.

stances of government intervention in economic matters. At times they even deemed it wise to make pronouncements on questions of abstract economic principles; and from these statements, together with their actual proposals of reform, it is possible to draw some conclusions concerning their solution to problems such as that of economic freedom. It would be foolish to draw a fine distinction between France's external economic relations and her internal economy. It is true, however, that in criticizing the economic legislation of the old régime the parlement found more to condemn in the legislation restricting economic activities within the nation than in that which dealt with external economic relations. To that extent, at least, the parlement favored principles of economic freedom within France and principles of regulation without.

3. ELEMENTS OF MERCANTILISM AND LAISSEZ-FAIRE

Now that the parlement's opinions on the subject of government intervention in economic affairs have been assembled, an attempt may be made to decide to what, if any, school of economic thought the magistrates of Provence belonged. Classification of the parlement's ideas, while not the main purpose of this study, is nevertheless of some importance, for as we have seen,[61] the decade following the Seven Years War was part of a period of transition when mercantilist, physiocratic, and laissez-faire doctrines were struggling to influence economic policies in France.

M. P. Albert Robert, in his study of the remonstrances and decrees of the Parlement of Provence in the eighteenth century, arrives at the conclusion that the magistrates' political aims were reactionary, in the sense that they sought a return to the ancient traditions of the monarchy, and that their economic aims were just the opposite: the judges believed, he says, that existing economic and fiscal arrangements were so faulty that it would be best to make a *tabula rasa* of what had existed in

61 See Chapter I, Section 2.

the past and to build on new foundations. M. Robert holds that the parlement wanted the old economic legislation to be swept away and to be replaced by the simple idea of economic liberty.[62]

This point of view is by no means supported in its entirety by the Provence memorials, which have been the basis of the present study.[63] The foregoing summary of the parlement's views on the relation of government to the economic system clearly indicates that there was in the parlement's economic thought a strong, and even a dominant, strain of mercantilism.[64] It is true that the parlement wished to sweep away much, though not all, of France's existing economic legislation, but an examination of the laws which the magistrates were willing to retain, of the new regulations which they desired to add, and of their purpose in accepting some legislation and rejecting the rest leads to the conclusion that the Parlement of Provence, while undoubtedly influenced by the liberal economic ideas cur-

62 Robert, *op. cit.*, p. 695.

63 And which, it will be remembered, Robert did not use in making his study. We have already seen that the parlement's political traditionalism actually had a revolutionary character. See Section 1 of this chapter.

64 There are many definitions of mercantilism, but it is safe to summarize the meaning of the term somewhat as follows: 1. It is a term which may be defined as a collection of economic "theories, policies, and practices" or as a "phase in the history of economic policy". 2. The term applies to the period between the Middle Ages and the age of laissez-faire. The extend to which mercantilist ideas were accepted varies from country to country during this period. 3. The aims of mercantilism were the unification, power, and wealth of the state. 4. Its methods were numerous and various but had as a lowest common denominator the belief in state intervention in economic matters where necessary for the carrying out of the above aims.

The content of this definition is taken from Eli F. Heckscher, *Mercantilism*, I, 19–28, and from Charles Woolsey Cole, *Colbert and a Century of French Mercantilism*, II, 558. Professor Heckscher has studied mercantilism as "a unifying system", a "system of power" and a "system of protection", a "monetary system", and "a conception of society". Professor Cole concludes his definitive study of Colbert with the following brief definition of mercantilism: "Mercantilism is a term which may be applied to those theories, policies, and practices, arising from the conditions of the time, by which the national state, acting in the economic sphere, sought to increase its own power, wealth, and prosperity."

rent in the second half of the eighteenth century, remained essentially mercantilist in their point of view.

To be sure, no conclusive proof of the judges' mercantilism is available in their statements concerning the *aims* of government and of economic policy, for these statements, few in number, may be interpreted as favoring either mercantilism or laissez-faire. The magistrates' contention that government and economic policy should promote the welfare of the people suggests economic liberalism; but coupled with the idea of welfare in the parlement's thought is that of making good use of the people, which implies a mercantilist aim—the wealth and power of the state. Thus the question at issue is whether the people's well-being was an end in itself or merely a means to a greater end, the well-being of the state.[65] As we have seen, the parlement's explicit statements about the aims of government leave some doubt concerning the solution of this problem, and in their statements about the aims of economic policy the magistrates supported first one and then the other of the two alternatives. They often made use of the phrase "service to the state" when passing judgment on the activities of merchants, financiers, and nobles; indeed, they never lost sight of the state, and of the economy as a national economy, and they saw this state in competition with other states. This point of view is undoubtedly mercantilist. On the other hand, their chief interpretation of the treasury's plight was that the best way of increasing the government's income was to enable the people of France to become wealthy; thus one might argue that the parlement, by identifying the interests of the king with those of his subjects, was exhibiting a liberal point of view. There can be no doubt concerning the parlement's faith that the in-

65 Mercantilism subordinated the individual to the state and made him a tool for its aims. This was certainly not the case with laissez-faire, though it would be too much to say that laissez-faire did the exact opposite. Although state and society are by no means identical terms, it is useful to remember that laissez-faire reconciled the interests of the individual with those of society. Early laissez-faire thinking, moreover, tended to be humanitarian, while mercantilists, in general, paid little attention to human values. See Heckscher, II, 318, 323, 327-329.

terests of king and subjects were the same. But an examination of the methods proposed by the judges for attaining these ends will cast further light upon the nature of the ends themselves, and will show the inadvisability of rushing to conclusions concerning the parlement's economic liberalism.

Many, though not all, of the specific economic policies endorsed by the parlement may be considered mercantilist beyond the shadow of a doubt. Economic self-sufficiency, a favorable balance of trade, positive government aid to national shipping, a protective tariff, and colonies as part of what the judges evidently intended to be a closed commercial system may be considered mercantilist policies, for here *method,* as distinguished from *aim,* is the basis for judgment. To this list may be added the parlement's clearly stated desire for a strong fleet to protect the commerce which they felt was the most important single cause of warfare in their century. All of these forms of positive government action perhaps imply a strong and wealthy state as an aim of economic policy, but in view of the doubtful character of the parlement's statements concerning their aims, this point should perhaps not be stressed. It is enough to conclude that judged by the methods which the parlement advocated, their economic thought undoubtedly contained a large amount of mercantilism.

As already noted, most of the parlement's recommendations for government interference in economic matters pertained to France's relations with other nations, or to matters of internal economy, such as productivity, which might be considered to have a bearing on competition with the rest of the world. On the whole the judges asked for little government intervention in the internal economy of France, but they apparently did not hesitate to demand such intervention where they believed it necessary. Their recommendations that steps be taken to get people out of Paris and back to the countryside, and that mining be encouraged and carefully regulated, are in the mercantilist tradition. The parlement's belief in public works does not appear at first glance to be mercantilist in nature, but the large scale of the projects which they proposed, and especially their statements that state-owned enterprises were in some cases to be desired and might be used as a means of increasing the government's income, make it impossible to dismiss this possibility entirely.[66] The parlement's faith in a policy of government spending, which led them to assert that no expenditure useful to the state was to be regretted, may be considered a sign of mercantilism in their thought.

On the subjects of population and money the parlement's opinions are for the most part in the mercantilist tradition, though it is true that similar views might conceivably have been held by men whose allegiance was to principles of laissez-faire. In general, mercantilists believed that a nation should have as large a population as possible, that great numbers of people were beneficial to the wealth as well as to the power of the state, and that the quality of the people, as well as their quantity, was an important consideration.[67] These were precisely the views of the magistrates of Provence, whose concern over what they called the "relative" decline in the French population since the sixteenth century was shared by a good many of their "repopulationist" contemporaries.[68] Anxious as they were to increase the French population, however, the magistrates of Provence were sceptical of the government's ability to encourage population growth by direct methods, and believed that the best means to this end was an increase in national prosperity. At least this much of their population theory may be considered liberal, a kind of tribute to the growing currents of laissez-faire in their century.[69]

66 It is possible, of course, that the idea of public works for government income was bait which the parlement used to win the approval of the authorities at Versailles.

67 Heckscher, *Mercantilism*, II, 44, 159.

68 Joseph J. Spengler, *French Predecessors of Malthus, a Study in Eighteenth-Century Wage and Population Theory* (Durham, N. C.: Duke, 1942), p. 77.

69 That it was possible for populationist ideas like those of the parlement to be reconciled with economic liberalism can be shown by an examination

Most of the parlement's statements about money are of little help in classifying them either as mercantilists or as economic liberals. Their awareness that money and wealth were not identical, their appreciation of money as capital, and their eagerness to maintain the circulation of money within the kingdom were all sentiments similar to those entertained by many a good mercantilist before them,[70] and are also quite compatible with the doctrines of economic liberalism. As we have seen, however, the judges did believe in government intervention for the purpose of increasing circulation and causing money to flow into France from other countries, and these methods of handling money may be termed mercantilist.

The fact remains, however, that many of the parlment's economic ideas, and especially those concerned with France's domestic economy, were undoubtedly influenced by the currents of laissez-faire thinking which were gaining strength in the France of the 1760's. As already indicated, the parlement demanded a greatly increased amount of freedom for agriculture, industry, and commerce. Probably this demand for freedom was to a large extent motivated by disgust at the mass of existing legislation, some of it financial, some mercantilist, and some pre-mercantilist or medieval. A part of the freedom demanded by the parlement can be explained on mercantilist grounds, but others of the parlment's ideas resemble the doctrines of laissez-faire.

Mercantilism, it must be remembered, did not oppose freedom at all times, and did not regulate merely for the sake of regulating. Some of the typical mercantilist policies actually aimed at greater economic freedom; thus the fight against the medieval particularism of internal tariffs and tolls was a struggle not only for economic unification of the nation but

of the thought of the Marquis d'Argenson, who as we have seen (Chapter I, Section 2) was to a large extent a believer in laissez-faire. Argenson's ideas on population resemble those of the parlement in many respects.—Spengler, *op. cit.*, pp. 73–74. Later economic liberals, like Malthus and Ricardo, were to be much less optimistic about the growth of population.

70 Heckscher, *op. cit.*, II, 175, 186, 188–190, 199–200, 217.

also, in effect, for greater freedom for the merchant.[71] Some
of the most striking passages written by the Parlement of
Provence are their pleas for the total abolition of provincial
douanes and other barriers to trade within the French nation.
These recommendations would certainly have been made by men
who were economic liberals, but they may also be considered an
attempt by mercantilist thinkers to complete the economic unification of France.

In protesting against the vast amount of legislation which
they disliked, however, the parlement did make use of one or
two concepts of a philosophic nature, and it is in their use of
these concepts that the key to the liberal elements in their
economic thought is hidden. Like many defenders of laissez-
faire, the judges insisted that certain rights of the individual,
such as the right of property and the right to sell his goods, were
inviolable. Without attaching too much importance to this
evidence, or denying that mercantilists also respected certain
rights, it is nevertheless safe to say that the increased use of
such concepts as "natural rights" did undoubtedly aid in the
growth of laissez-faire thinking.[72] Whatever their intentions,
the parlement, in reaching for weapons of this kind, was to
some extent participating in this movement. Of more importance, however, is the parlement's use of the concept of natural law or of "a natural order", and here the important
point is not that the judges made use of the concept, but how
they used it. Although many mercantilists were conscious of
an order in nature, they were prepared, through government
interference, to see that those laws served human purposes,
much as a master builder makes use of the principles of physics.
The key to laissez-faire, on the other hand, is that its defenders
had faith in what Adam Smith called the "invisible hand", faith
that the natural order would serve mankind if freed from human interference.[73] The basic question concerning the elements

71 Heckscher, *op. cit.*, I, 21–22; II, 273.
72 Heckscher, *op. cit.*, II, 322.
73 Heckscher, *op. cit.*, II, 308, 312, 318, 321.

of economic liberalism in the thought of the Parlement of Provence is thus apparent. To what extent were they willing to rely on the natural order to serve France's ends, free from government interference?

Part of the answer to this question has of course been given, for we have seen that the parlement relied, in many important respects, on government interference with economic matters, and was to that extent mercantilist in its thought. In other respects, however, the judges were clearly willing to let the "invisible hand" do its work. Agriculture and industry were for the most part to be free, on the assumption that the self-seeking of those involved would in the long run serve the common good. There was to be very little interference with freedom of the professions and with competition, which could be counted upon to get the nation's work done, set fair prices, and find new means of subsistence. The judges, however, thought they had learned the futility of attacking some evils, such as luxury, and of attempting to promote some desirable activities, such as marriage, by means of legislation. To the extent that the parlement was willing to rely on the workings of economic laws, or in other words on the natural order, to serve the general welfare, especially in fields which had formerly been subject to regulation, their economic thought may be considered liberal. It was after all but a short step from the mercantilist view (nature and economic laws plus interference to attain human ends) to that of laissez-faire (nature and economic laws without interference serve human ends).[74] The Parlement of Provence, although still essentially mercantilist in outlook, had in some respects taken that step, and may thus be said to have partaken of the economic liberalism which by the 1760's was contesting the validity of the great mercantilist tradition.

In this period of transition the physiocrats were likewise liberal in much of their economic thinking, and the question arises, how much the parlement's ideas resembled those of

74 Heckscher, op. cit., II, 322.

Quesnay and his followers. In the all-important field of agriculture, as already indicated, the parlement's views were certainly not physiocratic, for the judges not only assigned the quality of productivity to industry, but also defended the case for medium-sized and small agricultural holdings. Nor did the parlement's ideas on population resemble those of the physiocrats, who held that undue population growth was undesirable, since it threatened the minimum living standard of the numerous poor.[75] The physiocratic desire for free trade certainly found no favor with the magistrates of Provence, who were busy planning a uniform protective tariff for use at France's borders. Both the physiocrats and the parlement, to be sure, advocated a considerable amount of laissez-faire in France's domestic economy, and while the magistrates of Provence may well have been influenced in this respect by their better known contemporaries, it is probably safe to say that both groups reacted to the same stimuli: annoyances with existing legislation and a growing faith in the natural order. In matters of taxation, the parlement may have been influenced by the physiocratic idea of a single tax on land; as we have seen, they appear to have been moving in the direction of some form of single tax, and certainly shared the physiocratic desire for simplification of the tax structure of France. It must be remembered, however, that the *impôt unique* was by no means the exclusive property of the physiocrats, and that the parlement's tentative gropings toward a single tax reveal a desire to tax other incomes than those from landed property. Moreover, despite the almost complete failure of the mercantilists to reform the tax structure of France, much of which had been inherited from the late Middle Ages, the desire for uniformity and simplicity in taxation may be considered a characteristic of mercantilism as an agent of economic unification, or state building.[76]

75 Spengler, *op. cit.*, p. 371.
76 Heckscher, *op. cit.*, I, 124-125.

4. Conclusions

The economic thought of the Parlement of Provence may therefore be classified as mercantilist in its general outlines, with certain definite elements of laissez-faire and few signs of physiocratic influence.[77] But again it must be remembered that the magistrates were not primarily theorists but men in close touch with practical affairs, who faced a particular problem, the need for a rational financial system in France, and seized the occasion to express their accumulated grievances against the economic legislation of their day. If the result was a set of recommendations which may be classified in terms of economic doctrines, this fact must not be allowed to obscure the real character of the authors. These were men of the world, with a substantial stake of their own in the economic life of Provence and of France,[78] men with ability to theorize, but whose awareness of specific interests seldom left them. Their ideas on political economy, like the theories of all such men, were a composite of disinterested and objective thinking, specific demands fought for with whatever weapons lay at hand, and traditional doctrines, some of which were perhaps accepted uncritically as eternal verities. The significance of the Provence memorials is not that they contain a remarkable body of doctrine, though the parlement's theories require no apologies, but that men such as the magistrates of Provence held those doctrines, and that they embody one of the great judgments of French economic legislation in the old régime.

77 The writer who influenced the magistrates the most was undoubtedly Forbonnais, who as we have seen (Chapter I, Section 2) was essentially a mercantilist, although sometimes called a neo-mercantilist because of certain tendencies toward economic liberalism in his thought. The parlement, as already indicated, was familiar with a rather wide range of economic literature, but most of their references to books are for the purpose of documenting statements of fact. This is true of most of their references to the work of Forbonnais, but in view of the number of these references and the general similarity of the parlement's thought to that of Forbonnais there can be no doubt that the magistrates were influenced by the author of the *Recherches et considérations sur les finances de France.*

78 See Chapter II, Section 1.

What, then, were the interests which the parlement had in mind when writing their memorials? Although the problem of motives has not been the concern of this study, a few tentative conclusions may be drawn from what the magistrates actually said. Certainly they had in mind the economic interests of Provence, for characteristic products of their native province— wine, oil, soap, playing cards, leather—appear again and again in their memorials, usually as the victims of antiquated legislation, insufferable taxes, or unscrupulous financiers. Of the various forms of economic activity the parlement seems to have favored agriculture first, commerce second, and manufacturing last, although as we have seen they did not neglect manufacturing and considered all three activities interdependent. This moderate view is not surprising, for Provence's agriculture was rather specialized, and in some respects poor, and the inhabitants of the province needed to supplement it with commerce and manufacturing.

Did the magistrates represent the interests of a particular social class? As already indicated,[79] the Parlement of Provence was made up of wealthy men, nobles of the robe who formed a judicial aristocracy of long standing and who successfully excluded men whose only qualification was wealth. It is clear that the parlement was anxious to preserve the social hierarchy in France and to rehabilitate the nobles politically and economically by "encouraging" agriculture, protecting it from undue taxation, recalling the provincial estates, and abandoning the outmoded view that for the nobility only the profession of arms was honorable. Yet the parlement's recommendations were almost as favorable to the bourgeoisie as to the nobles, despite the fact that they hated financial fortunes and considered landed property to be more important than other forms of wealth. In agriculture the parlement favored medium-sized holdings of land, managed by their owners, who were largely members of the bourgeoisie, and the small holdings of peasants, who formed a precious labor supply for both agriculture and domestic in-

79 See Chapter II, Section 1.

dustry; the magistrates' ideas on land-holding favored both nobles and bourgeoisie. Both of these classes, moreover, stood to profit from the freedom for agriculture, industry, and commerce within France and from the protection against foreign competition which the parlement desired for all Frenchmen. Judged solely by the reforms which they proposed, the magistrates of Provence, nobles themselves although of bourgeois origins, exhibited no noticeable preference for the economic prosperity of either nobles or bourgeoisie; rather, they may be said to have defended the interests of both wealthy groups against economic legislation which threatened their prosperity.

The parlement devoted little attention to the lot of peasants and artisans, except where these were associated with some interest, such as porcelain manufacturing in Marseilles, or some doctrine, such as populationism, which the judges wished to defend. They appear to have been more concerned over the well-being of the peasants, whom they considered an especially important part of the French population and whom they wished could become owners of the lands which they tilled, than over that of the artisans. In view of later developments in industry, the parlement's desire for a free labor supply and their statement that competition would keep down the cost of labor have an ominous appearance. It should be remembered, on the other hand, that in the second half of the eighteenth century the guilds, which were an obstacle in the way of the "freedom" of labor, were becoming more and more exclusive, and that for populationist reasons the parlement was anxious that poor families be aided wherever necessary.

Finally, what of the parlement's statesmanship? The role of France's sovereign courts in the last years of the old régime has been pictured by most historians as one of narrowminded, reactionary selfishness, a selfishness made all the worse by demagogic appeals to public opinion.[80] We have seen that two students of the Parlement of Provence in the eighteenth century, MM. P. A. Robert and L. Wolff, have given the magis-

80 See Chapter I, Sections 4 and 5.

trates at Aix credit for sincerity, ability, and integrity in the performance of their judicial duties.[81] Concerning the parlement's statesmanship, the Provence memorials in response to the Declaration of November 21, 1763, should furnish at least a tentative answer.

The issuing of this declaration was a political victory for the parlements of France, but at the same time it challenged them to prove that they, the government's critics, could plan an adequate and efficient system of finances. The Parlement of Provence accepted the challenge and undertook to do much more than they had been asked to do. There can be little doubt that they took the Declaration of November 21 seriously, for we have as evidence the amount of work they did, a project extended over several years, their reading of the works of political economists—for they were thoroughly competent—, and the progress which they made—they actually began to collect the information necessary for their master plan of reform. True, they never finished their task, but responsibility for this failure was not theirs alone. Louis XV and his ministers apparently cared little for the great tax inquiry, offspring of a political defeat for the crown, and most of the parlements shared the royal indifference. As far as this writer knows, the Parlement of Provence was the only sovereign court which took the Declaration of November 21 seriously and made a sustained effort to lay the foundations for financial reforms.

This behavior in a period when the other parlements accomplished little except obstruction must earn for the magistrates of Provence considerable respect. They may nevertheless be indicted on two counts. The magistrates, in the first place, took part in the activities of the "parliamentary league", led by the Parlement of Paris, and may therefore be considered as sharing the responsibility for the effects, whether good or bad, of that league's actions in weakening the monarchy and helping to bring about a kind of revolution which they never intended. This political activity furnishes the background for the

81 See Chapter II, Section 1.

writing of the Provence memorials, but is not the primary concern of the present study. In the second place, there is some reason for concluding that the parlement, even in undertaking the immense project which has left us the Provence memorials, were to some extent avoiding the basic problem presented by the Declaration of November 21, the need for a system of taxation that was both orderly and adequate to the needs of the state.

There can be no doubt concerning the parlement's acceptance in principle, of the ideal that everyone should contribute to the needs of the state according to his ability to pay, and very little doubt concerning the sincerity of their attempts to rationalize the ancient jumble that was the French tax structure. It is in the matter of the government's need for adequate revenues that the parlement's realism and statesmanship are open to question. Faced with the problem of reforming the nation's finances, the magistrates very quickly enlarged their project to include the wider issues of political economy, and in so doing made the problem of taxation subordinate to that of improving the national economy. This interpretation of France's needs was permissible, but in adopting it the judges were adopting a formula which allowed them to do what they were most anxious to do: to criticize existing taxes and economic legislation. The parlement did not abandon the project of planning a new tax structure, but they postponed it. They did not refuse to acknowledge the government's need for money, but by insisting that the needs of the national economy came first they removed the necessity for any immediate sacrifices on the part of the taxpayers of France. To this extent they may be accused of taking the easy way out of their difficulties and evading the issue of the treasury's need for money.

But the outcome of that evasion—the great set of reflections on the economic and fiscal legislation of France—must be judged on its own merits. Here the magistrates were at their best, for they were attacking the problems which interested them most, such as the effects of specific laws and taxes on the economic life of France and particularly that of Provence. The farther they strayed from such problems, the more tenuous, theoretical, and impractical their thoughts became; thus the tentative state of their proposals for a new tax system appears to indicate that their hearts were not in this part of their work, and it is probably significant that here the magistrates' suggestions begin to approach the summit of abstractness and impracticability in considering the *impôt unique*. The same is true of their plans for paying the nation's debt, which scarcely measure up to the parlement's theoretical statements about the need for removing all outstanding obligations.

But in the field of their true interest the Parlement of Provence must be given credit for a substantial accomplishment. It was no small matter to pass judgment on the bulk of the economic and fiscal legislation of old régime France. The parlement evaluated each law and tax, expressing opinions which, although indicative of their desire to preserve the social hierarchy, cannot be called excessively selfish in their relation to the interests either of their province or of their social class. From these opinions emerges a political economy, mercantilist in the main, but with unmistakable elements of laissez-faire thinking, the characteristic product of an age of transition.

BIBLIOGRAPHY

Des memoires envoïés à M. le Contrôleur Général des finances par le Parlement de Provence, en vertu de la Declaration du Roi du 21 N^bre 1763. These fourteen folio volumes of manuscript, written by a commission within the Parlement of Provence in the years between 1764 (when the commission was appointed) and 1766 or 1767, are the chief source for the material presented and the conclusions reached in the present study. For a more detailed discussion of the title and origin of these volumes, see Chapter II, and especially Notes 39, 40, 44, and 45. The manuscripts are now in the Seligman Collection at Columbia University.

Alem, André. Le Marquis d'Argenson et l'économie politique au début du XVIIIe siècle. Paris: Rousseau, 1900.

Aulard, A. The French Revolution, a Political History, 1789-1804. Translated from the French of the third edition by Bernard Miall. 4 Vols. Vol. I, The Revolution under the Monarchy, 1789-1792. London: T. Fisher Unwin, 1910.

Bickart, Roger. Les parlements et la notion de souveraineté nationale au XVIIIe siècle. Paris: Alcan, 1932.

Les Bouches du Rhône. Encyclopédie départmentale publiée par le Conseil Général avec le concours de la Ville de Marseille et de la Chambre de Commerce sous la direction de Paul Masson. 16 Vols. Paris: Librairie Honoré Champion, 1932-1937.

Busquet, Raoul. Histoire des institutions de la Provence de 1482 à 1790. Marseille: Typographie Barlatier, 1920.

Cantillon, Richard. Essai sur la nature du commerce en général. Reprinted for Harvard University. Boston: George H. Ellis, 1892.

Clamageran, J.-J. Histoire de l'impôt en France. 3 Vols. Vol. III, L'Epoque monarchique, depuis la mort de Colbert (1683) jusqu'à la mort de Louis XV (1774). Paris: Guillaumin, 1876.

Cole, Charles Woolsey. Colbert and a Century of French Mercantilism. 2 Vols. New York: Columbia University Press, 1939.

Condillac, Etienne Bonnot de. Le commerce et le gouvernement considérés relativement l'un à l'autre. Amsterdam, 1776.

Carré, Henri. La fin des parlements (1788-1790). Paris: Hachette, 1912.

——. Le règne de Louis XV, 1715-1774, in E. Lavisse (ed.), Histoire de France depuis les origines jusqu'à la révolution. Paris: Hachette, 1909.

Dakin, Douglas. Turgot and the *Ancien Régime* in France. London: Methuen and Co. Ltd., 1939.

Darigrand. L'anti-financier, ou relevé de quelques-unes des malversations dont se rendent journellement coupables les Fermiers-Généraux, et des vexations qu'ils commettent dans les provinces. Amsterdam, 1763.

Daire, Eugène (ed.) Economistes financiers du XVIIIe siècle. Paris: Guillaumin, 1851. Contains reprints of the works of various economists. The following were used: Vauban, Projet d'une dime royale; Boisguilbert, Détail de la France, and Traité de la nature, culture, commerce

et intérêt des grains; Melon, Essai politique sur le commerce; Dutot,
Réflexions politiques sur le commerce et les finances.

Depitre, Edgard. La toile peinte en France au XVIIe et au XVIIIe siècles.
Paris: Rivière et Cie., 1912.

Ducros, Louis. French Society in the Eighteenth Century. Translated from
the French by W. de Geijer. London: G. Bell and Sons, 1926.

Forbonnais, François Véron de. Elemens du commerce. 2 Vols. Leyden,
1754.

——. Recherches et considérations sur les finances de France, depuis 1595
Jusqu'à l'année 1721. 2 Vols. Basle: Frères Cramer, 1758.

Gide, Charles, and Rist, Charles. A History of Economic Doctrines from
the time of the Physiocrats to the Present Day. Authorized translation
from the second revised and augmented edition of 1913 by R. Richards.
Boston: D. C. Heath and Co., n. d.

Gomel, Charles. Les causes financières de la révolution française. Vol. I,
Les ministères de Turgot et de Necker. Paris: Guillaumin, 1892.

Gonnard, René. Histoire des doctrines économiques. 3 Vols. Paris:
Valois, 1921-22.

Harsin, Paul. Les doctrines monétaires et financières en France du XVIe
au XVIIIe siècle. Paris: Alcan, 1928.

Havard, H. and Vachon, M. Les manufactures nationales; les Gobelins,
la Savonnerie, Sèvres, Beauvais. Paris: Decaux, 1889.

Heckscher, Eli F. Mercantilism. Authorized translation by Mendel Shapiro.
2 Vols. London: George Allen and Unwin Ltd., 1935.

Jobez, Alphonse. La France sous Louis XV (1715-1774). 6 Vols. Vol. VI,
Paris: Librairie académique, 1873.

Labrousse, C.-E. Esquisse du mouvement des prix et des revenus en France
au XVIIIe siècle. Paris: Dalloz, 1932.

Marchand, J. "Provence", in La grande encyclopédie, inventaire raisonné
des sciences, des lettres et des arts, par une société de savants et de gens
de lettres sous la direction de MM. Berthelot, Ch. Langlois, and others.
2nd. ed. 32 Vols. Paris: Société anonyme de la grande encyclopédie,
1886-1902.

Marion, Marcel. Dictionnaire des institutions de la France au XVIIe et
XVIIIe siècles. Paris: Picard, 1923.

——. Histoire financière de la France depuis 1715. 6 Vols. Vol. I, 1715-
1789. Paris: Rousseau, 1914.

Mathiez, Albert. The French Revolution. Translated by Catherine Phillips.
New York: Knopf, 1929.

Mirabeau, Victor Riquetti, Marquis de. Théorie de l'impôt. 1761.

Robert, P. Albert. Les remontrances et arrêtés du Parlement de Provence
au XVIIIe siècle, 1715-1790. Paris: Rousseau, 1912.

Roberts, Hazel Van Dyke. Boisguilbert, Economist of the Reign of Louis
XIV. New York: Columbia University Press, 1935.

Roussel de la Tour. La richesse de l'état. 1763.

Schelle, G. Vincent de Gournay. Paris: Guillaumin, 1897.

Sée, Henri. Histoire économique de la France. Le moyen âge et l'ancien régime. Paris: A. Colin, 1939.

Spengler, Joseph J. French Predecessors of Malthus, a Study in Eighteenth Century Wage and Population Theory. Durham, N. C.: Duke University Press, 1942.

Turgot, A. R. J. Oeuvres de Turgot. Eugène Daire (ed.). 2 Vols. Paris: Guillaumin, 1844.

Vauban, Sébastien Le Prestre, le maréchal de. Projet d'une dixme royale. In Collection des principaux économistes, G. Pirou and F. Simiand (eds.). Paris: Alcan, 1939.

Vührer, A. Histoire de la dette publique en France. Paris: Berger-Levrault et Cie, 1886. 2 Vols.

Weulersse, Georges. Le mouvement physiocratique en France (de 1756 à 1770). 2 Vols. Paris: Félix Alcan, 1910.

Wolff, Louis. Le Parlement de Provence au XVIIIe siècle. Organisation, procédure. Aix: Impr. B. Niel, F. N. Nicollet, succ., 1920.

INDEX